Beyond the Deal

BEYOND THE DEAL

Optimizing Merger and Acquisition Value

Peter J. Clark

HarperBusiness
A Division of HarperCollins*Publishers*

Library of Congress Cataloging-in-Publication Data

Clark, Peter J., 1950–
Beyond the deal: optimizing merger and acquisition value/Peter J. Clark.
    p. cm.
  Includes index.
  ISBN 0-88730-440-0
  1. Consolidation and merger of corporations. 2. Organizational change.
3. Organizational effectiveness. I. Title.
HD2746.5.C55 1991
658.1'6–dc20   90-24367
                                                                      CIP

91 92 93 94 PS/HC 9 8 7 6 5 4 3 2 1

Dedicated to Dash, Stuart, and Paul

Contents

Preface

This book was written because most deals fail and because the consequences of deal failure are greater today than ever before.

Most Mergers Don't Succeed, But Who Cares?

Evaluating acquisition success often means assessing whether an acquisition transaction long since passed was advisable. Should a specific merger action have been taken? Should the deal have involved that target company, basis for acquisition, terms, and bid price? Before the arrival of the leveraged merger boom in the early 1980s, these were the key questions posed in assessing acquisition success.

Few raiders, acquirees, transaction intermediaries, or analysts were interested in determining whether an acquisition was indeed a success. Even if a deal that closed four years ago was clearly a flop and the buy decision was ill-advised, the consensus was that nothing could be done today to change the past. Moreover, the backward-looking analyses that were conducted provided little of worth to help acquiring company top executives seeking to improve their success chances for future acquisitions. Moreover there was little agreement about how to even define merger success (what is *your* definition of acquisition fit?). As a result, no common set of statistical measures emerged for gauging deal performance after the transaction's close.

Managing Perceptions about the Deal

Virtually any postclose acquisition assessment can be labeled subjective. Accordingly, the top manager of the acquiring firm has extensive latitude to shape perceptions about the deal's success. Without reliable, consistently applied bases for assessment, many acquisition success judgments have been based largely on subjective considerations—that is, the perspectives, objectives, and background of the evaluator. The acquiring firm's corporate public relations officer predictably approved of management's acquisition record. By contrast, an external human resources consultant would likely base his "success" assesment on the level of stress endured by acquiree company employees.

Unless the close of the deal was followed shortly afterward by a highly visible, nearly total collapse of the acquiree company, the acquirer CEO generally could explain away an under-performing or disappointing acquisition. If a sizable acquisition depressed a publicly traded acquirer's earnings per share (EPS) performance, top management could adroitly deflect concerns by referring to long-term wealth-creation objectives. In effect, management in the past defined acquisition success based on dynamics of the deal itself. Perceptions about a completed transaction could usually be shaped to be the same as those about a successful deal.

The High-Leverage Transaction (HLT)
Era Arrives

Once the high-leverage transaction (HLT) era arrived, the implications of acquisition success began to extend beyond the limitations of the immediate transaction. Acquisition success began to move beyond the deal.

Two key developments accompanied the arrival of the HLT era: (1) debt increasingly displaced equity as the center of the acquirer's capital structure; and (2) the focus of leveraged buyout (LBO) transactions shifted away from the acquirer's balance sheet and toward the acquiree's balance sheet and operating performance. Not only did increasing use of debt raise the stakes of the acquisition game for these transactions, but once a substantial balance sheet and income statement were no longer the price of admission, new entrants could join the game.

Early HLT acquisitions of undervalued companies seemed to confirm that the issue of acquisition success was still not a key concern. To the contrary, the spectacular success of some early LBOs suggested that a new mechanism for instant wealth creation had been discovered. The allure of the LBO's simplicity was undeniable: the success of the transaction was tied to the acquiree's ability to pay back the mountain of acquisition debt incurred in the transaction from the assets or operations of the acquired firm itself.

No magical wealth formula for successful leverage exists, however. Leverage can work to either the acquirer's advantage or disadvantage. As the underpriced LBO deals of 1983 became the overpriced transactions of 1987, excessive acquisition borrowing began to put into motion forces that eventually caused the LBO world to shake. At first these signals of danger were faint. As long as the number of quality acquisition candidates remained plentiful, after all, the increased borrowing necessary to culminate the deal was seen as merely a necessary price to pay for success. Even if profits of the newly acquired company later turned out be insufficient to service acquisition debt, that might not necessarily mean that the deal was doomed. Indeed, the acquiree could generate cash flow to service the deal through a variety of liquidity instruments and mechanisms. Such mechanisms included noninvestment-quality LBO securities, some with and some without provision for interest adjustment in later periods, and for a limited portion of the LBO boom period, an initial public-offering (IPO) market for "LBOed" companies that had been taken private.

Postclose Value Improvement

As these and other liquidity sources faltered, the acquirer was left with a stark new reality: the easy ways to pay back acquisition debt through the assets, operations, or untapped borrowing capacity of the acquired firm had all been exhausted.

That left only improvements to the business itself as a means for generating the additional cash flow needed to prevent loan default. Repayment of acquisition borrowing and acquisition success now depended on achieving additional value in the acquired firm after the transaction was closed. As a result of this evolution, acquisition success changed from a transaction issue to an operating performance issue. Improving cash flow and augmenting the worth of a business was no longer a theoretical matter.

Changes in the nature of the acquisition success issue were paralleled by changes in concerns among the parties interested in the deal. These included directors of acquiring companies who grew anxious about their possible exposure in the event that a collapse of the acquired company could be linked to careless use of leverage by the acquirer group. Acquisition advisors worried about what was once unthinkable—possible recapture of fees if they could be proved to have been part and party to a reckless recapitalization or acquisition financing scheme. Lenders were concerned both with protecting second-stage refinancing of leveraged portfolios and deals that were previously funded as well as with establishing approaches to acquisition financing support that would protect both borrower and lender.

New Measures, New Approaches

The changing nature of acquisition success brought, in turn, renewed focus on the basics of new cash flow and value creation in the acquired firm after the close—the focus of this book. Looking *Beyond the Deal* requires executives to explore and understand the strategies and mechanisms of postclose value creation and to apply those principles to past acquisition situations as well as to ongoing corporate opportunities for worth creation.

I

SETTING THE
STAGE FOR
ACQUISITION-VALUE
DEVELOPMENT

1

Fact: Most Mergers Don't Work

This book was written to help parties involved in a merger ensure that their deal succeeds.

Most Deals Don't Work

Growing evidence suggests that many acquisitions *have not worked*. Academic researchers, management consultants, merger statistic reporting organizations, business writers, and securities analysts have all, from time to time, attempted to gauge the success (or failure) of a subject acquirer's acquisition attempts. The range of measures used has been as diverse as the evaluators. The list includes the speed at which investor's equity stake is paid back, the level of the acquisition price-to-earnings (PTE) ratio relative to historical norms, and the precedent established by other deals—financial returns to the acquirer's shareholders, appreciation of the acquiring corporation's market value, and the continuity of the relationship between acquirer and acquiree—but on one point these analyses tend to arrive at the same overall conclusion: *the majority of mergers don't work when objectively assessed in future years.* One study conducted in the mid-1980s indicated that two-thirds of all mergers examined failed to earn as much as commercial bank certificates of deposit (CDs). Other studies have found that one-third or more of all acquisitions eventually become undone.

McKinsey & Co.'s Analyses

The management consulting organization of McKinsey & Co. has been a pacesetter in analyzing acquisition performance. In November 1984, during the early stages of the 1980s merger boom, *Fortune's* Myron Magnet described the dilemma of acquisition underperformance as discovered by McKinsey consultants:

> A pioneering study by the consulting firm [McKinsey] shows that over two-thirds of the corporate diversification programs it examined never earned as much as the acquirer would have by investing the money in, say, certificates of deposit issued by a bank.[1]

Corporate acquisitions involve considerably greater risk than savings instruments issued by major financial institutions, and the offset to greater risk is supposed to be greater financial return—something that did not occur in these transactions. Another McKinsey & Co. staff study[2] examined 116 U.K. and U.S. acquisitions. In this analysis, the authors concluded that 61 percent of transactions examined failed to achieve a return equal to or exceeding the "cost of capital... on the funds invested in the program." The 61 percent statistic approaches the two-thirds figure cited in the earlier McKinsey analysis.

Acquisition Break-ups

Yet another way to gauge deal success is to measure how long it takes before the merger "marriage" ends in a separation or divorce.

[1]Myron Magnet, "Acquiring without Smothering," *Fortune* (November 12, 1984):22–28.
[2]Stephen C. Coley and Sigurd E. Reinton, " The Hint for Value," *The McKinsey Quarterly (Spring 1988): 29–34.*

In 1985 W. T. Grimm & Co., the Chicago-based acquisition statistical firm, estimated that one out of three merger marriages eventually comes unwound.[3] Some other merger scene observers have found even higher figures. In an examination of thirty-three U.S. corporate acquistion programs over the period from 1950 through 1980, Michael E. Porter concluded that more than half of the acquirers examined—53 percent—unloaded their acquisitions over that period.[4] This tendency to dispose of the deal if it is perceived as not working is supported by statistics showing a surge in corporate divestments as the 1980s merger boom progressed. Figure 1.1 shows that annual divestments by U.S.

[3] Magnet, 22.
[4] Michael E. Porter, "The State of Strategic Thinking," *The Economist* (May 23, 1987): 17–22.

Figure 1.1.   U.S. Divestiture Patterns 1982–1989

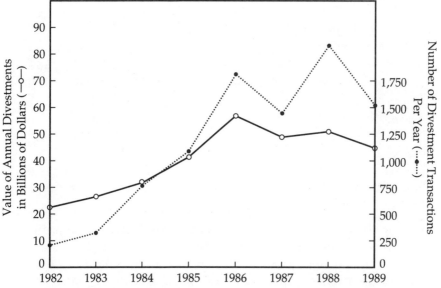

SOURCE: M&A Database, ADP/MLR, *Mergers & Acquisitions* (May–June 1990): 85.

publicly traded companies tripled from 1982 to 1986. Over that same period the value of divestments increased from $8.3 billion to $72.4 billion—more than eight times the 1982 reported amount.

Implications for the Merger Marketplace

The implications of these analyses of shattered merger "marriages" are significant for deals completed over the active merger boom period of the 1980s.

Either a modest percentage of "broken relationships" or a small base of completed deals over the 1982–90 period would mean modest financial consequences, as few deals would be expected to collapse in later years.

But instead, the opposite is now at hand: a huge base of recently completed transactions and stunning statistics on merger break-ups—regardless of whether the W. T. Grimm or the Porter estimations are used. Losses, even significant losses, are imminent. The merger boom that began in 1982 and peaked in mid-1989 was an unprecedented period of acquisition fervor. Even if acquisition failures remain at lower historical trend levels, potential dollar losses could be staggering because of a large transaction base.

Historical failure rates, moreover, may understate the loss potential for a sizable segment of the 1980s deals—the leveraged buyouts closed after the October 1987 crash. The combination of too many pursuers, too few quality acquisitions, bid prices that are too high, and too much debt for the acquired company to sustain may mean a high level of disappointing transactions.

The aftermath of the acquisition excess of the 1980s is felt first and most deeply, however, by individuals with vested interest in the transaction's completion:

- *By the lender*   who may face as yet undiscovered (or undisclosed) losses buried in his LBO loan portfolio. That lender must first diagnose the source of the possible LBO exposure early enough to be able to take effective corrective action.

- *By the prospective seller*   who wonders whether the passing of the boom merger cycle means that he has missed a one-time opportunity to sell his company at an attractive price.
- *By the limited portfolio LBO investor*   who wonders whether his prize deal can survive and thrive despite the alarming statistical data pointing in a different direction. In some instances, these are otherwise savvy businessmen who have invested both dollars and reputations.
- *By the long-term acquirer*   which refers to the continuing marketplace participant, and not just the one-time participant in the 1980s merger boom, who knows that high-leverage transactions are no longer considered magical but that leverage remains an important part of the acquisition environment of the 1990s. How should acquirers best pursue acquisition opportunities in the future months?
- *By the transaction intermediary*   whose financial lifeblood consists of the fees from completed transactions. True, a wave of divestitures creates additional fees for some. But a divestment is a one-way street with no follow-on revenue. While a single acquisition may spawn a whole series of related transactions, a divestment often signals the end of the line.

The "bad" news is that it is reasonable to anticipate a significant increase in acquisition failures measured on a total dollar basis as well as on a percentage basis. At first, second, and third look, these indications of merger disappointments are not positive to those hoping for acquisition success. But not all of the implications are adverse—if increased emphasis and attention on post-deal operations improvement of the involved companies is seen as a positive.

The "good" news, then, may be that intensified analysis of the causes and consequences of acquisition failure has produced knowledge about what can be done to make acquisitions *succeed*. This knowledge has been translated into new tools and techniques which may be applied to increase the chances for success of *all* acquisitions and in all stages of the acquisition, including the prospective bid, the transaction that closed a few months ago, and the deals that closed a few years ago but that can still be salvaged.

Acquisition-Market Participants and Uses and Users of This Book

Acquisition-market participants—acquirers, lenders and advisors—seek a better way to evaluate potential deal opportunities. These transaction intermediaries understand that a successfully completed transaction is different from a successful acquisition and guide their clients based on that understanding. Acquisition market participants entering the 1990s have recently experienced a period of ultraleveraged deal making and want to know how *continuing* acquisition success can be achieved in debt-financed transactions.

This book seeks to assist a broad range of users and uses:

- *Bidders*—prospective corporate acquirers and investor groups—can learn how to replace static candidate pricing approaches with a more practical and flexible approach that centers on the two commonsense questions that every acquirer faces in practically every deal: "What is the company worth?" and "What will it take to acquire it?"

- *Due-diligence investigators* can learn the advantages of beginning their postacquisition value-creation activity well before the close.

- *Acquirers and their senior lenders* can use the systematic programs described in this book to create postacquisition value that can service the debt undertaken to acquire the target company.

- *Senior and mezzanine lenders* can use the diagnostic and action-oriented strategies presented here to develop operations-based early warning indicators that distinguish the acquiree with resolvable problems from companies with problems that cannot be fixed.

- *Operating managers* can learn to apply some of the performance-enhancing characteristics of LBOs to their own daily businesses without changing ownership and without unbalancing their company's balance sheet.

Defining Acquisition Success: What Does It Mean?

Transaction Success versus Acquisition Success

Definitions of *acquisition success* tend to involve a high degree of subjective judgment. One company's acquisition disaster, after all, may be another's triumph. Consider a Korean heavy equipment manufacturer that wants to be viewed by potential customers and suppliers as a new global player. The Asian company acquires an American distributor at a price that U.S. competitors consider ridiculously high. The Korean manufacturer, however, sees this acquisition in a different light. Because U.S. market entry is a prerequisite to competing in the world market, it evaluates the high cost of purchasing the distributorship against the possible opportunity to make global profits and not profits solely in North America.

Given these varying interpretations of success, however, it is often easier to define what acquisition success does *not* mean. Acquisition success does not mean transaction success. The acquirer, lender, or advisor that develops its ongoing acquisition program with these differences in mind can avoid disappointments.

Transaction Success

Transaction success is event based: no deal, no yield. To consummate the transaction successfully, the investor closes the deal promptly, with a minimum of required follow-up, and at realistic terms given prevailing market conditions. Different parties have differing perspectives about and interests in the transaction, but buyer, seller, and intermediary share one interest—ensuring that a successful and swift completion of the transaction results.

- *Acquiring company chief executives* want to enhance their standing as business leaders.
- *Sellers* want to optimize their return—to sustain the momentum and continue progress to date, but not so fast that actions are regretted later.
- *Lenders* seek a high-yield home for sizable amounts of lendable bank or institutional funds. An appealing LBO proposition, financed largely by bank debt, offers bankers an opportunity to earn fees, interest, and perhaps even an equity kicker.
- *Deal intermediaries* seek performance fees or payment based on work hours for roles such as matchmaker, evaluator, legal advisor, or market investigator.

Acquisition Success

Acquisition success is a performance-based concept: it depends on how quickly and effectively the acquiree becomes integrated with its new parent. This integration is financial or operational or both, depending on the nature of the new business combination and objectives of participants:

- If the acquirer is a passive investor and the acquiree a portfolio investment, then the postacquisition integration extends only to finances.
- If the two firms are similar or complementary, the postacquisition integration involves both operations and finances. Collections, joint procurement, banking relationships, plants and their workers, salespersons, and products—all are possible combination opportunities for the new enterprise.

Integration is mere activity unless focused on a goal. One goal is to create sufficient value in the new enterprise to cover the *acquisition purchase premium*—that is, the difference between the price paid and the preacquisition value. Acquisitions almost always sell for somewhat more than the prevailing market value of the target company before acquisition pursuit itself boosted prices. The historical pattern of purchase premiums for acquisitions of publicly traded target companies is shown in Table 1.1.

High-leverage transactions brought the performance imperative out of hiding. An acquisition financed substantially with equity lacks the urgency of the same deal financed with debt. The underperformance of a new equity-financed acquisition is likely to show up only on paper in the combined companies' earnings-per-share (EPS) results. If that same acquisition is debt financed, however, then underperformance may mark the first step toward insolvency. If the acquired company's subpar results mean that principal and interest payments are missed, the acquiring company risks default on its acquisition debt.

Acquisition success can even occur without a transaction. If the acquirer has decided to walk away from a bidding race that has unreasonably inflated prices, then future losses probably have been avoided.

Hiding the Evidence

New methods for measuring acquisition success are emerging, but until they are adopted, acquisition success will be defined

Table 1.1.   Purchase Premiums Paid Over Market
Value, 1982–89

Year	Average Percentage	Number of Transactions
1982	47.4%	176
1983	37.7	168
1984	37.9	199
1985	37.1	331
1986	38.2	333
1987	38.3	237
1988	41.9	410
1989	41.0	303

SOURCE: *Mergerstat Review*

NOTE: Premium calculations and transactions are for publicly traded companies. Purchase premiums are based on stock prices five days before an acquisition announcement.

subjectively. The acquiring company CEO still enjoys wide latitude in shaping perceptions about the success of acquisitions and continues to avoid having all but the most conspicuous acquisition flops labeled failures. Unless the deal unravels almost immediately following the close, underperforming acquisitions usually can be camouflaged.

One tactic is for the acquiring company chief executive officer to split the operations and assets of the problem investment, scattering staff and resources among several of his other separate business units (SBUs), and rendering postacquisition performance assessments virtually impossible. Another tactic is to twist the logic of shareholder-value creation and thereby deflect attention away from money-losing acquisitions. The person questioning the wisdom of the acquisition or its price finds himself characterized by the CEO as an opponent of progress and new shareholder-value creation, who "obviously doesn't recognize the long-term benefits to shareholders that we expect from this acquisition."

Further Evolution of Acquisition Performance Measures

The possible definitions for acquisition success are as numerous and as diverse as the perspectives of acquisition parties:

- *The social activist* measures acquisition success in people terms—that is, based on the severity and length of trauma endured by employees who are displaced as a direct consequence of the merger.
- *The credit agency budget analyst* considers the financial resiliency of the acquirer and acquiree. By combining, have the two companies increased or decreased their ability to withstand unexpected shocks?
- *The acquiring company's attorney* concentrates on overcoming possible antitrust and fair-trade obstacles so that no court challenges interfere with the deal.

Gradually, acquisition measures for performance have evolved from the earnings-per-share dilution concerns of the 1960s and toward statistical comparatives.

The 1960s and 1970s: Equity Purchases

The acquisition world was simpler in the 1960s, when players were fewer and the rules of the game seemed to change less frequently. In 1969 an acquiring company's board of directors usually limited its questions concerning completed deals to earnings-per-share dilution concerns—if indeed, it raised any questions at all. Lenders to the acquirer were concerned about the possible effect of hemorrhaging operations on their client and the strain added by term debt used for interim acquisition financing.

Acquisition financing was ultimately supported by the acquirer's balance sheet and income statement, which meant that acquiring firms of this era were usually large, publicly traded concerns. The acquirer's access to public capital usually provided lenders with some assurance of additional protection if the acquisition or its parent later experienced difficulties. Moreover, Wall Street dictated how acquisition performance would be measured. To support a growth stock image—and the accompanying price-to-earnings multiple—the acquirer needed to display a consistent pattern of quarterly earnings per share growth.

The 1980s: Acquisition Debt, Shareholder-Value Creation, and Management Agency

When the 1980s arrived, the number and nature of acquisition market participants changed, as did the marketplace itself. Some saw the need for new measures that would keep pace with new realities. The key acquisition concern moved away from whether the acquiring firm's earnings per share would increase or decline in the months following the acquisition. Many of these new-era acquirers were private companies, and thus the public firm contest of EPS growth was avoided. No longer did these acquirers need to have a billion dollars in

sales and be publicly traded to complete their deals. Encouraged by the successful experiments with ultraleverage by some
of the early LBO acquirers, some mid-range and marginally
capitalized acquisition groups eagerly attempted to enter the
LBO game as the 1980s boom progressed. For some of these
firms, the emergence of the LBO vehicle meant that their buying group could, in effect, attempt to finance their deal based
largely on the current strength and future potential of the *acquired company's* operations and balance sheet.

Not surprisingly, the availability of seemingly unlimited
credit tends to boost the prices paid for hotly pursued acquisition targets in desirable fields. Thus, as the 1980s merger boom
began to show its age, concerns began to shift to the issue of
repayment—that is, how and from what sources the mountain
of acquisition debt taken on by the investor group to complete
the deal and then designated to the acquiree would be repaid.

Two additional issues of importance also emerged in this
period. Shareholder-value creation and management agency
issues accelerated the movement toward statistical measures
based on the returns actually received by the owners of the
business.

The key thrust of the shareholder-value issue is that the primary purpose of the corporation—and by inference, the mandate for corporate management—is to optimize the long-term
wealth position of company shareholders. The equity investors
in the acquiring company are the owners of the company. They
are the ones who provide captial to operate, who absorb the
risk of operations. If it is assumed that rewards are, or should
be, commeasurable with risk, these are the individuals who
logically should benefit first from acquisition success.

But the idea of "optimizing shareholder value" lends itself
to broad interpretation. This, in turn, means a broad range of
perspectives when applied to deals.

"Creating value for our shareholders" was the sole rationale for many acquisitions in the 1970s. Its goal of generating
long-term wealth, after all, was highly subjective and open to
different interpretations.

The concept of "long-term," for example, was particularly
subject to differing interpretation. To a paper company exec-

utive concerned with the availability of timber, the time perspective may be ten to twenty years. For the minicomputer software producer, by comparison, the time spectrum may be twelve to eighteen *months.*

When the LBO era arrived, the concept of *long-term* almost immediately became compressed. The faster the acquirer moved, he reasoned, the more likely that hidden values could result in a fast turn of his money. Some raiders attempted to transform themselves into protectors of individual shareholder rights, in order to shorten *their* perspective of time, as well. Spurred by T. Boone Pickens and other self-appointed protectors of owners' interests, shareholders in some acquisition-target companies began asking public company shareholders, in effect, instead of waiting for long-term wealth *someday*, why not get it *today*?

If the effects of this cheerleading had ended here, perhaps no secondary effects would have resulted. But a shareholder is a shareholder, and those putting up the money for the acquiring investor groups were likely to want to have part of the action, as well. It was only a matter of time.

Some shareholders in acquiring companies—the purchasing firms—soon began to wonder about their return from the acquisition movement, as well. By the mid 1980s, when the questions first arose, LBOs were in full swing, and some acquiring company shareholders thought that only a small number of parties were getting rich from the acquirer company's actions— and that the enriched group didn't include them.

A second development which contributed to changing the course of acquisition success definition was the concept of management agency. One observer refers to the agency issue as involving the actions and motivations of company executives who have negligible or no ownership interests in the companies they manage.

In theory managers *should* act to optimize owners'—that is, the shareholders'—wealth position, as the *agents* for those owners. But this ideal is sometimes hard to achieve. Sometimes the agent-managers will act instead to fortify their own power positions, and be tentative in responding to business opportunities.

The agent-manager has only position, salary, and bonus to protect. Not suprisingly, protecting these may become the executive's overriding concern.[5]

In an active acquisition program, the result can be stalemate, or worse. This agent-manager may not pursue business expansion or diversification opportunities with otherwise acceptable business risks for fear of making a mistake that could justify termination and loss of position and salary.

The arrival of the merger boom helped activate this issue, particularly at acquiring companies where shareholders asked "What's the payback for us?"

Acquisition Success Defined: Three Measures

Three widely accepted measures of acquisition success have emerged: total return to acquirer company shareholders, coverage of financial servicing, and coverage of acquisition value difference.

Total Return to Acquirer-Company Shareholders

To determine the total return to the acquiring company shareholders, the prior acquisition or acquisitions are evaluated as if they were passive investments of equivalent risk and payback period, made by the acquired company management. To estimate this equivalent return, financial proceeds to acquirer company shareholders made by the acquirer group are calculated. For purposes of the discussion that follows, *"total return"* refers to after-tax distributions actually received by shareholders, plus actual or potential appreciation of the actual or presumed market value of acquiring company shareholders' equity. All calculations in this exercise should exclude nonrecurring or extraordinary items.

"Total return," as calculated in this fashion, can then be compared with applicable alternative investments for which, in the-

---

[5] Professor Michael Jensen of Harvard Business School has been prominent in the development of the concept of the agent-manager and its implications. See his "Eclipse of the Public Corporation," *Harvard Business Review* (September–October 1989): 61–74.

Table 1.2.   Total Return to Acquirer Shareholders: One Approach

Step 1:	Select the value analysis period.
Step 2:	Estimate net after-tax proceeds from distributions actually received by shareholders.
Step 3:	Estimate actual or potential increase in market value. Add steps 2 and 3 (Net after-tax proceeds and increase in market value), which become total return to acquirer company shareholders from acquisition or acquisitions.
Step 4:	Calculate investment.
Step 5:	Determine net return (as a dollar figure or ratio).
Step 6 (optional):	Compare return with investment alternatives assumed to be available to acquirer shareholders.

SOURCE: The sequence represents a combination of several approaches. The McKinsey & Co. analysis noted earlier in this chapter is recognized as encompassing one of the important approaches in this area.

ory, it is assumed the acquiring company shareholders could have made instead (see Table 1.2).

If the term and relative risk are similar, shareholders in the acquiring company and others now have one basis for gauging the wisdom of acquiring company management's acquisition moves: Did they make money for us, or not?

Admittedly, the exercise is illustrative in some instances. Although a shareholder in an acquisition-active public firm has ample opportunities to choose investment alternatives, the capital source to a small, closely held investment group has less latitude. Nonetheless, a capital investment decision was made at some point in time, and even the private acquisition company can be assumed to have had a choice at some point in the past. Steps in the development of such a comparison follow:

Step 1:   Select the Value-Analysis Period

The time period selected for evaluating the acquisition or acquisitions should exclude the immediate postacquisition period, which is a transition stage that allows the new company to adjust to the change in ownership. The analysis period should be long enough to provide an accurate gauge of ongoing performance. We recommend an analysis period covering the acquiree's first six years following the close but excluding the first year.

Step 2:   Estimate Dollar Returns—
Distributions

One source of the returns received by shareholders of the acquiring firm is distributions—the after-tax effect of cash dividends and other applicable disbursements declared and paid to shareholders of the acquiring company:

1. Sum applicable distributions. Credit nonapplicable distributions, such as returns of capital, against investment.
2. Calculate the after-tax effect of the applicable distributions.
3. Multiply the amounts in 1 and 2 by a factor representing the portion of the net distributions attributed to the acquisition or acquisitions.

Calculating the ratio for item 3 may be problematic in high-leverage acquisitions where the debt-servicing schedule is usually skewed toward the early years of the transaction so that lenders can be paid off quickly. Most or all of the cash flow generated by the acquiree in the initial years following an acquisition close may flow to lenders and not owners. If distributions to shareholders are calculated for the first three to five years, they may be zero, but that number would not depict the underlying worth of the business. We suggest adjusting the debt load of LBO acquirees back to preacquisition levels for analysis purposes, and assuming prevailing interest rates for the analysis period. Assume that ten-year financing fully amortizes principal over that period.

Step 3:   Estimate Returns—Appreciation
in Market Value

The second element in the total-return formula is market-value appreciation of the shareholders' equity interest, calculated in either of two ways—as stand-alone market-value appreciation, or as the analyzed portion of the acquirers' total market-value appreciation.

The stand-alone market-value appreciation is made on the basis of market-value appreciation of the specific acquisition or acquisitions being examined. Because most of these acquirees are private, this approach uses public-market comparables in order to estimate the unit's "if public" value.

Estimating returns based on the analyzed portion of acquirer's total market-value appreciation basis may be more accurate than the stand-alone approach, particularly if the parent–operating company regularly makes acquisitions as part of its corporate growth strategy. Philip Morris, the tobacco company, has made acquisitions in beer (Miller), soft drinks (Seven-Up), and foods (General Foods and Kraft) (see Figure 1.2). Instead of untangling the individual returns from various acquirees—a formidable if not impossible task—the overall market-value appreciation for the parent company and all subsidiaries and divisions is first calculated. Then the market-value appreciation effects due to ongoing operations are calculated and that number is subtracted from the previous total. The result provides a usable estimate for the portion of market-value appreciation developed from acquisitions. The results for applicable distributions and market-value appreciation are summed, representing the gross total dollar return for the acquisition under consideration.

Step 4:   Calculate Investment

Calculating equity capital requires determining the amounts invested originally to acquire the acquiree. The investment amount also includes the present value of any additions to net working capital (current assets minus current liabilities) or permanent fixed investment made since the company was acquired.

Step 5:   Determine Net Return
to Acquirer-Company Shareholders

Estimating distributions and appreciation in market value (steps 2 and 3) results in the total return that is realized by

Figure 1.2. Acquisition Performance Evaluation on a Total Company Basis: The Example of Phillip Morris Companies. For an active acquirer with a series of past and prospective deals, the total acquiring-company's return to shareholders may be the only means of assessing acquisition-program success.

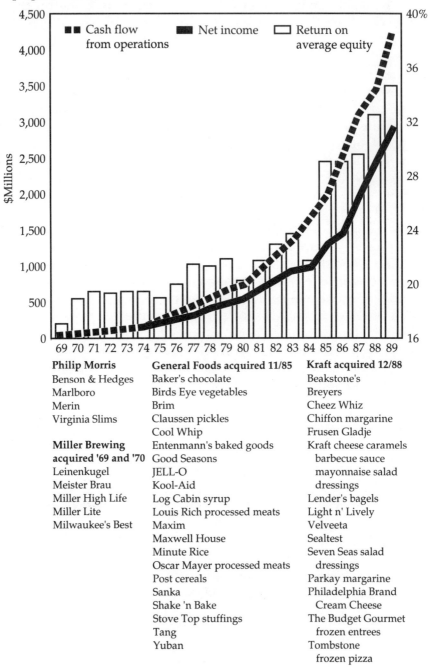

Philip Morris	General Foods acquired 11/85	Kraft acquired 12/88
Benson & Hedges	Baker's chocolate	Beakstone's
Marlboro	Birds Eye vegetables	Breyers
Merin	Brim	Cheez Whiz
Virginia Slims	Claussen pickles	Chiffon margarine
	Cool Whip	Frusen Gladje
Miller Brewing	Entenmann's baked goods	Kraft cheese caramels
acquired '69 and '70	Good Seasons	barbecue sauce
Leinenkugel	JELL-O	mayonnaise salad
Meister Brau	Kool-Aid	dressings
Miller High Life	Log Cabin syrup	Lender's bagels
Miller Lite	Louis Rich processed meats	Light n' Lively
Milwaukee's Best	Maxim	Velveeta
	Maxwell House	Sealtest
	Minute Rice	Seven Seas salad
	Oscar Mayer processed meats	dressings
	Post cereals	Parkay margarine
	Sanka	Philadelphia Brand
	Shake 'n Bake	Cream Cheese
	Stove Top stuffings	The Budget Gourmet
	Tang	frozen entrees
	Yuban	Tombstone
		frozen pizza

SOURCE: *Business Week* (April 2, 1990): 101.

the acquiring company's shareholders, or the *gross dollar return*. Equity capital—that is, investment (step 4)—represents the concluding element in developing *net return to shareholders*:

- *Net return to shareholders, expressed as a dollar amount:* To calculate the net as a sum, subtract investment (step 4) from the gross dollar return, which results in the *net dollar return measure.*

- *Net return to shareholders, expressed as a ratio:* To produce a ratio for performance measurement purposes, use investment as the numerator of that ratio and gross total dollar return to shareholders as the denominator.

Step 6 (Optional): Compare Return with Investment Alternatives

An optional step is to compare this total return with other investments which acquirer-group or company shareholders could theoretically have made. Comparing acquiring company management's acquisition performance to alternative investments of comparable term, risk, and appreciation potential may provide additional insights into the acquisition performance of management.

Instead of subjective observations about deal success developed by corporate public relations, providers of capital face an opportunity to judge deal consequences for themselves.

Care must be taken by the evaluator to come as close as possible to equivalent timing and risk in selecting the passive instrument used for comparison purposes. But since business acquisitions normally carry greater risk than passive investments, comparison may by necessity have to be with an investment alternative of *lesser* risk. In such an instance, the success (or lack of success) of the acquirer's acquisition program should be judged by the size of the dollar or ratio return difference. The ideal comparable is a stock or composite with high relative-earnings potential. A debt issue is less attractive for comparison purposes because of the risk and value-appreciation differences between debt and equities.

Coverage of Financial Servicing

A potential supplemental measure of acquisition performance, suitable for some LBO performance evaluations, is assessing how well the acquirer covers its financial-servicing obligation. Most LBOs are structured so that the maximum amount of acquisition debt is repaid to lenders virtually as fast as the acquiree generates enough cash. This focus on early debt repayment is a characteristic of high-leverage-financed acquisitions and a key disciplining attribute cited by LBO supporters. That repayment goal also means that—for purposes of assessing the success or failure of the acquisition, at least—debt servicing becomes the ultimate performance measure. The reasoning: If the company's debt obligations cannot be met, then nothing else matters, because lender will close the company down and liquidate. But an acquired company that is meeting or can meet its servicing obligations with some margin for contingencies may indicate a probable acquisition "success"—that is, an acquisition well on its way towards putting extra effort and capital into achieving market advantage—*thriving*, not just surviving.

As an acquisition-performance measure, debt servicing as described here should be used with caution. Servicing levels and repayment terms of the specific acquisition and related financing hardly represent a constant. For debt repayment to be used as a measure of acquisition success, repayment must be achievable. In one transaction, the debt-to-equity percentage and terms allow for acquisition debt to be serviced even if plan performance is only 80 percent achieved.

But what if acquisition debt starts off as excessive, or if terms immediately cause the acquired firm to be hard pressed from the beginning of the acquisition period? This deal and acquiree may be equivalent in all ways, yet debt repayment prospects are slim to nil.

The evaluator also must understand *how* debt-servicing requirements are met. Simply generating enough cash flow does not automatically indicate that no problems exist. Consider the acquiree that meets several scheduled acquisition debt payments with no visible difficulties—with funds for the first payment totally from the business, for the next payment from the sale of some unused property, and for the third payment from the sale of part of the acquiree's delivery fleet. Even though its debt-service payments are being met, this acquired company is going through a staged liquidation. An acquiree management that sells off needed assets to conduct future business or loses critical people resources due to a shortage of funds faces future problems even though everything appears to be in order today.

Coverage of Value Difference

The value difference is the gap between what the acquirer pays for the company and what that company is worth, calculated on a conservative basis. As with debt servicing as a supplemental performance measure, value-difference coverage is a matter of absolutes: either the acquirer develops additional sources of corporate value and makes up the gap—and succeeds—or it does not. (Value difference and related concepts such as operations valuation and financial market valuation are covered at greater length in Chapters 2, 3, and 4. This chapter examines value difference only as a possible acquisition-performance measure.)

As the Boom Wanes

The explosion of acquisition activity in the 1980s means that even a moderate failure rate, if applied to that sizable base, will result in significant losses to investors and others. The large dollar volume of acquisition transactions from the 1982–89 expansion period and, in particular, the possibility of a particularly high failure percentage for high-leverage transactions closed in the latter stages of the 1980s boom present the prospects of a potentially alarming loss period, probably occurring in the early 1990s. Despite the dwindling number of quality acquisition candidates, acquisition purchase premiums remained robust throughout the 1982–89 period: in 1988–89 LBOs represented about 27 percent of the total dollar volume of merger activity.

The 1980s Merger Surge

The storied late 1960s conglomeration activity of James Ling, Harold Geneen, and Royal Little pales in comparison to the volume generated in the 1980s. As Figure 1.3 shows, transaction dollar values in 1984 approach $26 billion per year, which eclipses comparable statistics from other merger cycles. The

Figure 1.3.   Constant-Dollar Volume of Manufacturing and Mineral Company Acquisitions, 1895–1985

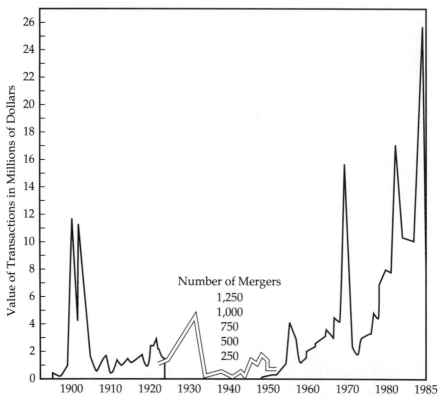

SOURCE: F. M. Scherer, "Takeovers' Present and Future Dangers," *Brookings Review* (Winter–Spring 1986): 16; F. M. Scherer, *Industrial Market Structure and Economic Performance*, 2nd ed.(Boston: Houghton Mifflin, 1980), 120; extended using Federal Trade Commission and W. T. Grimm Co. data.

NOTE: Data on the value of manufacturing and mineral company acquisitions are not available for the years 1921–1947. The white line reflects the number of acquisitions in those years. Amounts have been adjusted for 1972 constant dollars.

Table 1.3. Selected Acquisition Statistics, 1980–89

Year	Number of Deals	Dollar-Value Transactions ($ billions)	Indicated Average Purchase Premium (percentage)
1980	1,588	$ 34.8	49.9%
1982	2,298	60.7	47.4
1985	3,486	146	37.1
1987	4,015	178.3	38.3
1989	3,412	230.7	41

SOURCE: M&A Database, ADP/MLR, *Mergerstat*

NOTE: Premium calculations and transactions are for publicly traded companies. Purchase premiums are based on stock price five days before an acquisition announcement. The average acquisition premium is based on a smaller number of transactions, as shown in Table 1.1.

figure also shows that the 1980s surge gained much of its momentum during the mid-1970s. As Table 1.3 indicates, selected statistics from the 1982–89 expansion reveal that the dollar value of annual transactions in 1989 exceeded $200 billion dollars. Even when adjusted back to 1972 dollar terms, this amount is several times the peak value shown in Figure 1.3.

The Late-Phase LBO Question

Although the possibility of loss exists with any business combination, some transactions present a great risk of collapse during the first half of the 1990s. We refer to these transactions as late-phase LBOs—the leveraged buyouts that closed in 1988 and 1989 after and despite the warning signal provided by the October 1987 U.S. stock market crash.

1988–89: The Boom Gets a Second Wind

During the months following the record decline in the Dow-Jones industrial average the U.S. acquisition market rebounded within weeks, roughly in step with the U.S. securities markets. In part, this fast rebound was a factor in rekindling acquisition enthusiasm as the decade of the 1980s came to a close. New investor groups saw the bounce, judged that merger market-place conditions were stabilized, and jumped in. Foreign acquirers and small investor groups that missed all or most of the 1982–86 surge also saw an opportunity to enter; concern about higher prices was neutralized for some by their stated objective of making long-term investments in the United States. In some instances the impetus came from new partners of earlier LBO leader firms. A new generation of investors became anxious to make their own names and fortunes and saw their opportunity to achieve their own profits.

When the acquisition cycle reached the 1980s, however, observers warned of the risks posed by excessive corporate debt on practically a daily basis. Nevertheless, indications of constraint were few and far between. As Table 1.3 shows, overall acquisition premiums remained robust after 1987, even though the major portion of the 1980s boom had already passed. Table 1.4 and Table 1.5 show that the dollar value of LBOs over the two-year 1988–89 period amounted to $108 billion, which comes close to the $120 billion total for the *four* previous years.

Table 1.4.   Leveraged Buyouts from 1984–87 Compared to 1988–89

Year	Number of Transactions	Dollar Value Transactions ($ billions)	Average Value per Transaction ($ millions)
1984	254	$ 18.7	$ 73.6
1985	255	19.7	77.3
1986	337	45.2	134.1
1987	279	36.2	129.7
Subtotal 1984–87	1,125	119.8	106.5
1988	377	46.6	123.6
1989	338	61.6	182.2
Subtotal 1988–89	715	108.2	151.3
Total 1984–89	1,840	228	123.9

SOURCE: M&A Database, ADP/ MLR, Mergerstat, *Mergers & Acquisitions* (May–June 1990): 71.

Table 1.5.   Leveraged Buyouts Compared to Total Acquisitions, 1988–89

	1988	1989	1988 and 1989 Combined
Total number of mergers	4,001	3,412	7,413
Number of LBOs	377	338	715
LBO as percentage	9.4%	9.9%	9.6%
Total value of mergers ($ billion)	$236.4	$230.7	$467.1
Value of LBOs ($ billion)	$ 46.6	$ 61.6	$108.2
LBO as percentage	19.5%	26.7%	23.2%

SOURCE: M&A Database, ADP/ MLR, Mergerstat

Unrelated Diversification

As the merger expansion period began its decline, acquirers began to pursue unrelated deals—that is, acquisitions in fields and industries in which they had limited, if any, hands-on knowledge. This tendency toward diversification into unrelated areas increases as the merger cycle ages, as quality related-industry candidates become scarce. Whenever it occurs, unrelated diversification ends with predictable disappointment. Coley-Reinton of McKinsey & Co. have concluded that large, comparable-size acquisition transactions between related parties were twice as likely to succeed as were transactions between unrelated parties.

Possible Outcomes

Two plausible outcomes for late-stage LBOs are depicted in Table 1.6. The first alternative assumes a very low failure rate of about 5 percent, applied against a dollar base of $108.2 billion. This is below the percentage level of high-yield unsecured ("junk") bonds that are in jeopardy. Such a percentage also assumes that managers of LBOs are able to take extraordinary steps to improve profitability and cash flow from operations after the acquisition. If the 5 percent level is maintained throughout the first half of the 1990s, losses will amount to about $5.4 billion.

Table 1.6.   Two Alternative Failure Scenarios for Late-Phase LBOs, 1988–89

	Dollar Value* ($ billion)	Percentage of Failure	Indicated Loss ($ billion)	Comments
Low historical	$108.2	5%	$5.4	Assumes that increased leverage doesn't increase failure rate
Elevated	108.2	20	21.6	Percentage is less than one-half Porter unravel level or 1988 McKinsey study of underperformance

*Sum of 1988 and 1989 amounts (Table 1.4).

The elevated scenario in the table assumes a 20 percent loss on the total dollar volume of the 1988–89 deals, resulting in a loss of $21.6 billion. The percentage may seem high, and the possibility of total loss on a transaction may seem remote, but 20 percent is less than half the failure rate cited by some researchers and largely excludes the effect of ultrahigh leverage.

The Participants' Perspectives

To the target company, merger success may mean that no deal takes place—wishful thinking in an acquisition environment in which almost any public company can be acquired by another with necessary persistance and resources. Moreover, the financial cost of rebuffing an unwanted suitor may be worse than the acquisition, as Harcourt Brace Jovanovich discovered while parrying Robert Maxwell's acquisition attempts. To satisfy its desire to remain independent at almost any cost, HBJ absorbed its own mountain of debt rather than a raider's, spun into decline, and was forced to divest several profitable operations.

Merger success has significant implications for *all* parties involved in acquisition transactions—target companies,

corporate managements, dealmakers, and transaction intermediaries. Within their own organizations, investment and
merchant bankers, deal intermediaries, and corporate acquisition advisors are likely to view acquisition success in terms
of fees generated. As a saying goes, the fastest way to create a small mergers and acquisitions group is to start with
a large m&a organization and then fail to achieve quota
for two quarters. Corrective action tends to be swift and
unambiguous.

The Principals

The transaction principals are the acquirer and the acquiree,
and their level of activity tends to be influenced by a number of factors, including perception of prevailing deal quality,
other companies' acquisition activities, and acquisition market
liquidity.

Quality, as used here, is the acquiring company's chief executive officer's or acquisitions officer's sense of potential acquisition candidates still available to be acquired. At some point in
every acquisition expansion cycle, deals are so totally undistin-
guished that the acquirer decides to withdraw from the marketplace. The challenge is in the timing—determining *when* to
act. When one CEO decides to switch from purchase mode to
a wait mode or a divest mode, others are probably doing the
same. *Other companies' acquisition activities*, especially in an flat
to up acquisitions market, may encourage action by managers
and directors that admire those acquirers.

If investable funds are readily available, this *liquidity* may
inspire an active acquisition program, particularly if those
funds do not show directly on the principal company's balance sheet. Borrowing to finance the major portion of an
acquisition carries a particular appeal—one called "other peo-
ples' money" by some. Funds eventually must be repaid,
but these are funds that the principal previously neither controlled nor used. For some, ample availability of new funds
may be the difference between acquisition-market activity
and inaction. Consider the situation brought to MetalliCo, a
hypothetical metalcutting LBO movement acquirer.

This firm owns a midsize machining center operation. Favorable contracts, tight expense controls, and skillful long-term financing policies have helped that business to survive and to turn a profit in an industry where many others lose money.

MetalliCo's chief executive and some expansion-hungry board members want to become an acquiring company. Despite this enthusiasm, that decision may lead not to riches, but to disappointment. Few of MetalliCo's capabilities are transferable to other companies in a way that can boost the operating and financial results of an acquiree. MetalliCo "doesn't bring anything to the party" in terms of partially paying for a target company through improved operations. This would-be acquirer may be well advised to cool down its merger enthusiasm.

The Transaction Intermediaries

The market reputation of intermediaries ultimately rests on their ability to assemble and direct the components of the deal. One or even two flopped deals can be blamed on rising interest rates or mismanagement in the acquiree, but beyond that some may fear that bad luck is contagious. Sellers look elsewhere, as do potential equity partners and lenders.

During the early years of the 1980s boom—from 1982 through 1985—some intermediaries found that they could complete one deal, jump to the next, then land in the next while never looking back. In terms of fee generation, the approach made sense. Why waste time with one almost-done deal, while there's another transaction waiting in line? The line became shorter in the boom's subsequent stages, however, until it eventually disappeared. Future success of completed acquisitions began to look less assured. As the acquisition cycle progressed, higher transaction prices and somewhat lower deal quality dictated closer involvement by the intermediary in the future of the deal *after* the close.

After the LBO movement had picked up steam—there is no threshold year, but we will use 1985 here—few high-leverage deals could be assured future success by simply paying down their LBO-incurred acquisition debt through the untapped resources of the acquiree. Additional sources of profits and value needed to be generated to fill the gap. Without a systematic approach for creating the additional sources of postacquisition cash flow and profits, the tendency is to grab for an instant solution—but there aren't any instant solutions, just expediencies. To support their merger marketplace standing and to avoid the negative consequences of a losing streak of deteriorating deals, intermediaries are beginning to search out structured approaches to successful postacquisition integration.

Merger Momentum in the 1990s: Where Next?

Despite the decelerating trend of merger momentum, acquisition interest remains high among several groups of current and prospective participants. Streamlined U.S. investment and merchant banks are competing in the newly globalized acquisition marketplace, operating corporations are taking a more active role as purchasers, lending to well-run acquirees continues to be a high priority for major commercial banks and other financing institutions, and deal finders and brokers are redoubling their efforts to unearth transactions that can be closed and financed quickly.

Increasing Asian Presence

The increasing globilization of the U.S. mergers and acquisitions marketplace is an unmistakable emerging factor of the 1990s, and much of that new investment impetus comes from Asia—specifically, from Japan. Foreign deals accounted for 343 U.S. transactions in 1989, valued at $51.2 billion, compared to 299 transactions valued at $50 billion for 1988. Britain led all foreign purchasers of American corporations in 1989 with 132 deals, but Japan's share is increasing: It acquired forty-one companies worth $9.3 billion in 1989. Assuming a supportive Tokyo stock market, the early 1990s should see a marked increase in the percentage of total U.S. transactions undertaken by Japanese trading houses and investment banking houses. There have been three major factors contributing to this development:

- *Minority investment* The acquisition approach of the Japanese in the latter half of the 1980s called for gradually increasing minority investments in major U.S. industries and companies.
- *Advantageous financing* Low interest rates helped to fuel the Japanese economic miracle, and the same advantage probably will be applied to the U.S. acquisition marketplace.
- *Politics* Economic power has been translated into lobbying influence in Washington, D.C., that overcomes obstacles to Japanese diversification programs before those obstacles become barriers.

Deal Origins: Swing Toward the Divestiture Side?

Most acquisitions that closed during the 1980s boom originated with a buyer group. Acquirer groups were eager for deals at their own bid-up prices. Transaction volume rose along with prices, and a boomish price-volume spiral was in place.

When acquisition volume plunged in the second half of 1989, however, so did transaction prices. This was not a temporary price break such as the period immediately following the 1987 crash, but represented a key turning point in the market. Although there are few indications that the overall acquisition period is over, evidence mounts that the acquisition environment of the early 1990s will be characterized by a growing importance for divestitures.

Buyers will need to carefully plan strategies for determining which acquisitions to proceed with today and which to defer until more advantageous market conditions. Sellers will need to prevent a rush to the market (and decreased sales proceeds) as the reality of reduced market prices becomes widely known. They need to devise portfolio strategy for all possible divestee candidates to determine which should be held and developed and which sold today as quickly as possible.

2

Six Foundations
for Acquisition Success

Many successful business combinations share similar characteristics and have taken similar approaches and steps to achieve
their success. They have recognized the critical difference between correct-*sounding* merger advice (such as "avoid over-
paying") and correct *guidance* ("create postacquisition value").
Most important, they have learned that acquisition success is
achieved one business combination at a time.

Although the prospects for acquisition success are sober-
ing, not all acquisitions fail. Acquisition success still can be
achieved.

Managers or advisors who know which steps must be
taken—and who have the persistence to see that those steps *are*
completed—still can make a significant difference in individual transactions. They need to understand what has worked—
and what has not worked—in past business combinations.
Six foundations for acquisition success are described in this
chapter—pricing and structure, timing, related acquisition emphasis, a tough-minded acquisition agenda, financial-progress
indicators and backup actions, and a supportive asset and divestment program (see Table 2.1).

Table 2.1.   Six Foundations for Acquisition Success

Pricing and Structure	Develop a bid valuation from the head and not from the heart.
	Develop a financial and operational structure that anticipates value and liquidity issues.
Timing	Adjust strategies and actions to be consistent with the merger cycle.
Related acquisition emphasis	Limit expansion to industries, processes, and markets in which acquirer expertise can be applied effectively.
A tough-minded postacquisition agenda	Isolate critical areas for improvement; fix these and leave other areas alone.
	Resolve to act and not simply analyze.
	Inflict pain today to ensure satisfaction tomorrow.
Financial progress indicators and backup actions	Monitor early measures of acquisition problems to deflect problems before they arise.
	Develop contingency measures to address unexpected problems.
	Revert to contingency actions if early indications show that the acquisition is floundering.
A supportive asset and divestment program	Develop effective asset and business sales programs.
	Use timely sales and divestments to sustain integration momentum.

Pricing and Structure

Pricing and structure refer to the amount paid for the acquisition and how that payment is structured to anticipate value and liquidity issues that may emerge.

Overpayment: Separating Apparent and Actual Issues

The principal problem for many struggling acquisitions may at first seem to be overpayment by the acquiring company. The word defies definition, however, particularly in a rigorous bidding contest. What does *overpayment* mean, after all, when the acquirer's bid price (and presumably, the assessment of target-company value) is sometimes adjusted upward two or three times over the course of the contest? Which of these values is the "right" one? From an acquisition success determination perspective, more meaningful than overpayment is the principle of value creation: the key issue evolves from the amount paid to whether the difference between payment amount and value of the target can be bridged by actions undertaken later. (The issue of corporate value is considered extensively in Chapter 3. The discussion here is limited to the issue of overpayment prompted by upward revisions in assessments of target-company worth.)

Payment and Overpayment

As the bidding contest for a target acquisition heats up, the acquirer encounters conflicting opinions about the value of the company it is pursuing. The acquirer's original bid for a hotly pursued target of $20 per share is first judged to be fair, then another would-be acquirer chases the bid level up to $30 per share and the competitor's bid is seen as justified. The acquirer bidding $30 per share has the highest bid and wins the chase. The LBO transaction progresses from the agreement-in-principle stage to the close of the deal and into the postacquisition period, and finally, several months after the close, the "winning" acquiree encounters problems in servicing the debt from the transaction. In response, one analyst comments that the $30 per share bid represented an overpayment.

Categories of Overpayment

Just saying that management paid too much for their acquiree doesn't make it so, however. The bid that first seems exorbitant may later appear to be reasonable, given new information about the untapped value of the acquired enterprise. The key is to understand the different types of apparent overpayment circumstances (see Table 2.2).

Table 2.2. Apparent Overpayment: Categories

	Acquisition Purch. Premium: Pct. of Pre-Bid MV	Comments
Minimal overbid	115%	Minimum premium for acquirer to win in a competitive situation
Achievable overbid	115–140%	Several bidders engaged in more than one bid series. Belief that premium can be covered by postacquisition value actions.
Unreachable overbid	Above 140%	May be too much of a burden for the acquirer to support. If LBO, acquiree cash flow may be insufficient to meet acquisition debt payments.

- *The minimal overbid* The minimal overbid approach means payment of a nominal premium over market value—a level necessary to win the target company. The minimal overbid may be up to 115 percent of the target's prebid market value. Despite the overbid label, this is probably not excessive payment. Acquiring company management should be able to identify readily the near-term opportunities to build value up to and beyond this level following the close.
- *The achievable overbid* An achievable overbid is a winning bid that requires a premium of up to 140 percent over market. If the prebid market value for the target company is $100 per share, the acquirer has to pay $140 per share to win the bidding race. To bridge a value gap of this level, the acquirer must go beyond the immediate value action such as simple staff consolidations and headquarters consolidations and take stronger actions to reduce expenses and create new revenue.
- *The unreachable overbid* The unreachable overbid dooms the transaction. When bidders are willing to pay any price

to acquire the desired company, they may lurch in hot pursuit of other bidders without understanding how much of the value gap can be made up after the acquisition. If the transaction is financed extensively with debt, excessive price becomes an excessive debt load, management finds it impossible to pay back borrowings, and debt-servicing dates pass.

Although there is no single numerical threshold point for how much value can be created from the acquisition, after the close, generally speaking, deals requiring more than 40 to 50 percent value improvement to "work" face a near impossible hurdle to success or must cover part of the price through proceeds from an initial public offering (IPO). Such a sequence of purchasing a company from public-market sellers, thus taking that concern private, and then reintroducing the company to the public market in an initial public offering is appropriately termed a "round turn."

If the IPO market is active, an aggressive acquirer may be able to use the round turn technique to counteract some effects of overpayment. The need to cover the difference between bid and underlying value from improvement to postacquisition may become less urgent. Availability of public securities market investors to become ultimate purchasers provides acquirers and their backers with additional assurance.

Consider the following sequence of events. On a per share basis, the "prebid market value" of Company A is $100 million. "Pre-bid value," as used here, refers to a conservative estimation of the business unit's worth. For a publicly traded company, that worth will reflect predictable, recurring earnings per share levels and price-to-earnings multiples—usually well below the maximum theoretical price under one-time high bidder conditions. Company B bids $175 million for Company A, wins a heated bidding war, and succeeds in its objective to acquire the company. Company B management's most optimistic estimation of the value improvement potential for A's operations is only $45 million, leaving $130 million in additional value that must be derived from other sources to achieve a fully "covered" bid. Thus Company B management adds a round-turn assumption to its unofficial financing rationale. To bridge the $75 million gap still separating its bid and Company A's prebid value, Company B management is counting on achieving the full $45 million of value in postacquisition operations improvements. Add to this $30 million from a round-turn sale of securities of Company A back to the public, and the acquirer figures that its bid amount is covered.

Form of Payment: Payment in Kind and the Reset Provision

At one time noncash purchase instruments were felt to increase the success of highly leveraged acquisitions. The reverse now appears to be true with the change in market conditions for ultrahigh debt.

During the peak years of the 1980s merger boom, noncash forms of debt supported aggressive purchase premiums. When noncash instruments are combined with cash and cash equivalents in bidding for a target firm, the result can be a bid that is less than face, or stated, value. An acquirer could issue an offer that had a $100 million face value but a somewhat lower actual value because the financing mix included payments bearing contingency provisions, seller's paper, or payment-in-kind (PIK) securities. A $100 million bid is worth only $95 million when today's value of all those noncash instruments used in the financing mix pulls the *real* value of the bid lower by $5 million.

PIKs are debt-financing instruments that call for interest — and sometimes principal and interest — payments by issuance of other securities rather than by cash. As used in acquisition chases in the latter phases of the 1980s merger boom, PIKs boosted bids and bidders over the top. Armed with a new source of liquidity, acquirers bid somewhat more for targets, reasoning that because immediate cash repayment would not be required, there would be negligible added burden to the cash flow of the LBOed acquiree.

PIKs represented a new financing mutation, stacked on top of a high-yield debt market that itself was immature. Accordingly, some additional engineering was required to assist lenders and the seller (and the seller's advisors and attorneys) to assign a finite value to these new instruments. When a reset provision is present, the PIK must be replaced by other instruments at a future specified date, with yield adjusted to prevailing marketplace conditions. Some issuers of reset PIKs later discover that they face an additional repayment obligation. When the collapse of the junk bond market ruled out easy rollovers of one PIK for another, some reset PIK issuers were confronted with the need to rollover using senior debt or cash.

Flexible Financing Structure

This refers to the terms and timing of the financing used to support the acquirer's bid in a debt-financed transaction. In an LBO the servicing burden is borne by the acquiree. A carefully planned and implemented financing structure increases chances for acquisition success—primarily by allowing management time to execute internal improvements. The potential role of structuring is illustrated in the following hypothetical example involving AcquireCo (purchaser) and TargetCo (acquiree).

The structure of AcquireCo's $175 million bid for TargetCo originally calls for investors to begin recouping their investment three years after the close of the deal. As originally structured, the deal calls for an eighteen-month fast repayment of all principal and interest following an initial three-year payment moratorium.

But then AcquireCo's management requests that the structure be revised with amended terms calling for a start date for principal and interest payments beginning at the sixty-month mark and repayment stretched over three years.

As a result, some debt calling for high fixed-interest rates throughout the term of the instrument is altered so that a somewhat lower rate will be charged in early years, balanced by a higher rate in future years as TargetCo's cash-flow–generating strength gains momentum. In addition, about $10 million of debt will be converted to equity.

These new arrangements changed the cash flow drain on the acquiree and provided additional time to make further improvements in TargetCo's operations, and improvements to Target Co support its debt servicing load with greater margin for unexpected events. The newly installed management team at TargetCo put in place by AcquireCo after the close estimates that the financing structure gives them at least four additional months to demonstrate that the deal is working.

Revised Performance Expectations

TargetCo's newly installed management group reviews the cash-flow projections developed during the due diligence period; that is, after the bid but before the close. They decide that the earlier projections were too optimistic. These projections assumed that TargetCo could begin achieving an operating profit within three months of the close.

Because TargetCo's new leaders consider these assumptions to be unrealistic, market penetration assumptions are scaled back, and assumed sales costs per newly captured account are increased, resulting in a six-month extension in the assumed profit breakthrough from three months out to nine months. The revised projections are accompanied by a new plan for achieving operating improvements, which boost TargetCo's cash flow and thus ease the acquiree's debt-servicing burden. The old projections simply showed an increase in available funds for financing, calculated on a percentage basis. Revised numbers identify *what* the revised cash flow levels will be and *how* the new projections will be achieved.

Revised Financing Structure

AcquireCo's chief executive is concerned that lenders might not change financing structure despite these changes. Such concerns are certainly understandable, since the lenders will now be paid back at a slower rate. Subsequent discussions with the senior lender help dispel this concern. AcquireCo and TargetCo management learn that the lender has already adjusted its own projections to delete some less defensible assumptions. With specific action programs to support the achievability of the new projections, the investor finds its audience receptive to many restructuring suggestions.

Restructuring Elements: Additional Considerations

The question shifts from whether restructuring actions will be taken to which actions are most suitable to meet the new operating realities that TargetCo faces. Deferral of interest, adjustments in front-end interest rates, and conversion to equity are three possible approaches that have been discussed in this chapter. Interest accruals are another possible approach. The most important refinancing issue in acquisition success, however, is to develop alternative sources of financing to supplement the tottering junk bond market.

The broad-based market for high-yield, non–investment-quality corporate securities—primarily debt securities of "LBOed" acquirees—emerged in the mid-1980s, and their liquidity sustained transaction momentum in the latter phases of the 1980s merger boom. The additional liquidity also fueled higher LBO prices, however, and the monumental corporate debt burdens associated with such prices. Acquirers, acquirees, and lenders had to live with the debt that was a consequence of high bids. In fact, as the acquisition cycle matured, corporate debt began to appear excessive to many (see Figure 2.1). Consistent with retrenchment in other overheated markets, the most volatile, least secured financing markets would be expected to be the first to feel the effects of a peaking market: in the late 1980s this meant the junk bond market. Later, new high-leverage transactions (HLTs) now face considerably more difficulty than before in securing funding, and some of the deals financed in periods of ample market liquidity will face difficult refinancing prospects in the early 1990s as initial financing matures or requires restructuring.

The Upcoming Refinancing Crisis

This crisis is real, and it will directly influence the level of acquisition success (and failure) in the early 1990s. How the crisis is resolved may mean the difference between a 5 percent failure rate for the late-phase (1988–89) LBOs that have financing due for repayment or rollover during the first half of the 1990s and a significantly higher failure percentage.

This refinancing imperative arises because of the high level of debt still in the junk bond market. When an LBO is involved, the need for refinancing is likely to be sooner rather than later, due to the nature and design of the LBO instrument itself, changing economic conditions, interest-rate variations, and competition:

- *LBO design: short-term focus*   By design, LBOs are blessed or damned (depending on your perspective) with a short-term bias. To maximize the potential of the LBO vehicle, you must quickly decide to acquire the target and take swift actions to generate new cash flow.

- *Changing overall economic conditions*   One of the most difficult forecasting challenges facing management is to look beyond present conditions and consider the effect of different, possibly less favorable general conditions. Financing projections for many late-stage LBOs that closed in the late

Figure 2.1.   Corporate Interest-Payment Burden, as Percentage of Pretax Profits, 1980–89

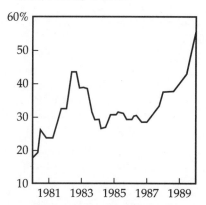

SOURCE: C. J. Lawrence, Morgan Grenfell Inc., *Wall Street Journal*, March 13,1990, p. A2.

1980s assumed that the business conditions present during the buoyant 1983–86 period would continue, but the 1990s will be less predictable than the preceding decade. Straight-line projections will be of questionable value, and unless the company is legitimately countercyclical (always rarer than many think), a turgid general economy will increase the pressure for LBO refinancing. Overly optimistic late 1980s numbers are changing and creating a growing urgency for financial restructuring.

- *Interest-rate variations*   Interest-rate fluctuations directly affect some LBOs because of variable-rate terms in their financing. All LBOs are influenced *indirectly* by the global pattern of capital flows into and out of U.S. securities markets. The issue is more than whether the discount rate will be within a few hundred basis points of the rates that were in place during the late 1980s. The greater issue is the pattern of world rates and the flow of funds into the United States. If Eastern European reconstruction or a retrenchment of Asian capital sources occurs, the most volatile markets will react first.

- *The competition*   An effective competitor can make confetti out of the future cash-flow projections of LBO management and thus accelerate the need for rescue capital (see Table 2.3). Competitors have learned how to cripple a cash-

Table 2.3.   The Competitor Pounces: Decreasing the Acquisition Success of a Competing LBO

Multiple-year investment program announced	Competitor announces sustained investment program aimed at lowering the costs of increasing customer satisfaction; cash-constrained LBO acquiree cannot match the move
Long-term warranties offered or extended	Subtle technique reminds mutual customers of the vulnerability of some LBOs
Opportunistic advertising and promotion	LBO reduces ad expenditures, leaving an impression gap for competitors to fill

flow–strained LBO by announcing a multiyear investment aimed at improving service or decreasing production costs (precisely the type of continuing commitment that the new LBO cannot afford to make), by offering long-term warranties as speculation arises about survival prospects of the LBOed firm, or by timing an intensive advertising surge to coincide with the LBO's ad cuts as the acquiree scrambles for cash sources.

Operations-Based Real Property Financing

As new financing approaches emerge following a period of rapid market expansion, the movement is back to quality. If lenders proceed in any other direction in an extended market, they risk becoming lenders of last resort—those that will take the brunt of bankruptcy.

One source of quality-upgrade supplemental financing is operations-based real property financing, which enhances the investment attractiveness of noninvestment-quality risks by identifying tangible sources of value within the company and then establishing a recurring refinancing structure that enables investor and lender to capitalize on that potential. Although this potentially cost-effective approach can work for LBOs with moderate rollover needs, it is not a cure-all for the looming general LBO-refinancing challenge. The approach is applied most effectively to LBOs that have been at least moderately effective at servicing debt and retaining share in principal markets since the close and LBOs that still maintain viable assets and staff. The underlying tangible asset foundation is real estate and attached improvements and unattached equipment. A productive plant, an occupied office building, or land that has multiple uses for more than one type of purchaser can serve as the core of a refinancing and restructuring program, if senior lenders concur.

Such financing played an important part in the successes of some of the earliest (and most successful) high-leverage transactions. William Polk Carey, chair of the Manhattan investment banking firm bearing his name, has described how his firm assisted Wesray Capital Corporation in financing its 1982 acquisition of Gibson Greeting Cards, Inc. The actual funding instrument was a sale and leaseback financing arrangement involving several carefully selected Gibson properties.

Despite the success of that financing, however, and the spectacular success of the related acquisition, Carey's approach was used less, not more, in the years that followed. As LBOs became more familiar, senior lenders and other institutional money sources sought to control all financing—and use the potential security to protect their position, as well.

In the face of continuing junk bond market woes, such an approach to noninvestment-quality financing may be primed for a comeback. As Carey explains, such financing may have particular usefulness today as the junk bond market is tested more with each successive week:

> Sale and leaseback of productive property offers possible advantages to the LBO acquirer, as well as to the acquiree—which is expected often to support the cost of its own financing in such arrangements. These advantages may come to involve the level of financing, the cost to borrowers, or both. Conventional financing of a given operating property might only raise seventy-five percent of market value. If the financing intermediary has flexibility and analytical ability, one-hundred percent financing might be achievable through an operations based financing approach including sale and leaseback—sometimes at rates considerably below those for unsecured financing.[1]

If an LBO has moderate rollover requirements and properties that can be split off into a separate refinancing vehicle, this approach might help that LBO succeed—by providing timely extended financing and possibly preventing premature liquidations and by possibly lowering interest costs and thus increasing cash flow available to repay the remaining debt principal. W. P. Carey & Co.'s George E. Stoddard cautions that such arrangements involve more than just property financing: "One must scrutinize the operations that are conducted on that prop-

---

[1]Discussion with William Polk Carey, W. P. Carey & Co., April 17, 1990.

erty, as well as the overall competitive health of the business. If, for example, the acquiree's main plant is operating at a high level of capacity utilization, but margins are pressured by price and the industry as a whole has an excess capacity problem, that property may not be as valuable for refinancing purposes as initially hoped."[2]

For operations-based real property financing and similar specific asset-secured approaches to play a role in future acquisition success, senior lenders with existing LBO loans must change their orientation to total financing. A meaningful number of financiers need to agree in principle with the concept of splitting out some secured assets for specific financing under some circumstances, but to make such a change they need an incentive. The potential reduction in borrowing cost cited by Carey is one possible motivator. The controller of the currency's position action on commercial bank identification of high-leverage transactions may be a second, particularly if such rollover approaches can help reduce theoretical HLT exposure.

Timing

The second acquisition success factor—timing—is of great interest and value to continuing acquisitions and divestitures marketplace participants. Acquirers, intermediaries, lenders, sellers, and other advisors are now looking beyond the 1988–90 disruptions in the acquisition marketplace. They see expansion through acquisition as a continuing program and are developing their acquisition programs for the future.

Timing is closely related to pricing; they are connected by the expected favorable results of a carefully planned and executed acquisition effort. Pricing should not be the acquirer's *sole* success consideration, but pursuit of the best possible price is always a high priority. Timing deserves special attention as an acquisition success factor for two important reasons beyond price:

[2] Discussion with George E. Stoddard, W. P. Carey & Co., April 17, 1990.

- *Emergence of the merger cycle*   The 1980s explosion in volume and participation has resulted in a U.S. acquisitions market that now displays many characteristics of securities markets. Signals of underbid and overbid markets can translate directly into greater acquisition success.

- *The two-decision approach*   The acquisition bid process is often more effective when approached as two separate decisions rather than one—the decision to acquire and the decision to act. This section examines what most companies do now and how a two-decision approach can help improve their level of acquisition success.

Timing's Role in Acquisition Success

Optimal timing is guided by the signals provided by the merger cycle and can help boost acquisition performance—sometimes substantially. It must be viewed as an important success factor, however, and not as an afterthought. Because examples of poor timing are rarely instructive—people often mislabel a series of acquisition miscues as poor timing—the acquirer must gain an understanding of what good timing means within the context of the merger cycle.

Many successful acquirers point to timing as a significant factor contributing to their substantial gains. Judicious pricing combined with opportunistic marketplace timing are a combination that can't be beaten, they attest. When acquirers are pressed further on how correct timing is achieved, however, they find it difficult to respond. Despite the importance of timing, few acquirers approach the issue in a systematic manner. Even fewer develop workable programs to pinpoint the appropriate time to acquire and perhaps more important when *not* to acquire.

Unless an acquirer knows the answers to the following three questions, then the chances for future acquisition success are small:

- *How* is the overall merger cycle positioned today in the context of the merger-cycle time continuum?

- *Where* is that cycle probably headed tomorrow, based on past patterns and current signals?
- *What* do those indications mean that management should do in terms of specific actions? Should the target company or an alternative in the same industry be rigorously pursued today, or should the acquirer wait until next month or even next year?

Everyone recognizes poor acquisition timing—but only after it has occurred. Southland Corporation buys a gasoline source as the oil-oversupply problem worsens. Former treasury secretary and 1980 presidential aspirant John Connally guesses wrong on an early rebound on Texas energy prices. Under Peter Cohen, Shearson Lehman Hutton tries to make up for its late entry into megadeals with overaggressiveness, and megasized costs go unrecovered.

Much less attention is paid to people who somehow— through luck or skill—exhibit excellent timing. Another former treasury secretary, William Simon, catches the early explosive profit growth of Wesray and then leaves the firm well before the peak. Willem deVogel, managing director of internationally oriented Three Cities Research, Inc., reduces its unofficial maximum for U.S. deals before the peak and proceeds with a balanced European investment policy.

The Cost of Poor Timing: Uptrend, Transition, Divestiture

During the uptrending (buy-side) portions of the merger cycle, it makes sense to pay a 20 percent acquisition-purchase premium when a company's market value is $50 per share, rather than wait to pay a 20 percent premium for that same concern based on a prevailing prebid market value of $70 per share.

During the transitional phase from a sellers' market to a mixed market, overall market characteristics give conflicting signals and must be disregarded—at least temporarily. The acquirer must focus solely on the individual potential transaction at hand and the "winnable" price for a desired target company relative to perception of value-improvement opportunities.

When the merger cycle shifts to divestment, the acquirer probably faces extreme opposition to most or all buy suggestions. Market news has turned negative, and the acquirer's base business may need attention. Nonetheless, this is often the best time to buy for the acquirer following a long-range expansion strategy.

The Merger Cycle

Market, cycle, phase, and *merger cycle* are central concepts that are important in considering the full potential role of timing in achieving improved acquisition performance. The working definitions that follow are for the purposes of this discussion only.

A&D Evolves from Activities to Market

During the 1980s merger boom—from approximately January 1982 to the present (and continuing into the future)—U.S. acquisition and divestiture activity has changed. It has evolved from the loosely clustered activities characteristic of 1970s, 1960s, and earlier to the stature of a true market. A market can be understood and tracked and thus can help guide acquirers toward optimal acquisition timing. This means a more successful transaction and greater profits from those deals that do excel.

As the word is used here, *market* refers to a process—that is, an open and free-exchange process with most (ideally, all) these characteristics:

- A sizable and growing number of past, present, and potential future participants;
- Sufficient transaction volume and knowledge for bid and asked prices to be reliable—and known by many;
- A reasonable level of participant entry and exit;
- Supportive external conditions (such as moderate interest rates, enough liquidity to allow quality deals to be closed,

manageable levels and forms of regulatory, political, and legal restrictions); and

• Extensive and timely communications.

Continuity

This newly evolved A&D market probably will be an ongoing fixture and a continuing element in future acquisition success, at least into the next century. Although the 1990s began with A&D volume off significantly—especially compared to the 1980s boom's second wind from the fourth quarter of 1987 to mid-1989—two factors in particular support continuing A&D activity in the years ahead:

• *Indications of persisting "buy-side" interest* As early as April 1990, a noticeable resurgence in possible purchase interest was observable shortly after some sellers reduced their asking prices by 20 to 30 percent. The number of participants remains high, although, admittedly, many are or must be inactive now—at least until better answers are developed for the junk bond question or prices decline another 15 to 20 percent or both.

• *Supportive role to be played by divestitures in the 1990s* We estimate four to six years of potential transaction volume at moderate levels, as the A&D pendulum swings back. A substantial reserve of future acquisition activity may lie within the portfolios of some commercial and investment bankers and some investors who were very active in HLTs after 1986. Ultrahigh leverage, mixed with the sheer volume of 1980s transactions, however, provides the ingredients to unleash another sustained A&D surge during the early to mid-1990s, and this time, ongoing transaction momentum will be sustained from the sell side. When the buyers of the 1980s wake up in the 1990s and look again at their prize purchases, they will begin to think about where next to proceed. This expected continuity represents good news for continuing A&D participants because as activities congeal and align to become freestanding markets, activities assume predictable patterns that should help acquirers pinpoint the timing for their next acquisition.

Cycles

Cycles are the patterns that activities and markets assume. They have beginnings and ends and are made up of sequenced *phases*. These phases are subperiods—parts of the *merger cycle*—and represent distinct periods of market and merger conditions. A change from one phase to another represents a threshold from one state to another. Phases characterize the past and future action of the market and help explain evolutionary changes within a maturing market cycle.

The types of merger cycles considered in this chapter follow a limited number of alternative courses, and their inherent predictability allows them to be used to help time acquisition actions optimally. When a delicate balancing of knowledge, risk, and reward is achieved, the acquisition is made at the earliest possible time in the cycle that does not subject acquirer shareholders to an unreasonable level of risk relative to the perceived reward involved.

The Classic Product-Adoption/Market-Penetration Cycle

The classic product-adoption/market-penetration cycle is a recurring cycle in many markets (see Figure 2.2). A version of the multiphase adoption cycle has been adapted for the merger market's cycle. The classic adoption cycle predicted the pattern of the 1980s merger boom and is still useful in the new decade. The overall sequence for a merger cycle, from inception to boom to bust, involves eight stages:

- *Introduction*   Some early adopters brave the apparent risk and enter the market on a test basis. Commitment is minimal, and the cycle progresses only slightly.

- *Active participation*   Business-risk and -reward takers enter the market when they observe that initial tests have succeeded. They are interested in moving faster and deeper on an orderly basis.

- *Major emphasis*   Business-risk participants experience substantial profits from market penetration. As they let out all

Figure 2.2. The Business-Expansion Cycle Applied to the 1980s Merger Boom

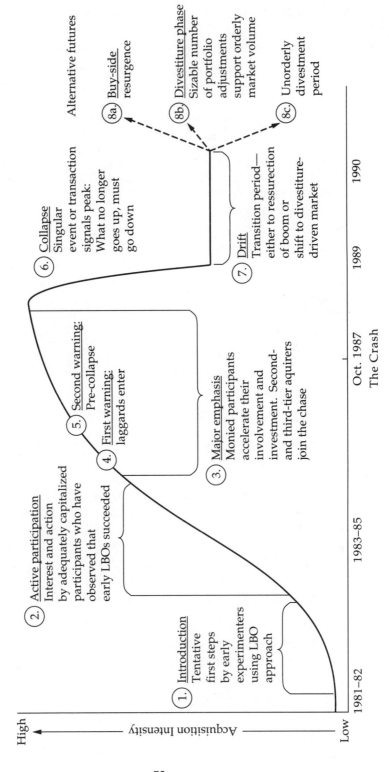

53

the stops, prices and acquisition purchase premiums soar.

- *First warning: the laggards enter*   Laggards who doubted the existence of the market from day one finally enter the fray, and undercapitalized investors also jump in. Deal quality declines, and new concepts are launched to broaden the field of bankable acquisitions.

- *Second warning: precollapse*   Pricing and purchase justifications reach their limits. New concepts that were laughed at two years earlier now are cited by acquirers to keep the buy-side momentum going. Savvy investors withdraw.

- *Collapse*   A watershed transaction marks the market peak. As with most markets, when momentum is no longer up, the market turns down suddenly. The shock period worsens as some late sellers try to act before the opportunity eludes them.

- *Drift*   A pause may be replaced with yet another surge, or the marketplace may prepare for the coming shift from a buy-side market to a sell-side market. Price drops of 20 to 30 percent or more occur.

- *Buy-side resurgence—last gasp*   or

- *Divestiture phase*   The final phase is usually abrupt and swift. This is the end phase of the merger cycle. The aftermath of the 1980s market, however, should produce an extended market.

This pattern of fear, procrastination, and finally action results in market whipsaw—entry into the market at almost precisely the wrong time. It happens in the securities market—the indicator is the odd-lot short index—and it regularly happens in the mergers and acquisitions market.

Opportunistic and Contrarian Approaches

With perfect hindsight, all acquirers would have completed their acquisitions programs by the summer of 1987, comfortably before the October 1987 crash. Observers may claim to have special advance knowledge, but no one has yet identified the guru who can tell exactly where the acquisition market is headed next.

Prevailing Acquisition Concepts as a Signal

Prevailing acquisition concepts may provide some insight into the current positioning in the M&A cycle. At the lowest-risk part of the acquisition expansion cycle, purchase emphasis is likely to be on asset-intensive basic-industry companies with cyclical demand characteristics. These companies have hard assets and hard demand. If the acquirer misjudges on operations, the contingency position is to sell the assets. As the merger cycle progresses, the easiest-to-turn cyclicals disappear. Acquirers are left to choose from troubled manufacturing concerns, non-industrial manufacturers/assemblers, and services companies. The M&A expansion progresses even more. The ratio of services acquisitions to total acquisitions increases to keep pace.

The Two-Decision Process

Acquisition-timing success requires that the decision to acquire and the decision to act be treated separately—with a period of time separating the two. But the customary practice is usually to treat the two as a single decision. Financial and job pressures encourage a would-be acquirer to proceed with the acquisition of a desirable acquisition as rapidly as possible— even if that means at a less advantageous price. Consider an up-and-coming vice president in a private investor organization who faces continual pressure to find and close new acquisition prospects on a regular basis. Such consistency, after all, is necessary for the firm to earn a steady stream of fees and for such officers to earn bonuses and carried interest participations in the acquisitions that they find. Consider also the corporate acquisitions manager who uncovers a quality target candidate and whose top management wants to move before any other acquirers catch the scent. The acquisitions manager's job security depends on generating new acquisition ideas now, and senior management is likely to be unreceptive to delays—even if a pause now might mean a more advantageous price later for the acquirer.

An alternative approach calls for treating selection and action as two discrete decisions. The impulse purchaser for a Mazda Miata falls in love with the spirit and 1950s grace of the car and pays thousands of dollars over list to get the car—*now*. The purchaser who is under control has just as much enthusiasm for the convertible sports car but waits to buy until a snowy, slushy day in January when most people's thoughts are on overcoats and not topless driving. Adopting a two-decision approach forces the acquirer to question whether its actions are the result of judgment or expediency. The two-step approach means that the selection must be the right purchase for the acquirer at any time—not just now because that's when the target appears to be available. The late-phase 1980s LBO failures emerging in 1991–93 will be well represented by the investor groups that acted on the basis of availability rather than quality.

This approach also requires patience—something rare when the company is in pursuit of an attractive candidate. Instead of pursuing a single candidate, the acquirer instead identifies several candidates with similar attractive characteristics and waits for the opportunity to act.

Changes provide opportunities for action. A change that affects the industry overall or alters conditions in the target company itself may provide the opportunity to proceed with rigorous pursuit. But this assumes that any adverse developments can be offset and that acquiring management's view about the basic investment attractiveness of the target remains unchanged. For individual companies changes include new management, the sudden loss of a top customer, or a competitor's new technology. Industries may experience an unexpected increase in interest costs or a change in the indices for purchasing intent indications.

Related Acquisitions

The oldest acquisition success rule is still the most ignored. When different types of combinations are compared several years after their closes, two key findings tend to recur:

- Mergers between complementary acquirers and acquirees usually are more successful than unrelated diversification; and

Figure 2.3. Comparison of Acquisition Performance of Related and Unrelated Acquisitions

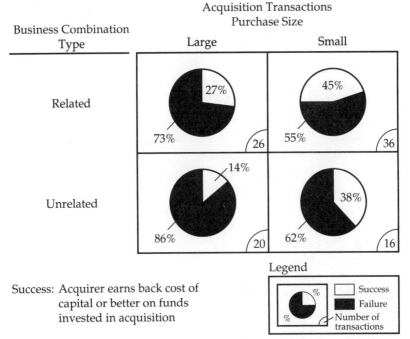

Acquisition Transactions
Purchase Size

Success: Acquirer earns back cost of
capital or better on funds
invested in acquisition

SOURCE: Stephen C. Coley and Sigurd E. Reinton, "Managing Value: The Hunt for Value," *The McKinsey Quarterly* (Spring 1988): 30.

- Mergers involving parallel or comparable companies—companies identical in most or all important aspects—in turn are more successful than corporate marriages between complementary concerns.

These findings are the oldest and most extensively documented among the six foundations discussed in this chapter. The link between merger performance and business similarity has been extensively documented by numerous firms over at least twenty years (see Figure 2.3). Unfortunately, this success foundation is bypassed or ignored as often as the other five success guidelines—perhaps more. Some disregard this success foundation. Financial acquirers, for example, add little more than the deal capital and later are shocked to discover that they cannot create sufficient new value in the acquired company to cover the value difference. Acquirer company leadership may be tired of a current business mix or the performance of the business that they know and manage well and move into an entirely new business direction, unsuccessfully.

Related Acquisition: A Working Definition

If two unlike businesses have not performed well postmerger, what can be done to make the enterprises more comparable? The conventional approach is to assess the degree of similarity of the base operations of the businesses. This rather narrow definition tends to be restricted to product similarities and occasionally to both product and technology. A more realistic approach, by contrast, studies the similarity of other factors including competitors, customers, manufacturing process, distribution network, and selling or salesforce similarities.

Despite the considerable base of research on this issue a basic question remains unanswered: How broadly should the word *related* be interpreted for acquisition-success evaluation purposes?

Definition 1: Most Limited Scope

At its most limited, *related* applies only to a target company with operations and product that are already intimately known to the acquirer before any bidding occurs: Chrysler acquires AMC/Jeep, MCI acquires smaller long-distance carriers, Sperry and Burroughs combine to form Unisys, a large car manufacturer integrates vertically with an electronic carburetors manufacturer, a manufacturer of glass jars purchases the company that makes the tops for its jars.

Consider, however, the many mergers that might be viewed as being outside these boundaries: IBM (data processing) and Rolm (business telephone systems/PBXs), Citicorp (commercial banking) and Quotron (securities on-line information), Infotechnology (best known as the company that owns the

Financial News Network) and United Press International (daily international scope news service). Should these acquisitions be considered unrelated? If *related* is interpreted *too* narrowly, then the number of acquisition candidates dries up quickly. Such a limited working definition could negate other considerations as well and might trigger an incorrect management decision. If GM acquires the carburetor company as a closely related acquisition, but profitability dissolves as the giant automaker adds allocated expenses for its own design and management bureaucracy to the acquiree's profit statement, a profitable statement quickly becomes a loss statement.

Definition 2: Extension to Processes and Technologies

In an alternative working definition, *related* is applied somewhat more broadly to include similar technologies or manufacturing processes.

Further Extension

Two forces—accelerating technology convergence and global competition—suggest a need to further extend the definitional boundaries of *related*. As the phrase is used here, "technology convergence" is the progressive march of different technologies toward interrelated and sometimes overlapping components, features, and operating characteristics. The need to be recognized as a technology leader in the marketplace is an important expansion motivation to many acquisition-minded firms. If these companies cannot lead, at a minimum they want to remain close enough to the recognized technology pacesetters so that they can be competitive in the marketplace.

Technology convergence has become increasingly significant because of the globalization of markets and supply sources. Customers look to the world—not just their own nation-market—for supply. For suppliers, the challenge is the mirror image: penetrating "credentializing" countries and customers facilitates other sales in volume.

For example, high-definition U.S. computer monitors are related to Japanese high-definition television products manufactured for home entertainment use. Technology and primary product use differ considerably between the two products but both products represent feasible HDTV approaches. The market convergence of the two products indicates that they are related.

The Tough-Minded
Postacquisition Agenda

Another axiom receiving attention but not much action is that "Successful acquisitions are made and not found." The key factor in acquisition success therefore is what new management does with the acquiree after the company is acquired. Chapters 4 through 8 of this book deal with the specific issues, challenges, and actions associated with creating postacquisition corporate value, but the issues of *focus* and *resolve* merit special attention in this chapter.

An LBO firm—called StatusCo for purposes of this illustration—completed an acquisition in a technology industry about one year ago. The dynamics of the acquired company—TekCo—and its market were and are exciting. Unlike many financial buyers StatusCo brought much to the table—keen analytical insight, an ability to inspire people to their maximum efforts, an appreciation for both the challenges and opportunities facing the industry in the future.

In fact, the acquiring company's smooth operating relationship with its acquirees was an important consideration in the selection of StatusCo over its bid rivals: flights to the acquiree's headquarters office were always preceded by a telephone message; opportunities for profit and operations improvement surfaced during the due-diligence period; and more issues were raised by two consulting studies conducted in the initial weeks after the close. A three-person postmerger action team comprised of the chair of StatusCo, the president of TekCo, and TekCo's financial officer, who was a former employee of StatusCo, appeared to be capable of developing and undertaking an active profit and operations improvement program, but little happened.

The Accelerated Time Clock of the Leveraged Acquisition

Although lenders and other investors had not begun to express concern, the TekCo deal was now a year old, and the acquiree was still operating considerably below its potential in both operations and cash-flow generation. The leverage in the deal accelerated the need for action. Easygoing StatusCo's inclination was to let the adjustment period sort itself out, but the acquiree's cash reserve had been taken out shortly after the close, leaving little cushion for contingencies. The acquirer lacked a finite postacquisition agenda identifying the most important things to be probed and changed, the quantitative and qualitative target improvements, timetable, and responsibility.

The Merger-Integration Team

Because the acquirer also lacked the resolve to implement tough decisions, the acquirer's action alternatives included using a substitute for the acquirer in the value-opportunity identification and action role. An outside merger-integration (MI) team is led by the MI team leader, who functions in a temporary officer capacity under the authorization of the lenders and equity holders of the acquiree. The team's action charter would be limited to the following postacquisition issues:

- *Implementing actions to avoid default* The team's first priority is to work with both management groups in developing default-avoidance actions. It presents action alternatives, establishes implementation schedules, identifies offsetting costs, and details timing considerations.

- *Beginning the operations improvement program* The team's second priority is to specify a limited number of key expansion opportunities for TekCo to pursue. Leverage in the deal increases the importance of pinpointing the correct market strategy the first time.

Financial Progress Indicators and Backup Actions

The Deal Is Done, But There's No Quality Information That Tells Us How We're Doing

The absence of financial progress indicators is an unpleasant surprise awaiting many acquirer senior managers in the first days following the close. It is often difficult to assess how things are going. Systems that the acquirer thought were installed and in place may not exist. Other reports may add little to the acquirer's base of knowledge about the acquiree's operations. Voluminous reports that management assumed were computer generated may be produced manually and take the time equivalent of a full clerk.

Early Warning Indicators

Chances for acquisition success are increased if acquirers have a set of indicators that indicate when the acquisition faces jeopardy. Because acquirers need to quickly grasp the financial and operating factors essential to the newly acquired enterprise, a comprehensive postacquisition program provides for contingency plans that are activated by specific warning signals:

- Cash coverage is dangerously thin.
- Too high a percentage of debt repayment is through dispositions of assets or businesses or through retrenchments in markets and businesses critical to the long-term success of the corporation.
- Ratio improvement in unit sales per administrative employee falls behind preclose projections.
- Churn of important accounts becomes visible.
- Transitional costs are *below* budget levels set at the time the postacquisition program was enacted.
- Executive recruiters designate the acquired company as a key area for concentration.

If acquiree information is reliable, timely, and—most importantly—verifiable, internal data in adapted form may suffice. In middle-range and smaller acquisitions, some form of independent backup is often needed. In some other instances, the acquirer must take a more active role in developing the early warning information, and must be directly satisfied that the report contains what it is supposed to contain.

Supportive Asset and Divestment Program

The best way to get a head start for acquisition success is to reduce the value difference between the amount paid and the acquired company's preacquisition worth. Quick sale of assets that are redundant, unneeded, or fully valued in the marketplace represents the possible opportunity here. But the acquirer should be aware that speed is only one of the considerations necessary for the program to be effective.

The Deal is Done: Now What Do We Have to Sell?

No acquirer who has endured the high acquisition price-to-earnings multiples of the past will need much prodding to get a team together to evaluate asset and business unit sales. Two categories are noted here: real property dispositions and business unit divestitures.

Real Property Dispositions

Real estate and operating facilities are often the first area of opportunity that gains management's attention. Store sales by Safeway halved the acquisition debt of the KKR acquisition from $6.2 billion to $3.1 billion and played an important role in R. H. Macy & Company's buyout. But an immediate sale does not always optimize the cash-flow benefit. Financing may produce more revenues than on outright sale would and without losing future use. If management fears that a sale announcement could lower the market, the finance-rather-than-sell alternative may be particularly attractive.

Business Unit Divestitures

Sales of ongoing entities to reduce the total value difference are frequently considered before the close. Most due-diligence examinations do not include at least some mention of business unit sales, particularly during periods of high acquisition price-to-earnings multiples (as in the late 1980s).

As with real property, management's immediate impulse may be to put the unit on the auction block immediately to gain maximum exposure along with maximum speed of execution. In some instances, however, a hold-and-improve approach may result in a greater price in present-value terms:

- *Remedial action needed*   If the intended divestee has been plagued by recent operating losses, an exodus of key employees, or high customer turnover, the quick-sale approach may not be best. Selling management may discover that remedial action must be taken before the divestee will receive a fair price in the marketplace.

- *Entities being developed*   A fast growing business that is out of step with the main business direction of the acquirer and acquiree may be particularly valued for its marketplace value, but that value may take time to develop, particularly in novel technologies. Again, a divestment approach that takes as much time and care as a major purchase may well make sense.

How to Optimize the Value Received
for a Divested Business

No single approach best optimizes the value of divested businesses. The three-stage approach described below summarizes key elements in the analysis approach used by Maplestar:

Stage 1: Business-Value Analysis

Each candidate divestee has an intrinsic value based on its sustainable profit-generation potential and competitive market ranking. External value indicators, such as recent acquisition premiums for comparable businesses, may suggest expected sales proceeds beyond intrinsic value. Accordingly, a comprehensive program includes value estimations developed on both bases. Selling management may then be advised on what *could*, or what *should*, be sold in the near term through auction or other techniques, and which businesses should undergo further value development before they are divested.

Stage 2: Acquirer Company's Search

Management is accustomed to pursuing intended *acquirees* through a systematic approach, beginning with criteria setting, risk measurement, and then estimation of anticipated cash flows, followed by an organized sequence of initial face-to-face contact, assessment, and follow-through. Why should a search for the target *acquirer* be any less thorough? The logical way to achieve the optimal price is through early identification of the synergistic buyer—the purchaser with the greatest substantive need for the business and its assets.

Stage 3: Divestment Strategy Development

Either divestment or further value development programs are prescribed for each business unit under evaluation. The sales programs are shaped by prevailing acquisition multiple ranges and market liquidity.

3

The Value and
Cash-Flow Linkage

Just as no single definition is universally accepted for *acquisition success*, no single approach is correct for valuing a company. Acquisition valuation, like merger success, lends itself to specific interpretation by the buyer and the seller based on their objectives and transaction dynamics. In theory, both buyer and seller understand the value boundaries of the bid range for the company: the buyer wants to purchase at a price close to the low end of that range, and the seller seeks to stretch the top of that boundary. Instead of a reasoned, orderly purchase sequence, however, the acquirer discovers that other competitors are fighting for the target. There is little chance to differentiate one bidder from another, except in terms of how much each will pay. Textbook value theory takes a back seat to brass-knuckles reality under such circumstances. To win the acquirer's bid must be sufficient to take competitors off the table—that is, to eliminate the other offers from consideration by the seller.

In an active market, the owner of a firm that *might* be for sale "at the right price" is playing a high-stakes game. The other contestants in this game are not other individuals or even firms: the opponents are time and the seller's own greed.

In 1988 through mid 1989—the late-phase LBO period— acquisition prices and premiums both continued to climb, to the delight of sellers, but the market was showing signs of topping out. Some deals that were cinches in early 1987 went unfunded in early 1989. Sellers may want to hold out for higher share prices, but knowledgable sellers know that boom markets have a disturbing tendency to end as quickly as they begin.

This chapter reviews a wide range of purchase-valuation philosophies and approaches. The acquirers who are best prepared for the bidding chase understand the key differences between valuation approaches and how those differences may unveil the underlying motivations of competing bidders. Valuation and success are also addressed in this chapter. The selected value approach can play a direct role in acquisition success planning *if* the basis for value calculation is based on future cash-flow generation. Care must be taken before selection. Many acquisition-valuation approaches purport to be acquiree-performance based, but 50 to 70 percent of the value in some of these formula approaches simply mirrors prevailing price-to-earnings multiples levels. The acquirer must understand the difference between today's value and the new worth that must be developed tomorrow to pay for the company to take the actions that will achieve acquisition success.

All in the Eye of the Beholder: Linking Value and Success

Understanding Acquirer Differences

In the U.S. acquisition arena, the differences among prospective purchasers that tend to be noticed first often relate directly to past deal-closure experience and future performance potential. These differences are based on characteristics such as reputation as a financial or a synergistic buyer, number and type of successful transactions closed successfully in the past, depth and permanence of equity and debt financing, management's skills in shaping, holding, and closing tricky deals, and even nation of origin of the investor's parent group.

Statistics and lists of attributes, however, reveal little about the true motivations of prospective competitors for quality acquisition targets. Unless such motivations can be understood, moderately capitalized acquirers will always lose out to the sheer tonnage of more money. Top management needs to understand where, when, and how bid competitors are likely to move. Public statements may offer clues, but statements to the business press may be designed to mislead market watchers and competing bidders. Investors that stand apart for their proficiency in quality deal development and closure keep their intentions as hidden as possible until the last possible moment, when they arrive with their winning offer.

New Concerns about the Single-Value Assumption

A Working Definition

An understanding of acquirer bid valuation approaches, principles, and motivations begins with the single-value assumption. When a successful bid is well above prebid market value, it may be *assumed* by many that true market value always equals purchase price. As applied by some, the single-value assumption can deter valuation accuracy and acquisition success:

- *Ignoring a basic characteristic about seller behavior*   Those with a tendency to automatically equate price paid with intrinsic worth disregard a simple characteristic about sellers' behavior: sellers rarely part with their investments except at prices perceived as being greater than current worth.

- *Confusing market-price action with intrinsic value* If the merger cycle is well established and the target's stock has risen substantially already, undervaluation in the 30 to 40 percent range—the level of acquisition purchase premiums customary during the 1980s merger boom period—seems hard to justify.

- *Having a false sense of security* The single-value assumption may jeopardize acquisition success if acquirers believe that the acquired company was undervalued and that new management will unleash its hidden value. If overconfident acquirers initiate a lethargic, ineffective postacquisition program, they may be surprised to find that their prize deal is in jeopardy only months after the close.

- *Increasing possible exposure* High-leverage transactions tend to compress the time needed for collapse. Instead of staggering along for seven years with balanced equity and debt-purchase financing, a HLT may face collapse in two. Arguably, the HLT acceleration effect adds to the visibility of the LBO collapse and thus boosts chances for shareholder or other action in the wake of a visible collapse. The possible risks to acquiring company management and directors should be apparent, but if suits arise, valuators, advisors, intermediaries, and others fueling the value-price spiral could find that they face unexpected exposure, as well.

Application and Misapplication

The parties to the transaction have a legitimate need for reassurance that a proposed purchase price is reasonably consistent with value of the intended acquiree. Bank lenders, for example, may require substantiation of a transaction's intrinsic financial worthiness before they provide even long-term clients with funds necessary to acquire businesses that are central to a carefully planned diversification program. Whether this requirement results from the bank's charter, its lending policies, or the exercise of senior executive supervisory responsibility, the bank's need probably increases if either (1) the acquirer-client's bid follows a significant increase in the price of the target's stock, culminating in a new high; or (2) the current merger-expansion cycle has been underway several years and now shows signs of exhaustion.

Value reassurance—and the instruments developed to meet that need—originally was intended as a security backup. It was a third layer of confirmation that the proposed purchase bid's relation to the intrinsic value of the company had been carefully examined *three* times—by the acquirers, by the lender, and finally by an outside party.

Unfortunately, value reassurance—and the underlying single-value assumption—can become part of the acquisition justification process instead of simply a check for that process. For an acquisition-oriented manager, this temptation may become difficult to resist, particularly in a soaring merger market. Consider the following sequence:

- *Acquisition urge strikes in the latter phases of a merger cycle* The chief executive who doubted that the merger boom would continue much longer in 1986 suddenly catches acquisition fever in 1988. The object of his urge to merge—a small publicly traded company in a related industry that is selling at $40 per share. Because the company could have been acquired for $20 per share just two years earlier and no changes of consequence occurred to explain the price increase, the CEO realizes that he would be hard pressed to prove that the target's doubling in market value was due to any factor other than general action of the overall market.

- *Justifying the deal* To win board approval for this transaction and obtain the necessary financing, the CEO needs to bid about 40% above the $40 value, for a total of $56 per share—stretching the value-justification problem even more. Involving others may help substantiate the reasonableness of the necessary purchase price.

- *Price bid equals value* There are enough valuation sources—and enough corporate fees to compensate them—to enable a convincing value argument to be constructed. The high-leverage acquisition is completed at $56 per share.

- *Acquisition aftermath* Expecting the market to later back up any enthusiasm for a higher price, the acquirer CEO limits postacquisition actions to cosmetic alterations that have little effect on operations or profit. About nine months after the close, however, it becomes apparent that these actions aren't enough. The target company misses two debt payments. The acquirer is forced to gradually liquidate the business—at a loss—because profits and cash flow remain at about the same level as before the deal.

The Value Difference Assumes a Price-Value Gap

Unlike the single-value assumption, the value difference (introduced in chapter 2) assumes that the price bid and the justified market value of the acquired company always differ and that the bid is greater. In fact, it brands nearly all deals as overpayments. Instead of assuming that bid equals value (single-value assumption), value difference assumes that a negative value gap confronts the acquirer as soon as the deal is closed.

To be successful with an acquisition, the acquirer has to put aside the single-value assumption and address the two basic questions confronting *all* acquirers: what must be paid to acquire the candidate (financial-market valuation), and what is the intrinsic value of the acquired company based on operations and continuing earning power (operations valuation)? Subtracting operations valuation from financial-market valuation results in the value difference—the new value that must be developed to make the acquisition work.

Differing Estimates of Acquiree Value

For the active acquirer, few issues exceed the importance of the value-price issue as it pertains to a potential acquiree. It affects decisions on whether to expand through internal projects or through external acquisitions and questions and priorities concerning what to acquire, what to divest, and how to allocate limited resources. No one deliberately wishes to overpay for an acquisition, and in an upward trending market the active acquirer probably can find a valuation or solvency source that, for a fee, will attest to the reasonableness of a bid, but an attractive acquisition candidate may attract bids that differ by as much as 15 to 20 percent and sometimes more.

Different Acquirers, Different Goals

Bid differences can be explained by differing degrees of information on the target and differing initial multiples for expressing a preliminary range of purchase interest. An acquirer with superior data on the target company is positioned to make a higher, more confident bid. Alternatively, if one bidder applies a four-times cash-flow multiple in establishing the lower boundary for its possible purchase interest and a different suitor applies a multiple of seven times, a considerable difference in bid ranges will occur.

In reality, neither of these two explanations appears to be the most common cause of bid differences. Information is remarkably similar for most target-bid situations because sellers want to avoid charges of preferential treatment. The bid-multiple argument is not convincing either because prevailing raider multiples for quick value estimations tend to be broadly known at virtually any time during the merger cycle.

These two explanations therefore can be eliminated leaving purchase-program objectives and limitations as the remaining plausible explanations for bid differences. A bidder that continually appears at the bottom end of the bid range in a multiple-round process may be signaling lack of adequate financing or a chief executive with a bottom-trawler (cheap asset-purchase) mentality. This bidder is eliminated from further consideration in the next round. A would-be purchaser that has dramatically increased its second-round bid level without visible reason may indicate a CEO who has been captured by the spirit of the chase. This bidder will stay in the race until the end of negotiations or until bankers or the board intervenes. Other bidders should try to determine why the difference came about. If the second bid represents a unilateral move by the CEO that might not be supported by the board, this bidder acts only as a spoiler.

Price Is Not Always the Same as Value

Price and value are not necessarily the same thing. Over the course of an active bidding contest involving an attractive prospective acquiree, price is often propelled primarily by the competitive bid dynamics in the market, but value is usually based on the ongoing cash-flow–generation potential of the business or on the net liquidated proceeds of assets if the going concern is questionable.

Valuation authorities contend that certain features distinguish a highly defensible approach. One such consideration is how much projections rely on market data about current prices rather than historical data. Generally, a projection based on current market data better reflects actual (and hopefully, future) performance results than projections built from historical accounting numbers. More accurate projections, in turn, should result in better-quality value estimations. Another quality-distinguishing feature is the knowledge of future projects presently under consideration by the target. Without at least some information about the target company's expected future priorities, projections can be little better than mathematical extrapolations.

The Case of Grommet International

Grommet International (GI) is a hypothetical manufacturer of grommets—those little metal rings that hold together everything from parachutes to sportscoats.

The Initial Stages of the Bid Process

April 1: The Breakfast Meeting

GI's president, Dave Gromeur, accepts a Monday morning breakfast invitation from the managing director of Stalkem, Inc., an East Coast leveraged buy out firm that has enjoyed a great deal of acquisition success and more than a little bit of notoriety. Gromeur has an idea of what is on Ted Stalkem's mind but waits for the investment banker to ask the question. When Ted inquires gently as to whether someday, somehow, under certain circumstances, Grommet International might consider becoming part of the Stalkem family, Gromeur asks,

"Why not now?" Stalkem and Gromeur are on the same wave-length. By the end of the meal Stalkem still knows nothing about Gromeur's selling price expectations, but it is agreed that Stalkem will have three weeks to develop and submit a bid to GI's board for Grommet International to be acquired by Stalkem, Inc. in a leveraged management buyout. Stalkem's right to pursue GI for the next three weeks is sealed by a hand-shake and not a piece of paper. Gromeur is wary of leaks and feels that a short time period will enable him to gauge Stalkem's sincerity while keeping the situation reasonably under control. Although several members of his board probably will support any move he proposes, the prospect of an LBO with manage-ment participation has never been presented to the board.

April 3–17: Stalkem Prepares

GI stock is presently trading on the exchange at $10 per share. Stalkem's analysts pour through the available projection data and estimate a bid range from a low of $13 per share to a high of $14.50, based on a future cash-flow–generation analy-sis of GI, the limited data provided by Gromeur himself, and what Stalkem management suspects can be sold or changed quickly after the acquisition. Stalkem chooses a price hovering near the low end of his analysts' range—$13.50—to take full advantage of his exclusive look. The prevailing acquisition pur-chase premium in the market is 43 percent, with a high in the fifties. Thus, by bidding somewhat below that premium level, Stalkem hopes to pare down his price through fast action. Ted advises Gromeur that his offer will be available on April 18, a couple of days ahead of schedule. GI's special board meeting is rescheduled for the new date.

Stalkem as Bidder

To both GI and other possible bidders Stalkem is a firm to be taken seriously: its resources are extensive, and it has al-ready established stand-by acquisition bank lines. Stalkem has a transaction mentality: its management has little time for con-cepts such as intrinsic worth when it wants a particular deal.

Nevertheless, Stalkem's management team understands that even at the bid price that they will be submitting, some additional cash flow and value must be generated by GI if a leveraged buyout is to be successful. Stalkem hopes that enough value can be squeezed from GI after the close to cover the $3.50 per share difference separating his bid from GI's prebid market price, but he fears that a recent run-up in GI stock price already has anticipated and absorbed any post-close value.

April 19: Stalkem's Bid Rejected

Stalkem submits its bid to the GI board, Grommet's board deliberates for about twice as long as expected. Spirits sink at Stalkem's headquarters because managers feel that the longer GI deliberates, the lower their chances for early success. That expectation proves correct. In a tersely worded communique. GI's board turns down Stalkem's bid and invites others to compete with Stalkem in a second round of bidding over the next four to six weeks.

April 20–May 5: GI's Board Reflects

Some members of GI's board suspect that Stalkem's fast bid is below prevailing acquisition-market price levels for companies comparable to GI and are able to squelch the Stalkem bid despite Gromeur's support. One board member suggests making a counter offer to Stalkem, but no one knows what price range to hint at because the board lacks a clear understanding of what their firm is worth. The GI board accepts the idea of a sale *if* bidders other than the Stalkem LBO group are also involved and *if* the resulting bid price is at a level that the board judges to be in the best interest of the company's shareholders.

What is GI Worth?

Adjusted Market Value

The board questions several different groups about Grommet International's worth. Some individuals with no interest in bidding on the company—such as a group of professors and graduate research assistants from the finance department at the university—call their valuation *adjusted market value*. It is not a bid but rather a value judgment. The university's efficient-market advocates argue that the market already has assimilated all the factors that result in an accurate estimation of worth and that the current market price of GI's stock—$10 per share—represents the maximum worth of the company. They assert that paying more than $10 per share for GI is overspending.

A subgroup within the finance department team contends that the maximum defensible value for GI is $9.75 per share—25 cents *less* than the current stock market price per share for Grommet International (see Table 3.1, row 1). A stunned GI board member asks how this could possibly be true and is told the following:

- *Adjustments to market value*   To be accurate, the indicated market value of $10 per share must be adjusted upward by any additional benefits that an acquirer assumes are not already reflected in the GI stock price and downward as necessary to adjust for nonrecoverable costs that an acquirer cannot reasonably expect to offset through its future operation of GI. The university team finds no positive adjustments but uncovered an important nonrecurring and thus nonrecoverable cost.

- *Unrecoverable control and consolidation costs*   Control and consolidation costs are the additional cost that an acquirer has to pay to control enough shares to force an acquisition. If present shareholders don't want to give up their shares, prospective acquirers can pay more, initiate a special contact program, and advertise—all actions that involve additional costs. The university team suggests that this control cost would amount to at least 25 cents per share.

- *Adjustment costs subtracted from market value*   If control and consolidation costs are recoverable through Grommet International's future operations or if the expenditures increase the value of GI's business, the additional cost per share could be added to GI's estimated market value. According to the university team neither circumstance exists,

Table 3.1. Grommet International: Alternative Bid Approaches and Alternative Valuations

Bid Approach	Illustrative Bid Amount per Share	Calculation Basis	Other Considerations
1. Adjusted market valuation	$9.75[a]	Current market equals current worth Adjustment for control cost	Never results in completed acquisition
2. Operations valuation	$14.13	Current market equals current worth Additional value for future improvements	Strategic-valuation approach—what it is worth is based on how acquiree is run
3. Financing acquirer value	$14.13	Same as operations valuation	Future improvement assumptions limited— acquirer doesn't know business
4. Synergistic-acquirer value	$17.00	Same as financial acquirer value, with greater performance assumptions	Incorporates capacity of research consolidation assumptions
5. Strategic-imperative value	$18.00	Bid deliberately at higher level than justified by internal analysis	Most probably global competitor with need for U.S. base, or company with business in permanent decline
6. Financial-market value	$23.00	Not a value but an overbid resolve	Answer to the question, "What price will be required to assure that we win the bid war?"

[a] Value indication rather than a bid.

so the team *reduces* the adjustment amount from the $10 per share value amount.

Grommet International's board, shaken by the suggestion that the company's value is less than Stalkem had bid and less than the common stock's current price, proceeds briskly to the next value indicator.

Operations Valuation

The next value indicator comes from another GI suitor, Seekem, Inc., which responds quickly to the board's invitation on April 19 to consider a possible bid to acquire GI. Seekem offers to acquire all the assets and business of GI for $14.125 per share (fourteen and one-eighth dollars) (see Table 3.1, row 2). The bid is submitted to the board on May 3. Asked to explain how the bid was determined; a Seekem spokesperson describes what he calls an *operations valuation* approach—that is, a discounted approach focusing on tangible improvement in cash flow generated from operations. Future after-tax net-cash flows of the company are discounted back to the present based on the company's cost for funds to sustain operations.

Key Principles of the Value and Cash-Flow Relationship

The foundation for the value linkage between corporate worth and corporate cash flow is the principle of the *time value of money*, and that linkage is further supported by Modigliani's and Miller's discounted cash-flow (DCF) formula, often referred to simply as the *MM formula*. The MM formula, in turn, establishes a direct connection between the value of the unit and changes in free cash flow generated in future periods by that entity.

According to the time-value-of-money principle a dollar received today is worth more than the same dollar received in the future. The reasons for that difference are interest and opportunity cost. Controlling and investing a dollar today at a 5 percent interest rate results in $1.05 in one year. For a dollar received one year from today to be worth the same as one dollar is today, that $1.05 must be matched. Converted into discount form, the factor is 0.952—that is, $1.00 divided by $1.05.

It becomes cumbersome and inaccurate to calculate a different investment interest rate for each incremental amount of investable cash flow received, so a simplifying assumption is made: the reinvestment rate will be the same as the corporation's own cost of funds. Using after-tax cash flows and discounting rates, the resulting value formulation is:

$$\text{Value} = \frac{\text{After-Tax Cash Flow}}{\text{After-Tax Discount Rate}}$$

The Miller-Modigliani discounted cash-flow formula builds on the principle of the time value of wealth received in terms of business-unit value. According to the MM formula the value of a business is comprised of two different components—the present value of the business and assets now in place at the company combined with the present value of the company's future growth. The base formula is[1]

$$\begin{array}{c}\text{Value of} \\ \text{business unit}\end{array} = \begin{array}{c}\text{Present worth of} \\ \text{unit's business and} \\ \text{assets now in} \\ \text{place}\end{array} + \begin{array}{c}\text{Present value} \\ \text{of unit's projected} \\ \text{future growth}\end{array}$$

The first value component of the MM formula—the present value of the business and assets now in place—is determined by dividing subject business unit's expected level of after-tax cash of capital, also on an after-tax basis:

$$\begin{array}{c}\text{Present worth} \\ \text{of unit's business} \\ \text{and assets now} \\ \text{in place}\end{array} = \frac{E(\text{NOPLAT})}{\text{WACC}}$$

[1] Tom Copeland, Tim Koller, and Jack Murrin, *Valuation: Measuring and Managing the Value of Companies*, Wiley, PA: McKinsey & Co., 1990, 106. This book provides extensive insight into the application of Miller-Modigliani to corporate decision making and has been an important resource in the development of this chapter.

where

E   means expected.

NOPLAT   refers to net operating profit less adjusted taxes.

WACC   means weighted average cost of capital, after taxes.

The formula for the second component of the MM formula, the present value of unit's projected future growth, is shown below. Determination of the value of future growth requires consideration of several factors including the unit's level of investment in its own business; returns earned on these investments in excess of the after-tax internal cost of funds (WACC); and the expected time period during which those competitive advantage returns, or returns in excess of WACC, are expected to continue:

$$\text{Present value of unit's projected future growth} = K\,[E\,(\text{NOPLAT})]\,N \times \frac{r - \text{WACC}}{\text{WACC}(1 + \text{WACC})}$$

where

r   Represents the competitive advantage return rate, that is, the rate of return on internal investments (which exceeds internal after-tax cost of capital, or WACC.

K   Equals the level of those competitive advantage investments (percentage of available cash flow).

N   Represents the time period during which such competitive advantage returns are expected to be sustained.

The Business Value Cash Flow Triangle
Illustrations

Figures 3.1 through 3.4 depict the MM business unit value equations in graphic form. The first of the business value/cash flow triangle illustrations is shown in Figure 3.1. This is a graphic depiction of the basic MM equation that finds the total value of the business unit from the sum of two parts: (1)

**Figure 3.1.   The Corporate-Value Components
of the Miller-Modigliani Discounted Cash-Flow
Formula: The Business-Value and Cash-Flow
Triangle**

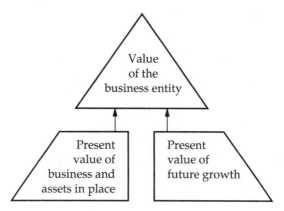

the present value of the business and embedded assets (assets presently in place in the company), and (2) the present
value of that unit's future growth.

Figure 3.2 focuses on the present value of the business and
embedded assets—the left side of the triangle illustration. That
value component is a function of the unit's estimated net operating profits less adjusted taxes (NOPLAT), divided by the
unit's internal cost of funds, as determined by applying the
weighted average cost of capital (WACC) methodology. Current NOPLAT is in turn determined by the level of the business
unit's embedded asset investment and by the rate of return
presently being achieved on the assets.

In Figure 3.3, attention switches to the right side of the
business value/cash flow triangle—the side pertaining to the
present value of future growth. As shown in equation form
earlier in this chapter, the future value results from four elements: the weighted average cost of corporate capital applicable to projected cash flows, the rate of return on new investment and the period that such a rate is expected to continue,

Figure 3.2.   The Corporate-Value Components of the Miller-Modigliani Discounted Cash-Flow Formula: The Present Value of the Business and Its Assets in Place

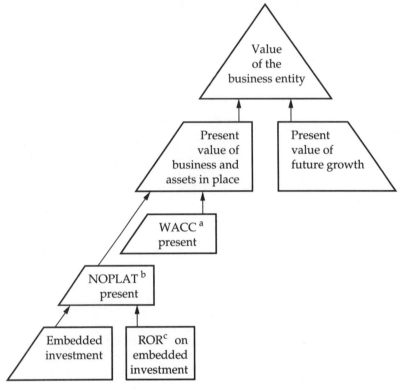

a. WACC : After tax weighed average cost of capital
b. NOPLAT : Net operating profit less adjusted tax
c. ROR : Rate of return

SOURCE: Copeland, Koller, and Murrin, *Valuation: Measuring and Managing the Value of Companies* (Wiley, PA: McKinsey & Co.), 105–121.

and the amount of net new investment that the management can afford to make in the business from internally generated sources. The latter, in turn, results from the future sustained level of NOPLAT generation and the rate of net new investments.

Figure 3.4 brings the right and left sides of the formula together and illustrates how fundamental improvements in

Figure 3.3. The Corporate-Value Components of the Miller-Modigliani Discounted Cash-Flow Formula:

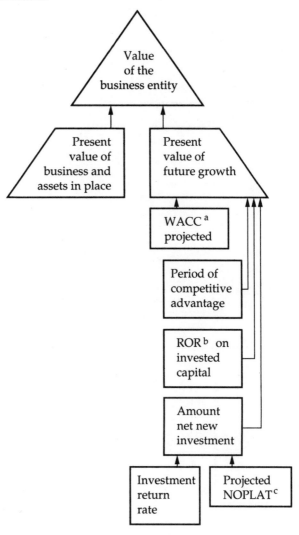

a. WACC : After tax weigh average cost of capital

b. ROR : Rate of return

c. NOPLAT : Net operating profit after tax

SOURCE: Copeland; Koller, and Murrin, *Valuation: Measuring and Managing the Value of Companies* (Wiley, PA: McKinsey & Co.), 105–121.

Figure 3.4.   The Corporate-Value Components of the Miller-Modigliani Discounted Cash-Flow Formula: Potential Opportunities

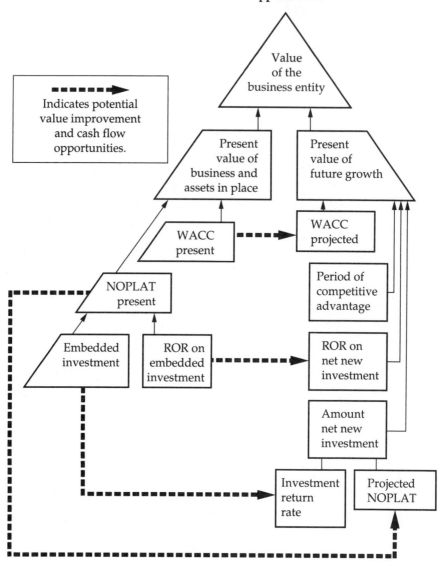

the business increase value. The arrow extending from WACC present to future represents the potential improvement in the business by operating the company with an optimal structure. Here, the term *optimal* means the mix of balance sheet debt and equity presenting the best balance between low total cost and risk, based on the expected performance of that business.

Poor return on equity (ROE) performance of American companies in the early 1970s did not merely indicate that profits were off. To some, ROE underperformance also suggested that many firms' balance sheets were burdened with too high a portion of equity in their capital mix. The after-tax cost of corporate equity may well be seven to ten percentage points above the after-tax cost of debt. If debt as a percentage of total capital is increased—either by transforming some equity to debt or by adding more debt—could result in a decrease in the after-tax WACC of, say, four full percentage points. A drop in the company's WACC, in turn, creates new value. The discounting example from earlier in this chapter showed the effects of changes in capital costs on value. One hundred dollars received one year in the future becomes the equivalent of $86.21 today when discounted at 16 percent. But if that discounting rate is dropped to 12 percent, the present value of that future $100 increases by more than three dollars, to $89.21. This helps show how low ROEs set the stage for the leverage buyout movement. But debt can also add to the overall risk of the company by adding yet another payment to the pile of obligations that are already in place. If more cash flow can be generated to support the higher debt-to-capital percentage, then a high debt percentage structure may be the most effecient. But if that is not the case, a less ambitious debt-to-capital percentage may instead be optimal.

The arrow in Figure 3.4 connecting the ROR boxes near the bottom represents the possible changes to the company's internal rate of return (ROR) achieved on net investments. Company management can do little or nothing about the level of external market interest charges, but internal returns are something else. The company's rate of return on its investments in itself may be improved by deleting administrative expenditures that bring no tangible improvement to company profitability, by dropping the bottom one or two projects or programs with the lowest internal rate of return (IRR) justification yields— even though the minimum investment hurdle rate has been exceeded and such projects would normally be approved for investment. Other possiblities for improving ROR are reducing the internal cost of administering the capital expenditure program by simplifying organizations and processes, and further reducing the mandatory payback time for new capital equipment purchases. (Additional suggestions for capital expenditure management in the postacquisition period are provided in Chapter 5).

The arrow from "embedded investment" to "investment rate" in Figure 3.4 connects the company's present embedded base of asset investments with the new level of internal investment projected by company management in future periods. Assuming that the company's rate of return on its internal investment has exceeded the cost of support funds, it makes sense that value is enhanced if *more* investment is made. For such an intention to be translated into action, however, management must make concerted efforts to reduce other uses of corporate funds, such as eliminating perquisites and bonuses that long ago ceased being performance incentives or even curtailing dividend payments to shareholders if it can be shown that the company's owners benefit more from having their funds being reinvested at high rates than being distributed too soon.

The arrow in Figure 3.4 connecting present and future NO-PLAT indicates that an increase in profits and cash flows increases value.

Applying the Value/Cash Flow Linkage to the Bid Strategy

Tables 3.2 and 3.3 depict Seekem, Inc.'s two-step process for applying the value/cash flow linkage to its operating valuation (OV) offer to acquire Grommet International. Seekem's initial bid for GI was for $14.13 per share. That initial bid is shown in Table 3.1, row 2.

Overview of the OV Approach Bid

The acquirer's goal in the operating valuation bid should be to discover the maximum justified bid level, as determined by the sum of current and future operating performance. Applied correctly, the approach relates closely to the MM DCF formula, with one calculation for the value of the target company's business and assets presently in place, and a second for the present value of future operations.

The OV approach emphasizes the target's justifiable performance-based value and not the bid dynamics of the

Table 3.2. Grommet International: Present Value

	GI Present
Value of business and assets in place	
1. NOPLAT[a]	$60,320
2. WACC[b]	16%
3. Subtotal	$52,000[a] (40%)
Present value of future growth	
4. E(NOPLAT)[a]	$1,809,745
5. Competitive-advantage period[c]	2 yrs.
6. Rate of return on investment[b]	17%
7. WACC[b]	16%
8. Investment rate (%)[b] into new projects	40%
9. Subtotal[c]	$78,000[a] (60%)[c]
10. Total value of entity[a]	$130,000 (100%)
11. Less: value of debt[b]	30,000
12. Total value of entity to equity holders[b]	$100,000
13. Number of common shares[b]	10,000
14. Price per share[b]	$10.00

[a] Information derived
[b] Information already known from public market value data or company statistics
[c] Management assumptions

Table 3.3. Grommet International: Present and Future Value

	GI Present	Future—Assuming Achievable Improvements	Changes Explained, Other Comments
Values of business and assets in place			
1. NOPLAT	$60,320	$60,320	Assumed no near-term improvement possible
2. WACC	16%	12%	Ordinary annuity
3. Subtotal	52,000 (40%)	$53,857	
Present value of future growth			
4. E(NOPLAT)	$1,809,602	$1,809,602	No change
5. Competitive-advantage period	2 yrs.	1.5 yrs.	Reduction by half year.
6. Rate of return on investment	17%	17%	One-percentage-point improvement

88

7. WACC	16%	12%	Reflects recapitalization
8. Investment rate (%)	40%	40%	No change
9. Subtotal	$78,000 (60%)	$403,960	—
10. Total value of entity	$130,000 (100%)	$457,817	
11. Less: value of debt	30,000	316,687	Recapitalization: more debt (assumed)
12. Total value of entity to equity holders	$100,000	$141,130	
13. Number of common shares	10,000	10,000	Shares stay same for analysis
14. Price per share	$10.00	$14.13	

acquisition chase. The bidder's danger of overpayment may be mitigated if the bidder applies realistic assumptions about when and how to achieve particular improvements. The OV approach, however, is as good as the depth and thoroughness of underlying future-performance assumptions. Blanket improvement assumptions lacking analysis support can reduce the OV approach to a worthless number-crunching exercise. Unsubstantiated or excessive assumptions on the future cost of funds, future sustainable earnings, or internal return rates can contort an otherwise reasonable analysis into a flawed bid that disintegrates under close scrutiny. The hastily completed OV analysis also provides investor and lender with a false sense of assurance that an overpriced bid will work. Investor and lender both discover later that the price paid was too much and that acquisition debt cannot be serviced by the target's operations.

Establishing the OV Baseline

The first issue for the bidder to address is the level of net operating profit less adjusted tax (NOPLAT) implicitly reflected by current indications of the target company's value. The process shown in Table 3.2 is a build-up: NOPLAT is developed by applying the two MM equations and inserting known data and some assumptions. The prebid market value for the equity of the company is assumed to be correct—in other words, the price of the target's common stock is assumed to fully reflect present and future price considerations of the MM discounted cash-flow formula.

Assuming for illustration purposes that the only equity is GI's common stock, the value of Grommet International that is available to equity holders is $100,000 (see Table 3.2, lines 12 through 14). GI has 10,000 shares of common stock as measured on a fully diluted basis. Applying the prebid price per share of $10, the result is $100,000. Grommet International is assumed here to be a publicly traded company; if it were private, the bidder would need to calculate an equivalent price per share using comparables. Adding the $30,000 market value of present target-company debt (line 11) to the $100,000 amount attributed to equity holders (line 12) equals the $130,000 total current market value of the target company (line 10).

Table 3.2 also assumes a value split between present and future value. Without some sort of limit attributed to future value, the analyst making bid calculations in a boom market may find that 80 percent or more of the company's assumed value comes from what will be instead of what is. Such projections may rely too much on future improvements to substantiate the selected bid level. Here the assumed split is 60-40: 60 percent of GI's target value is attributable to future growth, and 40 percent to the value of the business and assets in place now (lines 3 and 9).

GI's after-tax weighed-average cost of capital (WACC) of 16 percent is derived from an analysis of the cost and yield of debt and equity securities in Grommet International's current capital mix (lines 2 and 7). The company's rate of internal investment (line 8) is derived from GI's statement of financial condition and is estimated at 17 percent by Seekem analysts. The period of competitive advantage—the future time period when it is assumed that the target will achieve a return rate on profit on internal reinvestment exceeding its WACC—is estimated to be two years.

Now, the bidder is prepared to calculate the two sources of NOPLAT that are represented by the company's current market price per share of $10. First, Seekem calculates NOPLAT for the business and assets already in place (line 1):[2]

$$\begin{matrix} \text{Present worth of} \\ \text{unit's business and} \\ \text{assets now in place} \end{matrix} = \frac{E(\text{NOPLAT})}{\text{WACC}}$$

$$\$52,000 = \text{NOPLAT discounted one year @ 16\%.}$$

$$\text{NOPLAT} = \$60,320$$

This is followed by a separate calculation for NOPLAT corresponding to the present value of future growth (line 9):

$$\begin{matrix} \text{Present value of} \\ \text{unit's projected} \\ \text{future growth} \end{matrix} = K[E(\text{NOPLAT})]N \times \frac{r - \text{WACC}}{\text{WACC}(1 + \text{WACC})}$$

---

[2] Copeland, Koller, and Marrin, p. 106. E(NOPLAT) denotes estimated net operating profit less adjusted taxes.

$$\$78,000 = .4\,[E(\text{NOPLAT})] \times 2 \times \frac{.17 - .16}{.16(1.16)}$$

Solving for estimated NOPLAT results in the following:

$$E(\text{NOPLAT}) = \$1,809,602$$

Extending the Operations Valuation Analysis

Table 3.2 probably underestimates the potential value of Grommet International, unless it is assumed that the acquirer will make no improvements to operations after the acquisition is completed. Seekem's management makes the following assumptions, which it considers to be realistic and highly achievable (see Table 3.3, column B):

- *Reduction in the after-tax weighed-average cost of capital from 16 to 12% (lines 2 and 7)*   A four-percentage-point reduction in the WACC is considered realistic based on the debt proposed to be added to Grommet International's balance sheet if Seekem wins the bidding chase.

- *Reduction in the competitive-advantage period by six months (line 5)*   Management reconsiders and now believes that the competitive-advantage period should reflect an even more highly competitive environment than previously assumed.

- *Increase in the market value of debt (line 11)*   The increase from \$30,000 to \$319,000 is in line with the additional debt incurred as a result of the acquisition.

The resulting changes result in a new operating valuation bid for GI of \$14.13 per share (line 14).

Financial-Acquirer Value

A financial acquirer is a prospective bidder that does not have related operations, activities, or technologies that can be combined with the target to create additional value. Seekem is assumed to be a financial buyer, so the bid level in line 2 in Table 3.1 also applies to line 3.

Synergistic-Acquirer Value

A competitor knows that Grommet's European plant has excess capacity and can be combined with its own operations. The additional assumed value from such a consolidation appears to be $2.87 per share. Added to the $14.13 from the operating analysis, the result is a bid from this would-be buyer of $17.00 per share (see Table 3.1, line 4).

Strategic-Imperative Value

Global Expansion, Ltd. is a fast-growing Eurasian conglomerate. Global's board has been seeking a U.S. subsidiary for years and views acquisition of Grommet International as a critical part of its world manufacturing, distribution, and product strategy. Global's strong currency position relative to the dollar and liberal accounting treatment for goodwill in its host nation increase the amount that Global will pay. Its ultimate bid: $18 per share (see Table 3.1, line 5).

Financial-Market Value

This is not a valuation approach as much as a bid philosophy: this acquirer will do and pay whatever is necessary to ensure that it wins the bidding race.

Seekem, Inc.'s chairperson becomes increasingly restless as higher bids exceed his company's bid based on the operating valuation approach of $14.50. Criticized by some for waiting this late in the acquisition period to make a move, the chair finally acts: the initial bid of $14.13 per share is replaced by one of $22 per share.

Value Creation as an
Acquisition Deterrent

To this point, the illustration has assumed that GI management is indifferent to who runs the company in the future, but GI's management and board may instead wish to resist these acquisition attempts. If so, GI's management must work fast and hard to apply the value and cash-flow linkage to deter unwanted acquisition interest. A high price-to-earnings multiple is a good deterrent to acquisition, and increasing the multiple requires improved operations. As Sir Jimmy Goldsmith once suggested, it is difficult for a raider to acquire a well-managed company. GI might consider the actions taken by the management of one U.S. telecommunications company that had a sad record of diversification into high-technology and service fields in the mid-1980s. As underperforming acquisitions depressed the company's stock price and the price-to-earnings multiple of its stock, analysts predicted that the company was vulnerable to a takeover. Improvements in operating performance were needed to boost the stock price, so management took the following actions: it discontinued several failing ventures (including the company's investment in a fiber-optic cable business), dramatically pared administrative and supervisory expenses and thereby boosting profits by more than 20 percent, and reexamined investment in plant and facilities to eliminate wasteful gold plating or unnecessary investment.

The Value Difference

The value difference is the gap between the financial-market valuation (purchase price) of the company and the operations valuation (actual worth); estimation of both values is required in a comprehensive acquisition approach. Market valuation equals operations valuation when no postacquisition improvement can be assumed to be possible in the intended acquiree.

The Need for Specific Value-Action Steps

The difference between operations value and financial-market value cannot be explained simply by assuming that new management is superior to the management that it replaces or that working harder and better will make the difference. A systematic approach makes the resulting valuation believable and bankable. It should include the following:

- *Reduced expenses and improved profit initiatives* If present revenue levels are maintained, expense reductions often have only a limited number of offsets. Reducing expenses and improving profit initiatives can increase operating profits.
- *Increased sales* Increasing sales can result in increased value, if increases in working capital and other investments do not negate the additional operating cash flow from expended operations.
- *Reduced weighed average cost of capital* The acquiree's WACC reflects the components in the acquiree's capital mix and the costs of those components. The after-tax cost of debt is normally considerably less than the cost of equity, and permanent change in the capital structure may reduce future expected WACC by a full percentage point or more. Capital restructuring may result in more value for the shareholders of the acquiring firm: a fixed number, discounted by a more modest factor, results in a greater present value.

A suggestion on how to proceed: begin with expense reduction to generate additional cash flow and help to buffer debt-servicing requirements, lowering the acquiree's exposure to loss from this source.

Covering the Value Difference: An Example

Increased ongoing profits and cash flow boost company value. Decreased business risk, decreased capital support required to sustain future growth, and substitution of debt for equity (assuming no offsetting risk or cash-flow change) may result in a greater corporate value. Consider the following hypothetical example reconstructed from a situation facing two companies in the mid-1980s:

- *November 2, 1984* Software Company (SC) is acquired by Technology Corporation Trading Group, an Asian concern. The acquirer contends that a 35 percent increase in SC's future net cash flow, or $35 million, must be achieved to meet acquisition debt-repayment requirements in the deal's initial years.

- *November 8, 1984*   SC's budget staff recommends an across-the-board reduction in the following year's administrative cost budgets. The remaining part of the debt-servicing shortfall must be covered by revenue increases, cost re-structuring, and outright cost reductions. Those actions have not yet been identified.

- *November 29, 1984*   Working with the heads of the SC's thirteen profit centers and seven administrative cost centers, the budget group issues revised expense and revenue projections for next year. The new numbers are described as bridging the remaining debt-servicing gap of 25 per-cent (35 percent minus 10 percent from blanket reductions). New product introductions, higher product prices, and in-creased unit sales to existing accounts are offered to sub-stantiate the revised numbers.

- *December 2, 1984*   The estimates are incorporated into a revised proposed budget for the acquiree that assumes that $23 million of the $35 million net cash-flow improvement goal can be obtained through revenue-related actions.

A merger-integration team is brought in by Technology's chief executive. The team leader reports back with some of the following suggestions for improvements:

- *Establish stretch dollar goals*   Aim *beyond* the target goal amount. To better ensure that the $35 million in new cash flow is generated, the team leader suggests a stretch target of $50 million.

- *Replan the cash-flow program, emphasizing expense reductions*   Quantum improvements in cash-flow generation don't happen just by working better and harder. Such significant leaps usually require that half or more of the targeted sav-ings come from expense reductions. Managers expecting to achieve substantial cash-flow gains from sources *other than* expense reductions probably will discover that those savings are difficult to secure: price increases encounter pressure from competitors; operating profits from new-unit sales yield negligible profits because of the added expense of introductory pricing, special promotions, and extensive sampling.

- *Change the baseline period for evaluating expense reductions to the previous budget year* Assuming an upward pattern of corporate administrative expenses, next year's expense reductions already include some normal increases, based on corporate guidelines for grossing up prior year data. The use of prior year data helps ensure that cuts are made against actual expenses, rather than against year-to-year inflation.

The postacquisition team's analysis inspires a rigorous program of value creation, including the following changes: halving the number of combined profit and cost centers and reflecting the acquiree headcount reductions from those department eliminations in revised budgets; scaling back pricing and revenue assumptions so that revenue improvements cover no more than 15 percent of the net cash-flow increase requirement; and making all expense reductions from 1984 actuals rather than 1985 projections.

The Merger-Integration Time Spectrum

A third principle of merger integration is the merger-integration (MI) time spectrum. Although value creation may be most visible after the close, merger integration also applies to the weeks and months *before* the deal closes. As Figure 3.5 shows, day zero—the point at which the acquisition clock begins—is the day that the deal is closed; preacquisition planning (stage one), bid preparation (stage two), and due diligence (stage three) are designated in negative days; they precede the closing date. Postacquisition value creation (stage four) is shown to the right of the closing and is expressed in positive dates signifying the number of days following the date that the deal is done.

Figure 3.5. The Merger-Integration Time Spectrum

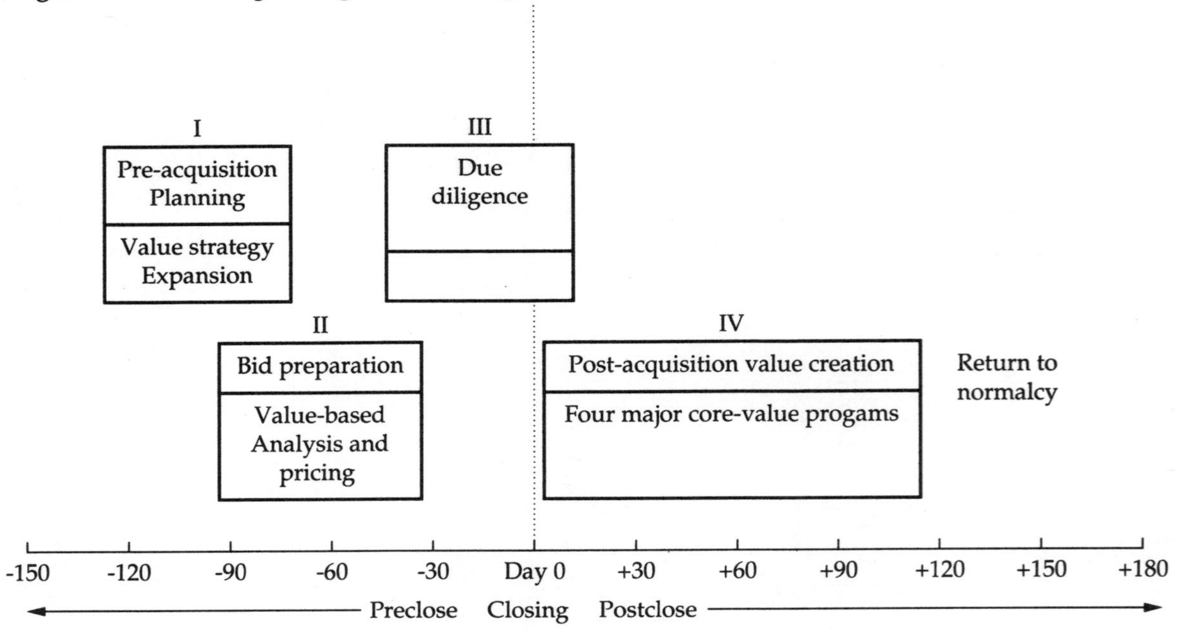

Postacquisition insight can be applied to earlier stages in the acquisition process. One approach is *value comparatives*, which actively searches for similarities linking target investigations to a knowledge base built from past postmerger value experience. Such linkages tend to involve one of four common denominators:

- *Industry* Consultants from an acquirer's U.S. staff might be familiar with the marketing approach and costs structure of several foreign companies that entered the U.S. marketplace beginning in the 1970s. That composite information can be used to help estimate expected market-penetration rates, expenses and profits for a prebid (stage two) investigation of distribution companies for a niche machine tool manufacturer looking to expand its market.

- *Life-Cycle Stage* The life-cycle stage is a point in time in the development of the merger cycle. If two separate postacquisition value investigations are conducted over a two-year period—one for an acquirer of a highly recognizable household brand name packaged foods company and one for a prospective acquirer in related start-up niches—data on costs, productivity per work hour, and other factors can be used to determine achievable dollar savings from streamlined operations in a due diligence (stage three) investigation for an international acquirer.

- *Process or technology* A company seeking to become a leader in the database acquisition field might be seeking strategic planning (stage one) advice for expanding into a third industry. If the prospective acquirer's decisions are made by committee, with little direct individual accountability and slow market responsiveness, the recommendation to the would-be acquirer might be to avoid acquisitions in the third industry unless made through a totally detached subsidiary.

- *Organization or Leadership Style* Advance knowledge of management's style and its beliefs allows the acquirer to anticipate what can be accomplished—and what may need to be deferred to future periods. Acquirer Robert Maxwell planned an aggressive initial target goal for scaling back

Macmillan, Inc.'s headquarters administrative costs. Five months following the acquisition of Macmillan by Maxwell Communications Corp. reductions were limited to head-quarters administrative staff reductions. Macmillan's and MCC's more than thirty separate reporting entities largely escaped staff cuts, in part due to Macmillan president William Reilly's advocacy of Macmillan's decentralization policy in the early 1980s. The firm's decline in competi-tiveness in the years before Reilly's arrival was reversed when Reilly returned operating autonomy to the business unit manager, even at the cost of incurring some duplica-tive expenses in the field organizations and at Macmillan headquarters.

II

MERGER INTEGRATION: CREATING POSTACQUISITION CORPORATE VALUE

4

Postacquisition Issues and Challenges

The closing ceremony marks the formal end of the deal process. For principals and intermediaries concerned primarily with the culmination of the deal itself, transaction success is achieved when the seller signs the agreement of purchase. Weeks of due-diligence analysis and haggling end with a signed and executed document. Fees are paid, and dealmakers proceed to their next transaction.

The closing ceremony does not necessarily mean the success of the acquisition, however. For the merger to work, the acquiring investor must achieve additional value in the newly created business combination. By winning the acquiree with an offer substantially above prebid market value, the investor has predicted the amount of additional corporate value that it can add to the new enterprise. In the postacquisition period these assurances must be transformed into effective action.

The Winning Bid and Postacquisition-Value Performance

The acquiring company's winning bid is linked to value creation following the close of the deal:

- *Bid determines purchase premium*   The acquirer's winning bid sets the amount of the transaction's value difference—that is, the gap between the financial-market valuation established by the accepted bid and the intrinsic value of the target determined on an operating-valuation basis. The value difference must be covered for the acquisition to succeed.

- *Purchase premium determines debt-servicing levels*   If the transaction is financed primarily or substantially with borrowed funds, the bid also sets the amount of acquisition debt, which, in turn, establishes the amount of debt servicing that management of the new enterprise must meet.

- *Bid needs to be justified to investors and lenders*   Lenders and other investors want the acquirer to create enough new acquisition value to cover the value difference and thus make the acquisition work, and the postclose period becomes the critical test of the acquirer's ability to prove that the bid was responsible and achievable.

Merger integration (MI)—the continuum connecting different phases of the acquisition process—represents the ongoing process of creating corporate value through effective business-combination activities. Value is created before the bid during the business expansion and preliminary acquisition analysis phase during the bidding process, during the acquisition due-diligence period, and during the postacquisition period after the deal has been signed.

The most important part of the postacquisition period begins with the close and ends about 120 to 140 days later. During this period the acquired organization and its employees tend to be the most receptive to the fundamental changes necessary to achieve substantial and sustainable value. A new enterprise has been established, and the leaders of the new business want to ensure its future success by implementing a logical and effective action plan:

- *Apply a structured approach*   A structured approach with a track record of prior success succeeds more often than intuitive approaches that assume that the easy-to-find value opportunities result in enough added value to cover the transaction's value difference.

- *Adapt the postacquisition program*   The postacquisition program must respond to the objectives, challenges, and limitations of a specific business combination.

- *Establish an effective organization and leadership structure*   No experience adequately prepares acquiree operating officers for the challenge of achieving twice the corporation's customary level of profits in half the required time, but these goals must emerge for the acquisition to work. Effective leadership and an equally effective organization allow the best value-creation ideas to surface and cut off unproductive courses of action. After the bulk of the postacquisition value-creation work is completed, effective management also leads the company back to normal operations.

- *Mitigate a postacquisition exodus of critical resources*   Despite the anxiety and insecurity that accompany change in ownership, critical assets, employees, and market standing do not have to be lost in the days immediately after the close. A comprehensive prevention plan minimizes damage to the new enterprise.

- *Address key acquiree employee issues in a balanced manner*   Concern for disrupted employees of the acquired company must be balanced by the new competitive spirit that must be developed among employees who will staff the new enterprise.

- *Establish clear postacquisition priorities*   Because there is always too much to do and too little time in which to do it in the postacquisition period, clear, precise priorities ensure that the most important opportunities are pursued first and that sufficient resources are applied to achieve those opportunities completely.

- *Reinvest part of the proceeds in the business*   Reinvesting helps the acquiree survive as a competitive factor in its industry and avoid slow liquidation.

The Morning After: The
Postacquisition Period Begins

In the weeks preceding the close, attention is riveted on due-diligence concerns, the closing ceremony, and related transaction dynamics. This is understandable because no business combination results without the completion of the close. When the transaction closes, attention shifts to building a new enterprise together, but acquirer and acquiree awake on "the morning after" realizing that each knows precious little about the other.

Acquirer and Acquiree Together

Acquirer Concerns

The acquiree's new owners have committed themselves to achieving an ambitious level of performance improvement in the new enterprise, but doubts persist among some of the acquirers and their lenders concerning the improvement potential of the newly acquired company and management's ability to achieve additional value. Acquirer management wonders whether present acquiree management will need to be supplemented in the coming weeks in order to get the job done or whether outright replacement will be necessary. Acquirers also worry about whether they will know that the time is right for change.

Some arguments favoring reliance on present acquiree management are compelling. It makes sense to presume that present management knows the acquired firm best and thus knows where the true value-creation opportunities reside in the company.

Despite weeks of due-diligence wrangling, acquirers have little knowledge about the operating capabilities of their new business partners, and some doubt that present acquiree management will take the requisite action. Incumbent acquiree company managers, after all, created the old order, and substantial value changes require nothing less than turning that order upside down.

Acquiree Concerns

Management and employees of the acquired company wonder about the future—both the company's and their own. During the closing top management from the acquirer firm assured them that postacquisition adjustments would be limited to those absolutely necessary to make the deal succeed. Early discussions designated several areas essential to the business as hands off. Nevertheless, today's hands-off issues have a curious tendency to become hands-on issues when the pressure mounts for additional sources of cash flow. The acquired company's officials are aware that a full price has been paid for their firm, and they fear that new value will be built on the backs of the employees of the acquiree.

As the Pace Slows

Deliberation

The pace of activity slows after the close, in part because the fervent period of contract negotiations has passed. Most of the deal intermediaries who inserted their personal opinions and haggled over three lines of contract text left immediately after the close. The pace also slows because acquirer and acquiree want to establish an effective future direction before proceeding further. Both sides sense that the time is right for careful reflection about what has occurred during the acquisition process and what remains to be done in the weeks ahead. The shared hope is that a brief period of reflection today may help prevent regrets tomorrow by anticipating the postclose slump that plagues some deals and acquirees.

Some acquirees seem to lose their momentum after being acquired. These companies simply do not breed well in captivity. Once a company relinquishes control of its own destiny, an essential element for success disappears. Sometimes that element can be identified readily, as when the acquiree chief executive officer retires without an adequate plan of succession and without an adequate successor, or when a plunge in the market share of an important product occurs because company salespersons are more attentive to acquirer-acquiree politics than to the competition. Postclose malaise may indicate deeper corporate problems as well. Some acquired companies never seem to regain their competitive momentum after the close. Customers, suppliers, and employees sense that something is missing as early as two months after the close as the once-confident organization becomes tentative and competitors who once feared the company now relish the competition. A sense of fatalism replaces the sense of destiny once conveyed by company management. Employees who once aspired to success now try to do as little as possible to avoid detection, reasoning that "If you don't do anything, then they may miss you in the next wave of downsizing."

Developing the Shared Agenda

One factor that differentiates a productive postclose pause from a mere delay in the value process is the emergence of a shared agenda. The chief executives of the acquirer and the acquiree can use the postclose pause to establish a shared understanding of goals of the business combination.

The first days following the close present a unique opportunity for developing such a shared agenda. The acquirer company CEO better understands the limits to postacquisition change from direct exchanges with the acquiree CEO about the people, units, and departments in the newly acquired firm. Although similar discussions were conducted during the due-diligence period, those may well have been clouded by negotiation considerations. Now the acquired company's CEO has the opportunity to become a full participant in the postacquisition value-creation effort. Some within the acquirer organization argue for their own value solutions on every point, but active, full involvement of the acquiree CEO at this point helps ensure that the acquired company will have a voice in its own future.

The Flawed Deal Structure

Comprehensive exchanges between chief executives cannot correct basic problems remaining in the deal structure. Consider General Motor's acquisition of Electronic Data Systems (EDS). That eventual breakup seemed to be caused by the pointed and increasingly personal conflict between GM's Roger Smith and EDS's Ross Perot, but probing beneath the surface reveals that the original GM-EDS structure did not specify how the acquiree would be credited for work on GM's systems-integration projects. The profitability of the GM work would directly influence profit calculations used in GM's issuance of additional E shares.

Before the EDS acquisition closed, GM chairperson Roger Smith complemented the can-do style and persistence of EDS's colorful chief executive officer, Ross Perot, but Smith and Perot never developed a joint agenda—that is, a shared set of expectations about the role to be played by each company and each company's CEO. Biases and misperceptions prevailed in both firms. Some at GM perceived the new acquisition as little more than another captive vendor that gradually would be assimilated into the larger firm, but some EDS employees misinterpreted Smith as authorizing radical reform from within—not simply changes to information systems and data integration but also how GM operated on a day-to-day basis, how executives were rewarded, and how the company competed in the marketplace. Perot's quips in the business press became more frequent, and tensions escalated between the two management camps of the sharp-pencil financial officer (Smith) and the charismatic salesperson (Perot).

The real problem was the deal structure itself—specifically, how EDS's profits from its work on GM projects would be accounted for. Payouts on the new and separate General Motors shares issued for the EDS acquisition were determined in part by the future profitability of EDS, but the purchase agreement indicated a lower level of profits for EDS work on GM projects than for work for other customers. GM negotiators erred in pressing for contract language more appropriate for the acquisition of a captive than for a full-status strategic partner, but EDS senior management also erred in failing to resolve the GM profit question before the close.

The Argument for a Structured
Postacquisition Approach

Instead of entering a postacquisition period of extended re-laxation the acquirer group finds itself playing a high-stakes game of management skill in which the ultimate success of the recently completed high-leverage acquisition is to be determined. The hectic pace of the due-diligence period seems tame by comparison with this intensive period. The acquirer's object in this game is to implement an effective postacquisition structure and program, which sometimes means nothing less than generating enough additional cash flow to meet the new servicing requirements resulting from the deal and its financing.

For the acquirer in a high-leverage acquisition neither go-slow nor intuitive approaches are likely to be sufficient. "Letting the two companies work out merger-integration specifics among themselves" may seem like an approach, but this go-slow course merely robs management of precious time that it needs to find an approach that *does* work. Intuitive, home-spun approaches are not really approaches either but are random actions aimed at changing whatever appears to deserve change.

A structured agenda can help the acquirer pace the overall merger-integration process and guide that process toward the logical, high-probability targets of value and cash-flow improvement. The structured approach described in this chapter—the four core approach—is based on past merger-integration experience and reflects an understanding of dependable sources of new postacquisition value creation.

The Acquirer's Challenge

The acquiring group's management team's challenge as the postacquisition period gets underway is to identify and secure substantial additional sources of corporate value in the new enterprise—at least enough to cover the value difference resulting from the transaction.

Moreover, this new value must be developed on an accelerated basis. Within weeks of the close, lenders and other investors expect to be presented with finite proof that shows that the potential for substantial new-value creation exists in the new enterprise and that this potential can be transformed readily into cash flow. The analysis must be complete and quick, or confidence in the acquisition success will erode. In extreme instances, confidence erodes so abruptly that acquisition failure becomes a self-fulfilling prophecy. Opportunities for error flourish:

- *Not enough answers and slow answers* Acquirers' assurances about the certainty of achieving additional value do not dispel fears about future illiquidity or bankruptcy, or those assurances are too late to neutralize growing concerns about the acquisition's viability.

- *Overreaching to buy time* Incessant pressure to produce more and better answers compels the acquirer to change its agenda and emphasize neutralizing concerns instead of proceeding with a fact-based value search. The acquirer's managers reason that no program will be approved unless the basic attractiveness of the acquisition is reaffirmed, so they retell the acquisition story developed during the due-diligence period, with enough additional positives to neutralize at least most of the concerns about viability: original projections are recalculated by analysts; the list of asset and business unit sales that might be sold is expanded; and each sale assumes optimistic proceeds in the event of a sale (even though potential buyers sense this fear and act slowly).

- *Missed projections* Hasty projections are not comprehensive analysis, however, and rarely gain enough additional time to find real answers to the value-creation problem. An independent inquiry by one of the acquiree's new board members may suggest that some projected sales proceeds are overstated and that some businesses and facilities cannot be sold under any circumstances because of impairments or obsolescence, or the new performance projections may appear less achievable in light of retrenchment in capital expenditures by competitors.

• *Consequences of missed projections*   The immediate consequence of missed projections may be limited to a brief period of finger pointing followed by changes in responsibility for implementing the postacquisition program. Future consequences may be more severe. Future second-stage financing may be jeopardized because of the overly optimistic expectations set in the past. Eventually, the acquiree rights itself and achieves moderate profitability, but because of unforseen changes in general business or competitive market conditions the acquired firm may require financial restructuring. Lenders that remember the projections that missed and the asset sale proceeds that didn't materialize may refuse to refinance, and the acquirer may be forced to liquidate its investment.

The Go-Slow Approach: Directionless Deliberation

Some acquirers and their advisors used to think that doing as little as possible to integrate acquirer and acquiree in the postacquisition period comprised a distinct approach to merger integration. Delegating critical postacquisition issues to involved participants may make many managers feel more secure, and such nonaction may help the acquirer company's chief executive to preserve a cordial tone for a few weeks, but a go-slow merger-integration process rarely succeeds at the primary goal for the selected postacquisition program—achieving requisite levels of new corporate value to ensure that the acquisition succeeds. Leaving the two companies to work out merger-integration specifics virtually always increases acquisition risk. Acquisitions transacted primarily through exchanges of stock and acquisitions centering on specific technology or luxury patents or licenses are two exceptions to this rule; in those cases if management faces no pressing urgency to repay acquisition debt, it may take a more deliberate approach to achieving value improvements.

For nearly all other acquisitions, go-slow is doubly danger-ous: it may cause the acquirer to squander time that could be applied in more productive ways, and it may foster a false sense that all is well with the acquisition because of a sense that most of the rancor accompanying other merger-integration ap-proaches has been minimized. Eventually acquirers discover the problem with go slow: a happy postacquisition program does not necessarily mean that the program is effective as mea-sured by new-value creation.

The Decision

After the recently concluded due-diligence investigations and in the spirit of the closing celebration, the acquiring group's CEO reassures his counterpart in the new subsidiary that only essential postacquisition changes will be undertaken. Although lenders and some acquirer company staff push for a vigorous, structured postacquisition approach, the acquirer group's CEO wants to satisfy himself that calmer options have been explored before authorizing another exhausting process. He questions whether the urgency really is required and whether affected departments and groups in the company and the new sub-sidiary should be allowed to work out their own integration agenda over time.

As a go-slow program emerges from discussions between the company leaders, those who lobby for a rigorous, struc-tured postacquisition approach find themselves outvoted by one vote—that of the acquirer group's CEO. The program calls for committees covering virtually every conceivable organiza-tional and operational issue likely to be encountered in the first year of the postacquisition period plus other issues as well. There are committees on the integration of medical benefits, information-systems, accounting procedures, and budget pro-cesses. Each committee is chaired by a middle manager from either the acquirer or the acquiree and develops its own action agenda. The thought is that only suggestions with broad-based support among employees will be adopted successfully.

Committee chairpersons receive little executive direction so that open expression and the committee members' sense of participation will be encouraged. The committee leaders are requested to develop their own list of the most important integration issues, along with proposed programs and implementation steps. If a subgroup within the committee disagrees with the majority report, minority position reports are to be submitted—again, in the spirit of open communication and full participation. Committees have eight weeks to report back with their recommendations and action steps.

The Reality

After eight weeks committee participation is reported as high, and individual contributions are spirited. Top management from both companies eagerly awaits the results of their committees' efforts, but after they have reviewed the committee reports the feeling is that time has been wasted. The two companies seem no closer to achieving their critical postacquisition goals. The go-slow effort has failed in many more ways than it has succeeded. Table 4.1 summarizes several of its most important shortcomings.

- *Few constructive new value ideas emerge* The employees' overriding concern is for self-preservation, but improving cash flow and value over a short time period requires expense reductions. Indeed, at least half of the improvement may have to come from expense reduction, which committee members are likely to interpret as meaning positions and discretionary disbursements.

- *Value opportunities already uncovered are forgotten* Improvement opportunities identified during the due-diligence phase or during the bid or qualifying-analysis phases may be treated as input rather than as value-improvement directives. A consultant's preclose report that calls for a simplified overall planning process, along with significant analyzed cutbacks in both the acquirer and acquiree companies, may be temporarily set aside, at least until the merger-integration team is designated and in place. The MI planning committee then may undermine the earlier report by raising fears about inadequate information for

Table 4.1. Why Go-Slow Merger Integration Is Likely to Fail

Few constructive new value ideas emerge.	Go-slow committees avoid making tough decisions about programs and staffing.
Value opportunities are forgotten.	Lenders and others become concerned that value-creation opportunities already identified will be deferred or forgotten.
A hands-off directive can be misinterpreted.	Some misinterpret encouragement of participation and creativity as a lack of concern for the new subsidiary's future.
Confidence drops.	Some wonder whether management has any control over the merger process.
Reports focus on process instead of data.	Committees explain how they developed lists of key concerns but avoid solutions.
Minority reports distract.	Minority reports address controversial issues. Excessive time is spent on positions that would have been disregarded in an executive-directed merger integration approach.
The rush is to differentiate.	Groups attempt to differentiate themselves to avoid comparison and cuts.
Productivity declines.	Committee meetings are well attended, but productivity declines.

executive decision making enacted and convincing senior management that the issue is too complex for action to be taken on the consultant's report now.

- *A hands-off directive can be misinterpreted* Management gives committee members considerable latitude to encourage a shared sense of participation in the postacquisition process. This means few directives and even fewer indications about hidden value that the groups are expected to find. In some instances, however, top management has few tangible value ideas to convey. Some may see top management's posture as indicating indifference about the future of the acquiree and its people.

- *Confidence drops*   Others view the hands-off posture as indicating that the acquirer has little control over the merger-integration process and fear that no direction has been provided because none exists.

- *Reports focus on process instead of data*   Comprehensive committee analysis is useful if the result is valuable new data that make the tough job of value creation easier. An open-agenda approach, however, encourages process output. Reports contain pages on how the list of key concerns was developed and how future answers can be developed, but staffers rarely prescribe a solution to these issues: the solution to the problem causes the elimination of their positions.

- *Minority reports distract*   Certain issues, such as system design and vendor selection, require single decisions and not debating societies. Unless minority reports are carefully controlled, a group that fears that it will eventually lose on an issue may misuse the minority report to prolong discussion and deliberation and delay the day of reckoning.

- *The rush is to differentiate*   Some groups and departments may attempt to avoid being categorized with other groups that have similar functions or responsibilities. Successful differentiation, they reason, makes it more difficult to compare operations and thus more difficult to enact cutbacks.

- *Productivity declines*   Committee meetings and report writing consume workhours, but productivity decline threatens both acquirer and acquiree.

The Homespun Approach: No Solution at All

If the go-slow approach actually means do nothing, what should the merger-integration team pursue instead? Some acquirers revert to intuition, which differs significantly from go-slow, but results are very likely to be the same—disappointment.

The intuitive approach is comprised of one part common sense and one part executive arrogance. Although no operating experience adequately prepares a corporate officer for the acute challenge of developing large amounts of new corporate value over a very short time period, the self-confident senior executive may attempt to lash together his own merger-integration approach. The acquirer CEO's sense of where and how to proceed will serve as a guide through the MI process. Merger-integration priorities may be based on personal bias or on something as complex as emerging technologies. A chief executive with a dislike for the accountants in his own company may make the new subsidiary's financial reporting and budgeting departments early targets for expense and staffing cutbacks as the MI process gains momentum. Some operations will remain out of bounds because the CEO feels that they provide the acquired firm with a defendable market position. The acquiree's research lab may have been flat in recent months in terms of new commercial product introductions, but the CEO may still discourage postacquisition expense cuts to research staff and projects.

Unfortunately, the emergence of hero CEOs may discourage consideration of systematic approaches. When chief executives want recognition as the Iacoccas of the early 1990s, their ambition may obscure the facts: correct moves are due as much to providence as to ability and insight. In a high-leverage acquisition, the cost of management missteps may be too great to consider any merger-integration approach except a systematic program.

Developing and Implementing the Appropriate Systematic Approach

Because no single merger-integration approach is right for all acquisitions and all circumstances, the challenge is to select the right MI program for the acquisition at hand. The selected merger-integration approach should meet the most important postacquisition concerns that management expects to face in the first months of the new enterprise and have enough resilience to identify new value-creation opportunities when initial prospects fall short of original expectations.

An effective merger-integration approach is built on a foundation of precisely defined, clearly understood assumptions. In theory, a postmerger program can be developed to emphasize any one of several goals: control, speed, and greatest number of potential value opportunities. Every merger-integration program represents a compromise. The fastest approach may not be the approach that surfaces the greatest number of value opportunities.

Four General Acquisition Archetypes

The number of potential types of acquisition approaches are as numerous as acquirers' reasons for acquiring, but four general types persist from year to year. Some of the advantages and disadvantages of each type are shown in Table 4.2. Understanding these recurring acquisition types helps the acquirer's managers fine tune their merger-integration approach. The acquiree's managers' understanding of these acquisition archetypes may help them prepare them for the future.

Takeovers

A takeover acquisition is a rapid, complete absorption of all operations and accounts of the acquiree. Practically speaking, the acquiree and most of its nonsales positions cease to exist. In dramatic takeovers virtually all redundant positions are eliminated within days—sometimes hours—of the official completion of the transaction. Sole survivors tend to be top salespersons and technicians in areas of short supply. Some refer to this approach as the neutron bomb.

The takeover approach is unquestionably fast. If two departments conduct similar functions, the acquirer's group remains. If the function is transaction-intensive, one or two positions temporarily may be filled by acquiree staff, but the hidden objective of the temporary assignment may be to learn about the acquiree's function and then switch staffing. Faced with the choice of hiring acquiree employees on a permanent basis or

Table 4.2. Four Acquisition Types

Type	Approach	Advantages	Disadvantages
Takeover	Acquirer absorbs acquiree's operations and identity	Implementation speed, uniform application, little ambiguity	Creates motivated enemies, skilled acquiree employees may lose out, possible repercussions in the community and courts
Makeover	Acquirer's approach is laid on acquiree's foundation	Preserves valuable acquiree resources, definite direction, implementation speed	Acquirer may impose inferior system, customer confusion as competitor differences fade, difficult period for acquiree employees
Restrategy	Best from each organization is combined	High sense of employee participation, establishes tough-to-beat combination of attributes	Slow to implement, may lead to analysis paralysis, may be impractical (who decides which approach is best)
Confederation	Each organization is facilitated or left alone	Only approach available for most financial acquirers, motivates entrepreneur who yearns to run own organization	Acquirer may never learn enough about the business to exert control effectively, cash-flow problems as debt-servicing burden rises

further automating the function, many takeover-style acquirers opt for the former.

Several problems may be encountered by those adopting this approach. The takeover humiliates people who are fired, demoted, or forced to succeed immediately at an unfamiliar job, and this mistreatment leads some employees to resolve to get even. Thefts are likely to occur with greater frequency, and data processing centers and other sensitive facilities are particularly vulnerable. Furthermore, a highly visible mass firing may create legal problems for the acquirer. The obsession with speed associated with the takeover approach brings with it the potential for staffing errors. Instead of staffing the position with the most qualified person the emphasis is on completing the postacquisiton process quickly. The result can be an acquiree made up of little more than shell-shocked employees with deficient skills.

Makeover

A makeover is a kinder, gentler type of takeover in which the acquiring company overlays its style and program on the acquiree's existing structure of systems, organizations, people, and facilities. The degree of retained acquiree operations distinguishes the makeover from the takeover. Changes usually are restricted to a limited number of issues essential to the ongoing goals of the acquirer, in contrast with the dramatic disruptions associated with the takeover type. A makeover acquisition is suggested by Chrysler Corporation's acquistion of Jeep/Eagle. Iaococca retained the identity and product distinctiveness of the newly acquired lines but transferred most of administration, production, and finance operations to his own staff.

As with the takeover, speed is an important advantage of this type. To avoid some of the problems associated with too much speed, however, some makeover acquirers maintain a review committee as a safeguard.

Many of the disadvantages associated with the makeover are similar to those associated with the takeover. In addition, when the makeover is used to consolidate several different companies in an industry, product differentiation dissolves. Before the series of consolidating makeover acquisitions, competitors staked out clearly different positions in the marketplace, but after the acquisitions few real differences separate former competitors. The confusion generated among many customers eventually may create a market-entry opportunity where none existed before.

Restrategy

In the restrategy acquisition the acquirer attempts to combine the best attributes of acquirer and acquiree—an approach easier to describe than to implement successfully. Companies that feel that developing a combined postmerger corporate culture is (or should be) a top MI priority may choose this approach. Its key advantage lies with people factors. Acquisitions using restrategy are characterized by participation by the individuals involved in the process. Overexpanding the participants' list is sometimes hard to avoid, but the restrategy process may become unwieldy and lead to paralysis by analysis. Because of this, the restrategy approach often evolves into one of the other three approaches described in this chapter.

Confederation

The confederation approach is used by financial acquirers—that is, acquirers without a product line, technology, customer group, or manufacturing process closely related to that of the acquiree. The acquirer functions primarily as a coordinator and a supplier of capital and sometimes as a provider of productive ideas. One example of a confederation arrangement that worked in the 1980s is Dover Corporation, a billion-plus multiple-company holding concern that grew its portfolio through the approach. Acquirees run their own operations, and their primary linkage to Dover is financial through the periodic capital budget.

One Systematic Approach: The Four Cores

Because each deal tends to have highly distinctive limitations and value requirements, an increasing number of acquirers look to the source of the potential future value when building their merger-integration approach instead of applying acquisition models. The following four merger-integration categories of potential opportunities are based on research into recurring sources of value in acquisitions that worked.

- *Core one: profit restructuring* Restructuring is the reconstruction of costs and cost-based relationships and processes to increase the company's profitability.
- *Core two: marketing and sales improvements (to operations)*
- *Core three: research, procurement, and manufacturing changes* Acquiree management needs to make fundamental decisions about what will be produced, where, and how. Profit-draining overcapacity must be addressed, possibly by cutting unused capacity either through an outright shutdown or consolidation.
- *Core four: systems restrategy*   In the aftermath of the acquisition, a wide-reaching integrated-systems program that is compatible with company expense-control goals must be developed and implemented. Information systems organization senior officers need to evaluate benefits and costs of a range of possible actions in the postacquisition period. Depending on the acquirer and acquiree organizations and their goals, these issues may include outplacement of some software maintenance costs, decentralized access to data, or facilities management.

Preventing the Loss of Key Resources

The greatest immediate threat to the acquisition following the close comes from instability. The downward spiral can be triggered even before the new enterprise begins its new existence as a subsidiary of another company. Account losses become amplified by competitors and the trade press, or the chief executive decides that he doesn't like his cut of the deal and departs abruptly. As soon as negative momentum is created, facts become secondary to perceptions. Eventually the threat of key employee departures may hang over the new company continually, suppliers talk about imposing restrictive terms, and key accounts face relentless sales pressure from the acquiree's competitors.

The Consequences of Resource Loss

In most organizations the most important assets return home in the evening. During the postacquisition period employees who once thought of their company as a permanent home now see their world disrupted. The acquisition of their company by another underscores to them that nothing is permanent, and they begin to consider a change. Moreover, the most talented people in the acquiree organization are pursued aggressively by opportunistic executive searchers and competitors. The acquirer organization often underestimates the importance of the people exodus, but waiting to act until the people exodus is confirmed may be too late. Preventative steps must be implemented in advance.

The acquiree's key accounts are romanced by motivated competitors. To these rivals, the acquisition presents a one-time opportunity to disrupt the acquiree's continuing relationship with its customers.

Suppliers to the acquiree also fear that the acquisition means a slower-paying account. The most aggressive of these suppliers may attempt to tighten terms almost at once on learning about the possible merger. If the acquisition succeeds, the supplier can appear to grant a concession when and if terms are returned to prior levels, but if the acquisition fails, the supplier's loss exposure has been reduced because of prompt action. Campeau's difficulties with its Federated Department Stores deal reportedly caused some suppliers to insist on cash payments for Christmas 1989 shipments to Bloomingdale's.

The Stabilization Response

Stabilization challenges vary by industry and circumstance, but one consideration doesn't change: the need for a program that immediately stops the exodus of top company talent, minimizes account losses, and resecures supplier relationships.

Retaining Key Employees

A progressive employer doesn't think twice about rewarding a top performer with a special bonus. Selected key individuals also should be paid a stay-put bonus for remaining with the company after the acquisition. Top performers are assured that they are foundation employees who are being counted on to continue to be top contributors in the future, and they cease observing the postacquisition process and begin being active agents of change.

Combined with an updated salary review, the stay-put bonus helps buy time for management of the postacquisition enterprise—time to make the right decisions about making changes in costs, revenues, administrative support, and processes. A thorough management review should precede implementation of any such program. If employee loyalty remains high after the acquisition and the threat of key employee loss is minimal, a stay-put bonus only increases the acquired company's expenses. When fully operational, the stay-put bonus arrangement should include the following features:

- *Bonuses limited to verified key contributors* Because payments are intended for those who directly influence the future value of the new enterprise, a certain amount of probing may be needed to distinguish the true achiever from those who try to take credit for the key contributor's accomplishments.

- *Emphasis on difficult-to-replace skills and knowledge* The recipient of the stay-put bonus should have few or no substitutes. The research technician who knows how to complete a new process critical to the company's future may be the first on the stay-put bonus priority list.

- *Future potential over current worth* It is sometimes difficult to compare future potential against present value, but if the stay-put program includes only today's key employees and overlooks tomorrow's, the company loses its future.

Rediscovering Key Customers and Markets

The close is a threshold event for the acquiree's customers. If the acquired company was an important supplier in the past, the customer wonders whether the change forces it to make changes in vendor arrangements. Moreover, the change in ownership has opened the door for competitors to approach the acquiree's best customers. Chances of permanent switches remain unlikely, however, unless the acquiree loses touch with its markets. Preventative action is to schedule face-to-face meetings with top revenue sources in the first week after the close. By listening to customers' concerns, acquiree management communicates that these accounts are important to the future of the new enterprise. The meetings also provide an opportunity for customers to understand the consequences of the acquisition in terms of prices, variety, and service.

Retaining Key Suppliers

The acquiree must juggle opposing supply objectives after the close: modifications to present procurement procedures could become a significant source of new-value cash flow, but the company must be sufficiently supplied to ensure that critical supplies and suppliers are available. To avoid a collision of these two divergent goals, the first step is to understand which item or line of items requires special purchase treatment. For practical purposes, these supplies usually are not subject to aggressive price bargaining, consolidation management, or preferred vendor programs. These and other value-related procurement tactics are explored in greater depth in Chapter 7 of this book. Critical supplies also refers to items that are either essential to key processes of the company, inventoried at or near minimum restock levels, or lack multiple sources. For practical purposes, this working definition becomes subject to the purchasing officer's own interpretation: the purchasing manager is likely to classify as critical anything in short supply at present. These supplies represent possible opportunity areas for future procurement improvement.

An additional way to avoid conflict between procurement savings and supplier special handling is to limit the period for special price reductions to a certain time period—say, one year. Acquiree management may announce that it will pay on more favorable terms but only for a preset period of time. For this approach to be worth the effort, savings should at a minimum be in the 20 to 30 percent range.

Balancing People Factors and Value

A comprehensive approach to postacquisition employee issues maintains a delicate balance between offering sympathy for displaced acquiree employees and inspiring positive performance by those who remain.

Corporate Culture as Corporate Resource

In the mid- to late-1980s corporate culture emerged as a key potential resource, as important to the company's future as patents, plants, and people. Corporate culture is a company's distinctive set of shared values and characteristic behavior—its identity. Corporate culture is the collective resolve of employees, suppliers, management, and customers about what the company represents. Each business unit develops and maintains its own distinctive culture.

The full test of corporate culture as a resource occurs after an acquisition. After the deal is closed, the founder—and his daily drive to excel—may retire. The acquired corporation with a strong sense of identity continues to know its place in the market even after the departures of the individuals who helped create it.

Some feel that emphasizing difficult-to-define concepts instead of new products and new-value creation lies at the root of the U.S. decline in world competitiveness. These pragmatists discount corporate America's penchant for introspection and claim that while Americans conduct their corporate-culture sensitivity sessions, Japanese companies take over the U.S. auto and steel industries. Still others feel that corporate cultures emerge as fast as the old order passes. According to this view, a venerable culture doesn't necessarily work to create new value: perhaps the former corporate culture wasn't so great, after all.

The aftermath of a traumatic acquisition often is tearful displaced employees and prosperous burgs that become ghost towns as new owners juggle job assignments. A corporate time past is often a poignant situation, but high sympathy at some point must be transformed to recovery for the employee and recovery from the merger-integration process.

Those requiring the most help are the employees who were forced to leave the acquiree, and they need help fast. To deal with their new circumstances they may need help in outplacement, securing severance pay and other benefits, or resumé preparation. Psychological counseling may be needed by employees who considered their employment a lifetime contract and cannot get on with their lives until they overcome a lingering sense of betrayal and hurt. Employees also may need to learn new skills, as well; downsizing at other corporations means that it is unlikely that a displaced administrator at one company can find a parallel job at another company.

Change Can Be Constructive

Management's first responsibility—even before helping employees—is ensuring that the company is viable and profitable. In a leveraged transaction that responsibility is likely to crowd out all other concerns. The debt-servicing overload usually begins to be felt within months of the close, and if management is not attentive to that issue, the transaction can be lost.

This attention to value, however, must be balanced by reassurances to the survivors who remain at the acquired company. They need to be reassured that they are valued employees and that another shoe will not drop, eliminating their jobs and destroying their careers. Those who would have survived but jumped to other companies should know that the new enterprise is stable and treats its employees humanely. They also need to know that they are welcome back if they later feel that they made a mistake.

Not all change is debilitating. Constructive stress can facilitate successful change in the new enterprise. When the acquisition happens, everything seems possible. Change replaces inertia. No longer will "not invented here" suffice as an excuse for subpar performance. No longer will territorial resistance prevail. Those who resist commonsense consolidations find themselves reassigned. Skilled, younger employees sense that their ideas will be listened to. The energies of these motivated employees are central to merger-integration success. Ideally, these emerging key drivers in the acquiree realize that they have not lost their independence but have gained the opportunity to shape their own destiny. Working with managers from the parent and new talent brought in to fill management gaps, they can forge a new direction for the new enterprise.

Establishing Postacquisition Priorities

The postacquisition period represents an opportunity to accomplish significant value-improvement change. Careful management is important:

- *Priorities must be set early and right*   Merger-integration success requires fast identification of the highest payback opportunities for new value creation.
- *Lower priorities must be put aside*   Pursue too much, and you may end up with nothing. The successful postacquisition program is limited to goals that can be accomplished realistically within 120 to 140 days after the close.

A rational approach calls for separate postacquisition efforts, directed at key areas of concern. Expense reduction, new-revenue creation, manufacturing, and systems emerge as four recurring program needs and are described in Chapters 5 through 8 of this book.

Return to Normalcy

At some point operations must return their productivity back to where it was before the close. Sometimes an operating company becomes so caught up in the motion and emotion of the acquisition and its aftermath that employees forget how to work. Two actions can speed the return to normalcy:

- *Fire the merger-integration consultants and disband the merger-integration implementing team*   Assuming that value-improvement goals are largely achieved, it's time to wrap up the postacquisition program. The consultants should not be given an opportunity to become part of the ongoing affairs of the corporation, and the acquiree should not become overly dependent on outsiders.

- *Add back some position reductions*   If the position reductions have been particularly severe in some areas, add them back. This establishes positive momentum and helps prevent the specter of an imploding acquiree.

5

MI Core One: Implementing the Value Partnership

Three words central to merger-integration (MI) success center are *how, which,* and *what*:

- *How* should investors-owners proceed in order to optimize MI program effectiveness—as manifested by increases in corporate net cash flow and by gains in value?
- *Which* value-creation opportunities should be given priority?
- *How* are opportunities and approaches best combined into effective, consistent programs?

The three sections of this chapter address these questions and cover forming the value partnership, selecting and empowering the appropriate merger-integration team, setting priorities for initial value-creation actions, assessing the potential value of each prospective opportunity, calculating the related costs of implementation, and understanding the follow-through actions critical to sustaining the new value each year.

Organizing for
Merger-Integration Effectiveness

One mark of the particularly effective merger-integration program is that it appears to function almost instinctively. A new department or a new issue is approached in the program. Shortly thereafter, logical insights for new corporate value creation appear to flow smoothly from their point of origination to other points for authorization and implementation. Substantial new sources of corporate value are accomplished in such a merger-integration program and apparently all without bureaucracy and the accompanying obstructions and distractions that stall attempts by permanent organizations to achieve fundamental change.

Appearances sometimes are deceiving, however. Merger-integration effectiveness does require the development of effective support organizations. Two organizations are described in this section—the value partnership and the merger-integration team.

Establishing the Value Partnership

The value partnership is the organization with ultimate responsibility for the success of the merger-integration program. The partnership must provide the continuing impetus to the MI program and its goals. It selects the day-to-day investigation team responsible for generating action recommendations and for ensuring that the group—called the merger-integration team later in this chapter—is effective. The value partnership is staffed with top executives from various organizations with a vested interest in MI success. Such senior-level involvement ensures that the group has the power necessary to remove obstacles.

Confronting the Forces Stacked against Merger Integration

The forces arrayed against merger integration are formidable and very persistent. A sufficiently rigorous core one profit restructuring program shows that this opposition is well deserved as the program mounts effective assaults against organizational, staffing, and budget sacred cows that stand in the way of a more profitable company. Some targets:

- *Automatically recurring department and separate business unit (SBU) expenditures*   These come under sharp-pencil scrutiny, sometimes for the first time.

- *The perceived corporate worth of the pure administrator and coordinator*   Paper-flow traffic cops are a luxury that the company can no longer afford, particularly considering debt-servicing pressures.

- *Organization charts*   Past rules concerning the number and types of staff needed to run the enterprise are discarded and replaced with leaner versions. Spans-of-control (that is, the number of positions reporting to a given supervisory position) are stretched to reduce the need for managers. Delayering—the elimination of whole layers of positions judged to be expendable—poses an unavoidable threat to those bureaucrats who have neither production nor sales roles. A new question arises: "Couldn't we operate just as effectively (or maybe even *more* effectively) with a simpler and leaner organization?"

Merger integration's initiatives strike at the fortress heart of the bureaucracy. Vigorous opposition is virtually guaranteed, and without sustained and energetic support by management with authority to make decisions stick—even if unpopular—the merger-integraton program may be in jeopardy. Resolve becomes replaced by debate. New recommendations are stacked like rush-hour air traffic, as opponents of MI attack previously submitted recommendations. Merger integration loses its way, and the acquirer company's chief executive is likely to discover that reestablishing this momentum is extremely difficult—some say impossible—once lost. MI slips in stature from a valued corporate-action program to a report that gathers dust on a planner's bookshelf.

The Value Partnership: A Working Definition

An effective and empowered decision and authorization body that succeeds in generating and sustaining MI momentum has become the value partnership. The central focus of the group is to create additional value in the new business enterprise through specific actions aimed at fundamental priorities, operations, and organization. The word partnership signifies unity of purpose to achieve merger-integration objectives once firm goals are established. Initially, members of the value partnership have their own perspectives on what should be accomplished over the course of the merger-integration period and what should be left alone, but later the group must come to a shared objective for MI to succeed. Once merger-integration program goals are set, value partnership members must sublimate their own goals to the agreed objectives of the program.

Sharing Postacquisition Decision Authority

The issue is whether the acquirer-investor should expand postacquisition decision authority beyond its own people or stick to the approach that predominates today: the acquirer reserves all real merger integration power for itself. Immediately on closing the deal, the value partnership is comprised of a single member—typically the chief executive officer of the acquirer-investor organization. The deal has been labeled as his. That designation, in turn, calls for a continuing involvement to preserve the image of success that came with winning the deal.

The working definition for the value partnership, however, clearly suggests an expanded membership roster, including the acquiree's senior officer, who has ongoing responsibility for the performance of the business. For transactions involving sizeable borrowing, add an officer from the senior lending institution. Whether before or after the close, it makes good business sense to accumulate the broadest base of knowledge and insight before making key decisions.

The advantages gained from diversifying the group outweigh possible risks. Admittedly, a larger postacquisition decision can become an ineffective debating group if the number of participants becomes too many, those assigned to the group are too junior, or the partnership lacks leadership, but offsetting actions can be taken if problems are recognized quickly. Careful attention to the interaction of group members along with assignment of specific MI value roles for each member go a long way toward heading off problems before they arise.

If expanded value partnership representation is a good idea for an acquisition financed with equal amounts of debt and equity, it is a great idea for the highly leveraged transaction. Debt restructuring doesn't change just the balance sheet. Such surgery also alters the operating conditions under which acquiree management conducts day-to-day business. Very few managers are accustomed to operating ultraleveraged companies successfully. The operating officer who ran companies with one-to-one or two-to-one debt-to-equity relationship enters unchartered territory when encountering a seven-to-one multiple. This suggests that the acquirer needs to pay even greater attention to the support that the acquiree management team receives to survive and thrive.

As depicted here, the value partnership may be an ideal. The acquirer-investor continues to dominate postacquisition decision making in many merger-integration programs, and little or no real authority is shared with others unless forced. Such situations are sometimes hard to spot. The following example of a merger-integration committee is called the Trojan horse:

- *Announcement*   The acquirer company CEO announces creation of a multicompany integration committee within hours of the closing ceremony, when spirits are buoyant.

- *Participation*   The committee is to include some officers who served the now-acquired firm in important functional roles before the acquisition, the statement continues.

- *Employee anxiety within the acquired company*   Anxiety is reduced somewhat because many employees believe that their concerns will be well represented on a postacquisition decision body that has real authority.

- *Acquiree officers*   Officers know that the acquirer knows little about their abilities and knowledge and see the committee appointment as a chance to secure positions of importance in the new enterprise.

- *Value knowledge* So motivated, acquiree executives reveal critical insights about what will work, what will not, and how to implement that later are used by the acquirer's team to reduce the value difference.
- *A sham committee* In some instances the acquirer uses the group to gather critical information that might otherwise be difficult to obtain. The group is next reduced to insignificance or eliminated altogether. Officers from the acquiree discover to their dismay that they have no real input into key issues concerning postacquisition facilities, staffing, and organization. They are powerless. As weeks pass, it becomes apparent that these decisions have already been made without them.

Control Retained: Reasons

An acquirer-investor may have three possible motivations for excluding the acquiree from a meaningful decision role during the postacquisition period—familiarity (or lack of it), fear of an obstructive role, and a 'spoils to the victor' mentality.

The acquirer chief executive officer knows his own staff and advisors and knows their capabilities and limitations. Years of working together translates into trust that they share values and the resolve to make the merger-integration program a success. That CEO probably cannot say the same about senior management from the new acquiree. Because prior familiarity is probably limited to the recently completed acquisition negotiations, the chief executive can hardly be blamed for not wishing to risk the success of the MI program on capabilities and people that are as yet unknown.

The absence of a prior working relationship also may mean that the acquirer CEO is concerned about active obstruction of the MI program or worse. Either of the following ploys by an empowered acquiree company officer could doom the MI program:

- *The delayer* This acquiree executive has knowledge about the company's operations that could be productively applied to create postacquisition value but instead undermines the acquirer's merger-integration progress. The de-

layer raises a stream of unsettling issues that require investigation, diverting the attention and efforts of the MI team.
The delayer's concerns are legitimate-sounding enough to
require follow-up investigation, which takes time away
from the development of new MI recommendations. The
delayer may note (helpfully) that the acquirer's plan to
close an underperforming plant must be cancelled because
of heavy penalties from a taxing authority that originally
granted the acquiree a sweetheart deal if it relocated there.
Likewise, the delayer may advise the acquirer that its plans
to boost the productivity of the salesforce by dropping several laggard salespersons cannot be implemented because
these employees are golfing buddies of the president of the
company's leading account.

- *The battler*   The highly vocal opponent to any and all of
  the acquirer's postacquisition actions claims that the new
  owners are destroying the value that has been built in the
  company over decades. The battler is irritating, and his
  overstatements may be a ploy to gain a better exit package
  in the acquirer's eagerness to put a disagreeable period behind them. Despite the formidable negatives, the battler
  may unknowingly spotlight some MI opportunities that
  might otherwise go undiscovered. The key: find the organizations, functions, and positions where opposition is
  most boisterous and where arguments are least supported
  by verifiable facts.

Finally, an acquirer sometimes treats the new acquiree as if
it were a reward of conquest—the victory of the bid. His
actions may simply reflect insensitivity, but such a conqueror
may later discover that he won the battle but lost the war. The
chest-pounder risks humiliating acquiree employees, which
may result in the fast departure of critical talent, increased
vandalism, and more postmerger lawsuits. Worse, a wronged
but brilliant employee may become filled with a tremendous
resolve to best the acquirer where it counts the most—in the
marketplace. Years later, the acquirer CEO may discover that
he created his own worst competitor or that a prize acquisition has deteriorated into a lifeless shell. That happened

to one European advertising mogul who envisioned himself—vocally and repeatedly—as the virtual emperor of his newly acquired American agency: one night key creative and account management simply left to form a new agency with more benign ownership—themselves.

Broadening the Base to Include Acquiree Top
Management

Based on these possible negatives the acquirer company CEO may well act on the belief that a solo approach is best. But that executive is making a terrible mistake. Regardless of the acquirer's concerns and fears, the value partnership must be structured to include meaningful participation by top acquiree management to improve overall merger-integration program performance, to better and faster implement recommended actions, and to effectively manage future risk and exposure.

The opportunity for improved merger-integration performance results when the right individual is selected and motivated. Assume that an expanded value partnership group has been set and will include a senior officer from the acquiree. Critical characteristics of that officer include

- *Relevant knowledge, effectively applied*   The right individual is drawn from the top management ranks and has the insight and experience to know where the top opportunities for MI value creation reside.
- *Greater goal orientation*   The officer is capable of sublimating personal concerns and loyalties for the agreed objectives of the MI period. Neither a delayer nor a battler is desired.
- *Forthrightness*   The officer cannot become only the implementation mechanism for the acquirer. If a given objective cannot be met, he has an obligation to point that out—as well as what the correct goal should be and how to get there.

It should be expected that merger-integration performance will improve when guided by knowledgeable insight. For the MI team member, probing a small number of prenoted opportunities is always preferable to looking for opportunities without assistance.

One of the toughest challenges for the MI team member is to distinguish the top value opportunities. Apparent opportunities are numerous, and imposters are often difficult to spot. Too many opportunities seem to be both substantial and achievable. The proficient outsider analyst has the skills to quickly identify possible opportunities and separate probables from possibles, but even the best job by an outsider can be made better when guided by the knowledgable source. The right acquiree executive knows where the real value opportunities are located, which helps the analyst dedicate more time to the higher-payoff prospects.

Including meaningful participation by top acquiree management also means accelerating the implementation of MI program recommendations. Ease of MI program implementation increases as more acquiree company employees view their company as involved in the postacquisition decision process, and appointment of a respected acquiree company officer to a role in the value partnership gives proof of that involvement. This does *not* mean that unpopular MI recommendations become popular overnight. Decisions that affect jobs, salaries, and reporting relationships are emotion-charged. Actions that would have been protested without meaningful involvement of the acquiree officer will be contested when such involvement does occur.

Finally, minimizing possible future risk exposure requires the involvement of more than just the acquirer CEO, particularly following the collapse of one or more of the acquiring company's acquisitions. If excessive acquisition debt is a factor in an acquiree's collapse, the acquiring company's management and directors may have good reason to be concerned: lenders that relied on the acquirer's assurance that the debt could be repaid before approving the loan now have to admit to imprudent lending practices or blame the acquirer and its acquisition advisors; employees jettisoned because of last-ditch efforts to preserve funds may also choose to join in the witch hunt because the acquirer failed to ensure that the acquiree would have the financial strength to survive. Other parties also may decide to join in the search for blame: taxing authorities may discover that they have lost a sizeable part of their revenue base, and antitrust agencies may find that the collapse of the acquiree has led to an unforeseen (and undesired) increase in industry concentration.

Failure of the LBOed acquiree may have been caused by overpayment—a too-high bid price that requires too much debt for financing—or by an inadequate postacquisition program, with few measures for increasing cash flow for debt servicing. In most instances, however, it becomes apparent that these two causes become intertwined as the acquiree stumbles down the slippery path to bankruptcy:

- *Overpayment* The winning bid aims high to beat out competition and only after the bid is secured is secondary consideration given to what the acquirer needs to boost cash flow to service the related acquisition debt.

- *Overestimation* To cut down the debt mountain, the acquirer overrelies on sale of certain assets and divisions, but proceeds disappoint. In an increasingly complex marketplace, some breakup value estimates now appear to be hopelessly overstated.

- *Underpreparation* Too much reliance on breakup value means too little preparation for a thorough merger-integration program. Some cosmetic actions are taken, but these are not enough to increase cash flow or reduce debt significantly.

Those looking to blame the acquirer for the acquiree's collapse may argue that both situations were in effect—that overpayment occurred and that the merger-integration program enacted after the closing was incomplete. The composition of the value partnership may become an important factor in the second consideration—the completeness of the MI program. If the value partnership includes meaningful participation by the acquiree, the acquirer is better able to assert that the merger-integration program was preplanned and rigorous because important postacquisition roles were played by officers who were knowledgeable about the best value opportunities in the acquiree.

Broadening the Value Partnership Further

Including senior lenders in the value partnership makes sense, particularly if the transaction required sizeable amounts of debt financing. The best time to negotiate a loan is *before* the need arises. If the senior lender is already part of the postacquisition senior decision body, the chances for a yes should increase.

Forging the Value Partnership Team

For the value partnership to function smoothly, three conditions must exist: value partnership members must share unambiguous goals to pursue; specific assignments for postacquisition value creation must be made for each value partnership member to ensure that all group participants maintain a personal interest in the success of the merger-integration program; and conflicts must be resolved by a tiebreaker mechanism that prevents stalemates.

Developing Unambiguous Goals

First, value partnership members must agree on priorities and resources. Developing a workable understanding of investors' and lenders' principal postacquisition objectives is key to merger-integration success. Without shared understanding, the merger-integration process drifts. In developing such a consensus, partnership members must wrestle with some difficult issues, including how the merger-integration process should be divided between pursuit of goals that can be quantified and those that cannot be quantified. Some target objectives can readily be translated into numbers: the number of staff can be counted; cost efficiencies usually can be measured; increases in sales can be recorded. But some other goals are more difficult to define: examples include the company's reputation among customers, research leadership, and the strength of customer and supplier relationships.

A balance must be established between these two considerations. If the value partnership group pursues only statistical goals to the exclusion of other considerations, attributes that are difficult or impossible to measure may be eliminated—a serious market misstep. The attributes that are most important to customers may not be measurable—at least not in customary terms. The service program that was the winning difference in capturing several new accounts last year might be eliminated because no one knows how to measure the contribution. On the other hand, without statistical guideposts, much of the discipline of the merger-integration program is lost. Remove the measure, and you also may remove the incentive to achieve that measure.

Making Specific Assignments

All members of the value partnership must be assigned responsibility for review of merger-integration recommendations, and reviewers must agree or disagree with the suggested actions as submitted by the merger-integration team. If a disagreement arises, the reviewer must provide analysis-based alternatives; simply stating that "the proposed action won't work" or "We've never done anything like that around here" does not suffice.

Resolving Conflict

The acquirer-investor chief executive wishes to broaden the participation of the value partnership—but not at the cost of strangling progress. Although the members of the value partnership agree to be bound by decisions of the group as a whole, that agreement may not prevent an impasse. Often, a tiebreaker process may be needed. If the partnership is comprised of just three representatives (acquirer, acquiree, senior lender), there may not be a need for departure from one representative/ one vote; the combination of lender and acquirer interests can prevail at any time. But if representation is broader (the value partnership should never exceed five members), an additional tiebreaking sequence may be needed to prevent bottlenecks.

Selecting the Appropriate Merger-Integration Team

Selecting the appropriate merger-integration team is a critical responsibility for the value partnership group. The successful MI program needs a team that develops and submits specific value creation recommendations to the senior decision group. Choosing the wrong team or selecting the right group but taking too much time to put them into place may jeopardize the overall MI program.

Prior Merger-Integration Experience

The range and number of possible selection criteria are numerous. Still, one factor stands out—the proposed team's prior MI experience. Members of the fully prepared merger-integration team exhibit relevant experience:

- They have wrestled with the challenge of selecting the best value prospects from among alternatives.
- They have devised analyses that support their recommended actions.
- They have confronted opposition from those in the acquiree company seeking to maintain status quo at virtually any cost.
- They have taken necessary actions to ensure that recommendations become actual value.

This is where acquirer and acquiree need help. That experience must come from the selected merger-integration team. Even a seasoned manager is unaccustomed to managing effectively under conditions of ultrahigh leverage. Fewer still know where to look and what to look for in order to separate apparent value opportunities from actual opportunities.

The MI Team Leader

The MI team functions no better than its leadership, but the skills and background of the merger-integration team *leader* are also central considerations in the selection of the appropriate MI team. The merger-integration team leader must be seen by all parties to the transaction as an equal. If the MI team leader is perceived to be middle management, the overall merger-integration process will likely be treated as a second-order priority. The political reality in most large corporations will be that every proposed dollar and position reduction action will be fought by more senior opponents to the bitter end.

Selection Alternatives

The merger-integration team may be selected from among several groups and individuals. The three possible choices discussed here are an emeritus executive with past operating experience from the acquirer company, internal task group leaders heading a combined team represented by both acquirer and acquiree, and outsider advisors.

An Emeritus Executive

An emeritus executive and his selected group may emerge as an appealing selection option. The corporate vice chairperson with a broad development charter or the former acquirer company chairman or president involved in expansion from a board position and perspective may leave day-to-day operating responsibilities to a assume a different role—to guide the future expansion course of the company. If he headed the board acquisition committee, he already may have been instrumental in the bid for the subject acquiree. In that case, the individual may have a particularly strong incentive to ensure that the acquisition works.

Assuming that the emeritus officer has remained close to the operations that he once ran, he maintains a deep understanding of what works and what doesn't in the acquiree company. The high level of respect he maintains reflects on recommendations as they are developed. The emeritus officer who remains current with his former post is positioned to excel in the MI program:

- He understands the capabilities and limitations of the acquiree's principal departments, functions, and individuals.
- He knows the key needs of the acquiree's internal operations.
- He understands how new outside resources are best combined with existing resources.

Moreover, if the emeritus officer has been involved with acquisition and expansion issues, he also may understand acquiree operations, strategy, and resources.

Some offsetting may arise with this selection, however—objectivity and energy. The executive understandably may feel a personal obligation toward former employees and past operations. That does not necessarily present a problem, if those relationships remain separate from the merger-integration analysis. Problems arise, however, if such a separation cannot be maintained.

A successful MI program calls for a high level of active involvement by the emeritus executive: direct digging and analysis capable of withstanding challenges. Unresearched, off-the-cuff observations and opinions will not hold up under tough questioning and neither will delegation. If the emeritus executive cannot, or will not, perform an active role and instead delegates his responsibilities, the power of this MI selection is wasted.

An Internal Officer

One advantage of having an internal officer from the acquirer company head an MI team is familiarity with the acquiree. If the proposed merger-integration team leader was involved in early identification of the candidate company, he probably has a head start toward uncovering value opportunities in the newly acquired company. Experience, however, shows that such a choice tends to be a mistake. Either as a result of delegation or direct assignment, this choice becomes the same as middle-management leadership of the MI program, which diminishes the effectiveness of the merger-integration effort. These MI teams lack the senior management perspective and the power to resolve the toughest MI resource allocation questions. Within both acquirer and acquiree organizations, the message is the same: "Wait long enough, and problems will go away." In response, the MI team limits itself to less offensive (and less important) concerns. Consider the following hypothetical sequence of events involving AcquireCo and TargetCo. An opportunity for delayering—that is, the elimination of one or two entire layers of positions from the new combined enterprise—emerges from the analysis conducted by AcquireCo's middle-management–led MI team. Savings and value-creation benefits from such a move could be substantial; but the internal political risk is too great for a middle-manager group, particularly since position reductions could effect AcquireCo. Because creating a permanent enemy with power is risky, incremented changes are pursued instead—position consolidation here, one or two process changes there. Diluting the MI effort helps keep the team out of trouble but prevents the MI group from being fully effective.

External Advisors or Consultants

Employing external advisors or consultants represents yet another merger-integration team selection alternative. This group is preferable to other alternatives if postacquisition experience is extensive and relevant and can be applied to the issues at hand in this upcoming MI program. In the best situations, the external advisor offers the following advantages:

- *A systematic value approach*   Prior merger-integration experience helps the advisor to look first where the greatest opportunities have resided in other MI programs. Such value-creation knowledge—about high-potential organizations, functions, and processes—is sometimes more important than operating knowledge about the two companies.

- *Methodology*   Some approaches are distilled into specific guidelines and tasks that provide members of the value partnership with a useful understanding about how much progress they have made in the merger-integration process and what they still have to do in the time available to meet value-creation objectives.

- *Speed*   Speed may be another advantage favoring external advisors. When in effect, the MI program resembles war: high intensity, constant anxiety, incomplete information for decisions, and limited approvals by necessity. The right kind of external team will be accustomed to operating under such conditions for weeks. The internal team may not be accustomed to this controlled chaos.

- *Independence and objectivity*   This external merger-integration team is not intended to be part of the present or future management of either the acquirer or the acquiree. This separation is intended so that recommendations pinpoint the best value opportunity and not those that are safest politically.

- *Return to normalcy*   Because the external merger-integration group is a transitional body, its involvement has a beginning and an end. Assuming that realistic MI goals have largely been achieved, disruption of day-to-day operations stops after the MI team leaves.

There are several possible pitfalls associated with using external advisors and consultants as the MI team. Most of these shortfalls arise from failure to achieve the performance noted above:

- *Using checklists rather than a pretested approach*   If the nominated team has questionable experience, or if its MI methodology turns out to be a little more than a "ten-things-to-know" checklist, be cautious before committing.

- *Presenting misleading qualifications*   Check out the breadth of experience cited for the proposed team. If additional investigation reveals that the leader is the only experienced individual on the team, confirm the actual time that the leader will spend on this MI work. Also confirm that qualifications apply to the specific members of the proposed MI team. Institutional qualifications often are impressive on paper but may be misleading if those who performed the leading role on the project are not on the team.

- *Assuming that outsiders will become permanent* A different sort of pitfall arises if the external group attempts to assume a permanent role in either the acquirer or acquiree organization. If this comes to be suspected by employees during the merger-integration program, the effectiveness of that MI group may be destroyed. Attention and energy become focused on discrediting the new political force rather than on creating postacquisition value.

Empowering the Merger-Integration Team

Selection of the best group for the job means little unless an empowered—albeit transitional—role is developed for the MI team and its leader during the postacquisition period.

Working with the Acquirer and Acquiree Chief Executives

Success for the profit-restructuring program relies to a great degree on the level, timing, and form of support provided to the MI team from top management of the acquirer and acquiree companies.

Reporting Level

The MI team should report directly to the value partnership group, assuming multicompany representation on that body. The partnership is the temporary organization developed specifically to empower the MI team and to examine action recommendations as they are submitted. Alternatively, the MI team can report to the acquiree company's board of directors. Board committees are sometimes formed to deal with specific issues of companywide importance, such as finance, management succession, and acquisitions. Assignment of a special committee at the board level for the MI program might be necessary if the value partnership turns out to be little more than a rubber stamp for acquiree company top management.

Timing

The timing of the merger-integration team selection announcement represents an important element in the initial empowerment of that team. If the selection process was in progress before the close, the MI team announcement should ideally be made at that ceremony to communicate that the merger-integration team is important and is a part of the postacquisition development in the weeks ahead.

Conversely, if the selection announcement could have been made at the time of close but is not, the perceived importance of the overall MI program may slump. The misperception may be that merger integration is solely an implementation matter that has little to do with the ultimate success of the deal. If the selection process continued into the postacquisition period, the logical time for announcement coincides with the time that the acquiree key drivers arrangements are announced (Chapter 4). That announcement will also command considerable attention.

Temporary Officer Equivalent

The merger-integration team needs some form of empowerment—implied or direct authority to get things done—or it faces challenge at every point; and formal—but temporary—empowerment appears to be the best approach. The MI team should be authorized to act as a result of specific proclamation or by assignment of the leader to a position with recognized responsibilities and authority.

Informal empowerment, by contrast, is usually more difficult to discern because employees and others have to *sense* that the merger-integration team and its leader have the power to undertake actions. Communicating this empowerment may be as subtle as the acquirer company CEO's proximity to the merger-integration team leader's place at the conference table. Admittedly, informal empowerment may be easier for employees to take—especially given the fast pace of changes to date. But such an approach takes time. The employees may not understand that the MI team has authority until weeks have passed, and considering the brevity of the the merger-integration program, there is not enough time to risk obstructions.

Working with Other Integration Groups

The working relationship between the designated merger-integration team and other groups within the acquirer and acquiree organizations that are expected to perform a postacquisition role will expectedly be strained. Merger integration is one activity in which more does not automatically mean better. In empowering the MI team, senior management also must communicate that no other group is permitted to submit position or expense recommendations to the value partnership.

Information Requirements and Requests

Access by the merger-integration team to complete information on a timely basis is critical to MI success. To be most effective, the merger-integration team must be able to cut through conventional channels to get needed data—and fast. A report that is 50 percent complete, or that is provided to the MI team leader two weeks late can slow MI to a halt. To help prevent this, the MI team leader can take several actions:

- *Set up the MI team's base at acquiree headquarters* An accessible location facilitates information gathering. It also allows MI team members to be available as needed for questions and comments.

- *Issue a top management directive* Acquirer and acquiree chief executives together communicate that information requests from the MI team must result in a full and complete response by a preestablished number of days. Actual performance is monitored on a spot basis, with greater frequency during the initial months of the merger-integration program period.

- *Assign an internal fact-gatherer to assist the MI team* Information-gathering is facilitated when the team has assistance from an insider. A knowledgable staffer from the acquiree is assigned on a full-time basis to help gather and interpret information. Decisions must be made with incomplete information, and substitutes or other analyses must be developed when it turns out that sought-after data simply do not exist. The appropriate individual knows what reports and information are available in the company today, as well as what is not available. He should be adept at developed or combined second-preference sources to come up with the best possible data support.

Profit-Restructuring Opportunities

Successful development of new corporate value through core one profit-restructuring actions may be tantamount to success for the overall merger-integration program. As a percentage of the overall new-value creation for the MI period, profit restructuring usually shoulders a significant part of the total value-difference coverage burden. Core one actions are highly visible to all of the parties interested in the ultimate success of the transaction. Many of these—organization restructurings, department and business unit consolidations, process modifications and changes in internal services—will be controversial. Core one establishes a momentum for the rest of the MI program. Early core one success can mean an unstoppable merger-integration juggernaut. But too-slow progress may encourage incessant sniping at the merger-integration team, jeopardizing this and the other MI core programs.

A Working Definition

Profit restructuring involves the identification, management, combination, and transformation of current and prospective expenses of the corporation to improve corporate efficiency and effectiveness. The true nature of this core is expense adjustment—adjustments between fixed and variable expenses; changes in the level and rate of growth of corporate support costs; simplification of cost-related processes; use of outside sourcing, either to spur greater efficiency or as a cost-effective alternative to company services or both.

The goal of profit restructuring is to recalibrate the enterprise's engine, enabling it to squeeze more cash flow from less revenue and with increased predictability. The engine analogy seems to be appropriate. The company's cash-flow mechanism generates a defined level of performance (cash flow) from its fuel (investment). But speed and other indications of performance may decline over time as the engine ages. Performance may be held back by excess weight, loose connections, or engine residue. Your vintage 1955 Ford Fairlane barely reaches 60 MPH without coughing, yet the kid down the street transforms the same model of the same car into a fire-breathing terror. You would like to believe that there are two engines under the hood of the revamped Ford, but you know in your heart that much of the performance answer lies in improving the efficiency and effectiveness of the engine—getting more from less.

How can the corporate engine be recalibrated to generate more cents of cash flow per each dollar of revenue? The principles are essentially the same as in merger-integration core 1. Lowering fixed costs and adjusting the relationship between some variable costs and revenues significantly reduces the subject company's break-even point—that is, the level of unit sales necessary to break even in profit terms.

In fact, it was an automaker, Lee Iacocca, who has provided one of the best examples of recent years of the corporate performance benefits from dramatically recalibrating key aspects of the corporate cash-flow engine. Cash flow was negative at the time Iacocca took the helm at Chrysler Corporation. A federal loan bailout and a reasonably acceptable series of new product introductions (K-Cars) played a critical role in the recovery. First, the former Ford executive had to reconfigure Chrysler's break-even level so that K-Car and other sales would be profitable. Several nonautomotive operations were divested. Expansive rooms that once held legions of design, promotion, and cost analysts at their desks now contained only desks. Chrysler Corporation was not a high-leverage acquisition, unless you consider a federal bailout to be the ultimate LBO, but it offers an example of how a unifying sense of intensity and urgency makes change happen.

Acquiree management facing their first possible cash-flow shortfalls as the economy spurts and sputters may wish to follow the Iacocca precedent. Yesterday, acquiree top management may have managed a company with equal amounts of debt and equity, but with the close the debt-to-equity ratio may have soared to five to one.

The Profit-Restructuring Imperative

Profit-restructuring actions should be taken in advance of need, but often they are not—at least not without an incentive—a profit-restructuring imperative. Initial divestments of assets and minor operations and (relatively) noncontroversial expense adjustments—such as eliminating shareholder relations staff and scaling back dual headquarters—are taken. These may actually generate enough cash flow in the initial months to allow acquirer and acquiree management to avoid tougher decisions later about positions, organizations, and operations.

But this is a damnation rather than a blessing. If effective profit restructuring actions are not taken in the initial weeks following the close, the new enterprise may lose its resiliency to make those changes in later periods. Moreover, some expense reductions may turn out to be illusory. Unless a structure exists for cutting out and keeping out unnecessary corporate weight, costs tend to return. Sometimes a threatened severe cash-flow shortfall is needed to spur management to take an overall action plan. Consider the following hypothetical example involving AcquireCo and TargetCo.

The Visit from TargetCo's CFO

Congratulatory euphoria following the close gave way to concern about the economic viability of the transaction. AcquireCo management and the financiers of the TargetCo transaction fear that both a cash-flow shortfall and a value shortfall could soon jeopardize the transaction. TargetCo's financial officer—let's call him Jim Greensleeve for this illustration—is in town to warn his boss/ counterpart, Cash Whoard, that TargetCo will soon be encountering tough times. The first few debt-servicing payments may be in jeopardy (Jim's boss and TargetCo's chief executive officer is also meeting separately with his opposite as the discussion with Cash begins). The disturbing news comes at a particularly inopportune time for the new acquiree. Cash notes that it was only three weeks ago that the closing took place, capped with a gala signing party. Nonetheless, Jim proceeds to explain the multiple problems that TargetCo faces:

- *Revenue mix in transition* Greensleeve describes how the outbreak of peace in Eastern Europe halved TargetCo's sales of its leading product to the military—a potassium compound added to pancakes by military cooks. The army was being cut back dramatically. New customers had to be developed. Developing alternative demand looks like a long-term endeavor. Military academies, certain corporate cafeterias, and surrogate operations of several types emerged as early prospects, but at this point marketing has virtually no understanding of these customers. Even if all those customer groups came through, TargetCo would still face a tonnage decline of one-half. The damage: at least $10 million in revenue, 30 percent of which drops down to operating profit. "It gets worse," Greensleeve warns.

- *Production* A conveyer-line snafu combined the lines for the TargetCo's one kiddie consumable—synthetic licorice whips—with deadly cyanide Q pills used by secret services.

- *Inventory* Then a competitor spread the word about the licorice disaster to the press and the product died in a fireball. Two weeks ago, the product was generating $8 million in annual revenues and a 20 percent operating profit margin; today, nothing. The product is trashed. It won't even work as cattle feed, since ranchers apparently don't cotton to their bulls having black teeth. The synthetic licorice whip inventory is soaring, drawing away cash that could otherwise be used for debt prepayment. The potassium inventory problem was caught early. The problem isn't as severe because those components can be sold individually as industrial chemicals.

- *Manufacturing* Capacity utilization overall now hovers around 65 percent, compared to a full twelve points higher one month earlier. No layoffs have occurred yet. Greensleeve is very aware that TargetCo's debt-servicing margin of safety has been wiped out. The interest payment due sixty days from now is $10 million. If everything goes right and there are no further problems, Jim's projections show that about $9 million will be available for servicing.

Cash paints an even darker picture, if that is possible:

- *Permanent cash-flow–value losses* He figures that the acquiree has lost permanent value, not just transitional costs that can be made up later. This further expands the postacquisition value difference that must be made up through value actions in the coming months. But no readily achievable sources of additional value are apparent—at least at this time. With one important product gone and another crippled, chances of covering the value difference decrease.

- *The licorice whip product appears to be dead forever* The spectacular adverse publicity has permanently damaged that product's customer franchise—obliterated it, as a matter of fact. This is value destroyed, without any offset in return.

- *The process of trying to generate replacement demand for the potassium compound abandoned by the military* raises a series of disturbing alternatives: any customer search would further drop product margins, just when every penny is needed to meet next quarter's debt-servicing obligation; and if TargetCo makes the investment, there's a high probability that much or all of it will be wasted. The company's mistake was thinking that a preferred vendor arrangement with a sizeable supplier could never go away. The military market for TargetCo was special—hardly the type of account relationship that can be offset with three months of customer and market investigation.

Cash and the other AcquireCo management are not afraid to act, but they don't want to jump in precipitously, either. The acquirer's dilemma, summarized:

- *Proportional reduction*   Unless the scope of TargetCo's operations are scaled back at least proportionally with the decrease in operating profits, TargetCo may never get close to meeting its servicing obligation.

- *Hesitation*   AcquireCo is reluctant to act prematurely. Unless the acquiree has people on hand to develop and maintain sales support materials, research, market analysis, and staff, there's little chance of gaining new customers (and product demand) to replace those that have been lost.

Explanations for the Cash-Flow Shortfall

How did the acquiree get into this predicament? Part of the answer lies with the pricing of the deal because that dictates the financing requirement. Another part involves the operating assumptions that indicated how the substantial debt load would be serviced and repaid.

Pricing

Assume that different acquisition groups pursuing TargetCo submitted bids ranging from a low of $90 million to a high of $120 million. The high bid was AcquireCo's. Assume for these purposes that all bidders were financial buyers—that is, buyers without related operations that they could directly integrate with TargetCo. Each prospective acquiree planned to manage TargetCo in a similar manner after the close.

Overbidding by AcquireCo became possible—some say, was encouraged—by the absence of a singular approach for determining what TargetCo was worth. AcquireCo was able to justify a "winning" price (which was substantially above competitors' bids) largely because of the latitude allowed by different numerical valuation approaches.

Deal Financing: Consequences

AcquireCo's financing was clinched by projections indicating that the high purchase price (and thus the equally high financing amount) could be supported by $30 million in added annual TargetCo cash flow. That additional cash flow, if real-ized, would be one-third more than TargetCo's current level of $90 million. About half of that additional amount, or $15 mil-lion, was identified at the time of financing. AcquireCo ana-lysts believed that extension of TargetCo's current market-share trendline into future periods would add about $5 million to the acquiree's annual net cash flow. About $10 million annually in additional net cash flow was projected from automatic merger-integration actions to be taken in the first few days after the deal. These automatics were highly visible actions recognized by virtually all of the bidders and even the financial press. Ac-tions on the automatic list included some headquarters staff consolidations and discontinuation of a new compound that had failed in three trials (but that had been a favorite of the chair). The difference between the improvement requirement and the sum of these amounts—that is, $15 million—remains to be covered by the new-value-creating actions of management.

Following the Close

Following the close TargetCo's cash-flow situation deteriorated more. AcquireCo top management was confident that projec-tions would solidify after the closing; but the close arrived and left, and no additional sources of net cash flow had been pin-pointed. Double trouble lurked on the horizon. In question were not only the original $15 million value difference but also other amounts that had previously been counted as sure things in financing the deal. The value difference was no longer $15 million but appeared to have increased by $25 million, to a $40 million total:

- *Bottom-line error*   The analysts preparing the original net cash-flow projections committed some critical errors that were not uncovered until now. They assumed that addi-tional revenues would result in added profits at the com-pany's gross profit margin (to sales), as contrasted with the operating margin. Net effect: overstatement of earn-ings from new revenue sources ($10 million impact).

- *Buy-in underestimation*   The assumption: TargetCo already participated in proposed markets, so no introductory expenditures were needed. The error: Market-entry outlays were needed. Sales coming anywhere near projections required special support and additional costs ($5 million impact).

- *Disappointing sale proceeds* Proceeds from a general auction sale of two business unit sales were considerably less than expected. The bankers conducting the auction blamed market conditions. Participants in the process complained about not receiving enough information to make a reasoned bid ($10 million impact).

Profit Restructuring:
Head-Count–Related Costs

AcquireCo management knows that something must be done and quickly. Although some financing payments and maturity dates might be rescheduled, AcquireCo management is reluctant to jump to that solution this early after the close. Such an action could jeopardize other AcquireCo deals, and financiers also might overreact to the TargetCo situation, pulling out funds before an effective solution can be devised. Consolidation of plants is a possible value source but will take too much time. The same goes for new product introductions—too little, not soon enough.

As the phrase is used here, *profit restructuring* means achievement of ongoing and significant improvements in the fundamental expense performance of the combined companies in the acquisition:

- *Ongoing* Emphasis is on actions and programs that create continuing profits and cash flow for several years and not just one. Selling unused land, boosting period earnings, and cutting company debt does not change day-to-day operations.
- *Significant* Profit restructuring emphasis is placed on programs that generate the greatest amounts in the shortest period of time.
- *Expense* Emphasis is on expense reduction as the primary source of profit and cash-flow improvements and thus

value increases. Experience suggests that 50 to 70 percent of a major profit-improvement hurdle must be met through expense reductions rather than by additional volume or pricing. Revenue-driven profit projections often underestimate full associated costs. More important, high support costs may become entrenched as management waits to see whether revenues are achieved. Once entrenched some of these costs prove to be particularly difficult to later cut.

Savings must be sought in *both* the acquirer and acquiree companies. Few acquirees have the untapped profit potential to cover the value difference by themselves, and pursuit of cash-flow improvements in the acquirer organization following the close—not just the acquiree—fosters a perception that the merger-integration program is neutral.

The principal target for profit restructuring is recurring corporate people costs—both apparent and hidden. *Apparent* people costs show up in the human resource department's head-count lists and company personnel records. These are compensation, benefits, and other direct costs relating to current employees of the company. In some organizations, analysis of people-related costs is extended to include some support costs on an allocated basis, such as space, telecommunications, and utilities. *Hidden* people costs include processes resulting from the interaction of too many or the wrong types of staff. Such costs are often difficult to uncover yet are significant drains on company profitability nonetheless. One example is paralysis by committee—the opportunity cost of an overly complex decision process made by committee at least in part because of excessive staffing. TargetCo's pricing apparatus may slow to a standstill because several layers of managers need to be informed about minor changes; competitors with a faster pricing process respond faster to market changes. Another example is an unbalanced supervisor-to-worker ratio. When the ratio of watchers to doers is out of synch, a seven-position rowing shell may have six seats manned by coxswains barking orders and a single rower doing all the work. Eleven profit restructuring categories are explored in the balance of this section.

Delayering the Organization

AcquireCo's MI team leader encounters a five-tier staff structure at TargetCo, and asks "Can TargetCo operate as well or better with two *fewer* layers?" That answer may go a long way toward achieving AcquireCo's postacquisition cash-flow improvement and value-creation objectives. Eliminating one or more total organization layers presents a singular opportunity to achieve significant postacquisition dollar savings:

- *Scope*   Staff reductions, when achievable, involve groups of employees, not just random individuals, and the same holds true for related costs.

- *Ongoing savings*   Direct and indirect extended head-count savings tend to be substantial—assuming that the head-count reductions are made in the layer identified and assuming that displaced executives are not automatically allowed to demote themselves to lower levels.

- *Process changes*   These changes may be approached in a systematic manner. Elimination of a full layer forces changes in corporate internal procedures.

Delayering tends to root out supervisors at all levels in the organization who function as traffic cops. Manager-level and higher executives may supervise, get along well, and communicate upward in the organization with great skill; but traffic cops add little or nothing to the operating profit line as a practical matter. They even may decrease cash flow in direct ways, such as by interjecting themselves into processes unnecessarily.

Delayering Breaks Through

Carefully planned and rigorously implemented, delayering slices through the obstructions created by organization complexity and position inflation. The company becomes more complex with growth, and over time conventional head-count-reduction attempts tend to be discouraged by structures already in place—dictated divisions of labor and responsibility, rigid span-of-control rules, and well-established dependencies between different departments.

Delayering cuts a swath through the organization that overcomes many of the obstacles to conventional position adjustment. Executive positions at the top layer and key customer positions tend to remain undisturbed. Often, it is *middle-layer* positions that come under intense scrutiny, perhaps for the first time. Delayering heads off any tendency to push head-count reductions down to the lowest paid staff. Issue a 10 percent head-count reduction goal to some department managers, and full-time secretaries and delivery boys lose their jobs. Such a "lowest person on the totem pole" head-count reduction approach is not only ineffective but may be illegal, as well.

Implementing the Delayering Approach

1. *Determine the number of organizational layers* First, the merger-integration team evaluates the opportunity and challenge at hand by devising an organizational depth chart with the customer shown at the top rather than the bottom. The key question is, How many layers separate the key customer from top management? If the organization is too complex for this exercise to be completed in a day, warning alarms should immediately be ringing. At one hierarchical organization that shrank slightly from ten layers to eight, the organization chart was a virtual encyclopedia. Each chart seemed to be tied to another, and another, and so on.

2. *Classify positions by broad functional category—executive, supervisory/coordinating, executional (implementing)* This is accomplished through interviews conducted at the next higher level, as direct discussions at this point can yield misleading findings. At this point, such discussions should concentrate on the subordinate's use of time rather than on a description of specific responsibilities.

3. *Coordinating activities are forced down, or alternatively, up, into other layers of the organization* Look at the pattern that emerges from the corporation's newly developed organization depth chart with customers at the top. Look for positions and layers in which coordination and supervision represent 40 percent or more of the indicated time spent

by the manager. Once a possible target organizational layer is identified, probe to fully understand functional responsibilities. Some specific functions and activities will probably become apparent as candidates for elimination at this point. The functions and activities that survive are, in turn, assigned to other layers of the organization, without additional staff. Whenever possible, the assignment of added responsibilities should be driven down, rather than up, in the organization. A lower-level employee will stretch time to enlarge a job, whereas a higher-tier staffer will likely assign a low priority to the newly assumed responsibilities.

4. *Factor in key driver designations from the postacquisition stabilization effort (Chapter 4)* By definition and designation, these are the employees that the future organization should be built around. Adjust organizations for these important contributors if necessary. Organizational layers with few key drivers are spotlighted and become possible candidates for elimination. If key drivers have two senior managers between themselves and top management, eliminate those blocking positions.

5. *Transform layer changes into specific head-count reductions* Specific positions and incumbents should be identified; otherwise acquirer management risks having the investigation become little more than a study. The current incumbent in the position in the eliminated layer is usually also the employee identified for reduction action. Pushing the incumbent lower in the organization is unfair for the organization and the individual; employees who perceive that they have been demoted to positions below their capabilities become underperforming employees. If the analysis has been conducted thoroughly, the corporate traffic cop is the coordinating individual that the company can *most* afford to lose. The alternative would be to dismiss a skilled but lower-tier employee. Such a decision is not best for the corporation. An across-the-board layer elimination is likely to be easier to justify on a reduction-in-force basis; citing overall corporate objectives avoids specific individual assessments or other decision criteria.

Individuals who have recently been promoted to positions in the layer or layers designated for elimination are excluded from this head-count reduction effort. Their dominant skills are probably not coordinative; they've just had the tough luck to be promoted into the wrong place in the organization, at the wrong time. No such exclusion is granted for the demoted employee; the decision to redirect "good old Fred" out of the headquarters and into a regional group supervisor position was probably made in recognition of Fred's coordinator role.

Aftermath

Humane, sympathetic treatment of employees affected by this action is critical to the success of other parts of the merger-integration process. Both for their own benefit and that of the employees who remain, it is important that the employees involved in the delayering are moved off-site to a full-service support location. This should happen as quickly as possible following the delayering announcement. Particular care should be taken to ensure that the outplacement firm is appropriate. These are often senior managers; the wrong outplacement program may generate considerable resentment if that program is designed for middle-tier employees.

Extending special early retirement provisions for this group may make great sense. Overall, these are likely to be older employees with sizeable reserves in company profit sharing, pension, and stock-purchase programs. Extending the early retirement age back to fifty years for this group, liberalizing terms for pension vesting, and transitional counseling for second careers provide the beginning foundation for a positive program.

Capital Expenditure Adjustment

Capital and project expenditures may represent a sizeable opportunity to increase net cash flow generated by the company or at least to change the timing of part of those disbursements, in order to make more funds available when acquisition debt-repayment pressures are the greatest. Despite the low percentage of capital investment in the United States compared to other industrialized countries, opportunities do exist, but the merger-integration team must know what to look for—such as the automatic expenditure that is never challenged or the excess of projects designed to preserve present market positions and shares rather than build new ones.

Careful planning, categorization, and follow-up are needed to get the most out of this opportunity, and the compelling appeal of easy answers must be resisted. Percentage reductions rarely succeed. The merger-integration effort calls for a systematic program rather than misleading quick fixes. Key actions examined in the following pages include categorizing opportunities into relevant categories, establishing priorities based on key strategic objectives, and using a competitive approach for allocating scarce capital—that capital suddenly becomes much scarcer after the company is LBOed.

Background: Recognizing the Signals

Opportunities exist, but to find them you need to know where to look.

Once the transaction has closed, the merger-integration team's sights are set on achieving the deepest possible cuts in acquiree company disbursements as quickly as possible. The biggest apparent targets are the capital and project budgets. The capital expenditure, or *capex*, line often dwarfs all other annual report entries listed under uses in the statement and sometimes exceeds the next highest use category by a two-to-one margin.

The funds flow entry does not even reflect the full extent of expenditures associated with capex and project expenditures; only the equipment cost of projects are shown in the formal financial statements. Coordination, administration, and implementation costs are buried in the staff budgets of departments and the acquiree's various separate business units (SBUs). A multiplier effect is at work. Calculate the full cost of these full-time staff spending all or a substantial amount of their time on present, past, or future capital issues. Then, determine the number and cost of the additional administrative and supervisory people justified by the need to support *those* staffers. Then add those sums to the recorded amounts for capital projects. This illustrates the pervasive influence of the capital expenditure budget on the corporation and how that influence multiplies.

Here are three suggestions for where the merger-integration team might find its best capital-expenditure opportunities:

- *The built-in annual corporate expense expenditure*   Review expenditures that are never challenged but defy a convincing argument or continuation. New releases of software programs should not be purchased if they face declining use in the company. Company cars, desks, and computers should not be periodically replaced according to a predetermined schedule that has not been reviewed for several years.

- *The "treading water" expenditure*   Review proposed expenditures that do not show additional revenues and profits if the decision is go but instead show the expected losses that are presumed to be avoided if the expenditure is approved. They don't enable the company to swim upstream but only cause the company to stay in the same place and (possibly) avoid loss. Instead of indicating an expenditure need, such expenditures may indicate a growing operating management problem. On an individual basis, the cutback opportunity may involve both the expenditure and its submitter.

- *Pursuing the capital-expenditure system and staffer*   Simplify the process so that it is appropriate for the most important requirements (as opposed to all) of the company and the marketplace—no more, no less—and then, as necessary, adjust the scope and complexity of capex, the organization, decision process, and the staffing levels to match this new simplicity. Some staffers concerned about retaining their positions in an era of LBO-induced cutbacks create unnecessary complexity to entrench themselves, which may signal a sizeable expense-reduction opportunity—particularly when the scope of the business changes.

Expenditure Categories: Distinguishing
Deferrals from Reductions

A key to effective postacquisition capital management is to separate prospective opportunities into appropriate categories. Candidate expenditures can and should be differentiated according to timing, stage (e.g., the end of a multiple-part project or the beginning), level of technology, and the basis of financial justification—new revenue and profit creation, retention of existing profits ("treading water" expenditures), reduction of expense generating, or expense reducing. For merger-integration program purposes, however, none is more important than the separation of expenditures that can be cut (reductions) from expenditures that can only be delayed until later (deferrals).

A pure deferral expenditure represents an opportunity for time period transfer, only. The manager of your Albuquerque plant insists that he must have that new cutting machine in the budget in place by the first quarter or he will lose three major orders. The need for the cutter is legitimate, but will the company's market standing in the Southwest evaporate if that outlay is put off for twelve months?

The pure reduction prospect, on the other hand, is an expenditure that can be eliminated or scaled back significantly. One method for identifying this candidate is to assess the outlay in terms of the key profit produces of the next few years. Is the outlay critical to achieving a key market objective? If the answer is no, perhaps the expenditure is not needed at all.

Few candidate opportunities are exclusively one category or the other. Many reduction candidates have some element that may—or should—be deferred instead of eliminated or eliminated instead of deferred. A choice must be made because the approach for dealing with the deferral differs so extensively from the reduction. The principal danger occurs when the deferral is treated as a reduction: the expense is eliminated in year 1 only to be added back at significantly greater cost in year 3.

The Case against Reduction Allocations

The allocated budget reduction is a venerable technique for attempting to squeeze the fat out of the budget. Some contend that allocations can be used effectively for capital and project budgets, as well, but this is potentially dangerous to the firm. Blanket percentage allocations made at the executive level may encourage department and unit managers to try the same thing, as they wrestle with their dictated 15 percent reduction cut. Projects that should be eliminated struggle along with reduced funding; they never achieve expected returns, but their contribution deteriorates so visibly that the expenditure disappears. The new American automobile model may beat the domestic competition in quality, but because of reduced outlays for certain tooling years ago—reductions caused by management's dictated percentage reductions—not all of the requested tooling in the expenditure request package was purchased. As a result, the new model still loses out to Asian competitors.

Comparative Internal Rates of Return

Another approach for identifying the reduction or deferral candidate early in the MI program is to evaluate transactions on a competitive basis instead of an investment hurdle basis. The traditional capital expenditure approach is to fund all projects achieving an internal rate of return level exceeding the company's investment hurdle rate. That hurdle rate is usually based on the company's estimated capital cost, plus some additional factor for risk. The theory is fine, but as applied in some companies the hurdle approach often encourages overfunding. Submitters know what number they must beat to gain approval for their prize project. Not surprisingly, all submissions to headquarters exceed that level. Besides the issue of control, this raises the additional issue of funds availability. There may simply not be enough money to fund all of the projects with paper projections exceeding the hurdle rate. One possible remedy is to reevaluate the largest proposed expenditures using a single evaluator. Returns are then compared, and the top return projects are funded in full, until the predetermined capital budget ceiling amount is reached.

Symbolic Activity Cutbacks

Every corporation has highly visible expenditures that generate widespread resentment but don't seem to contribute much to either the corporation's or employees' well-being. Examples include the third corporate jet, separate executive dining room privileges for executives, luxury car allowances for a few, and a Christmas bonus plan that long ago ceased functioning as a motivator. The dollar savings aren't significant, but prompt actions reinforce management's seriousness about deep expense cuts. Furthermore, the message is clear that pain is being shared throughout the organization: "They must be serious this time if they're finally firing the company pilot." Implemented in the first few days after the close, a visible cutback in a perquisite buys time for senior management for other expense reductions.

Executive Streamlining

Normally, the cost-reduction–value-creation program avoids the executive suite like the plague. There is after all a healthy streak of self-preservation in most people. Yet the corner office of the acquiree's organization is where the cost structure of the organization is set, as well as the actual costs in many instances. Few acquisitions programs today can afford to overlook this potential source of additional value. In terms of recurring savings, a reduction of one senior manager may represent two or even three middle managers because of salary differentials, space usage, and perquisites.

- *Readjust the numbers and types of top executives*   Compare the number of top managers to the performance leaders in the acquiree's industry and also to comparables in other industries. Redesign the corporation: what should a small, responsive, and competent LBO acquiree organization look like? With inescapable cost reduction and cash-flow improvement pressures, management may need to retreat from its conventional staffing approaches and instead place spot emphasis in areas of greatest future perceived need. A new LBO acquiree in the locomotive rebuilding and leasing/ renting business doesn't have a human relations department, or a planning unit, or a separate management information systems (MIS) officer, but finance is essential to the future, so the treasury and credit departments are both three-deep. A highly decentralized travel services business has a lot of separate business units and thus a lot of presidents, but it has been determined that a centralized approach is the way that the company will go in the future.

- *Resist the temptation to implement an overly complex new management information system*   Instead of taking active steps to improve profitability, top management may delegate responsibility for developing a system that "provides everything I need to know" in on-line format. An overly complex control system response to merger integration is doubly dangerous. First, the overly complex control system fosters an illusion that something is being done, while, in reality, the same old data is just being redisplayed in many instances. Second, the agenda of the systems department becomes distorted to meet a short-term time schedule. Instead of debugging the existing order-entry system or developing new sales territory performance analysis software, resources are drained to meet the perceived need in the corner office.

- *Make temporary positions temporary—once again*   New top executive perches were created in TargetCo over the years, which allowed management to attract new talent in critical areas. Multiple planning and administrative officer positions exist, however. The vice chairperson position was once an emeritus position for a cofounder of the company, but now there are three vice chairs, each with special strategic responsibilities. Another form of position inflation occurs as midlevel positions rise in importance with their incumbents' seniority. The treasury function used to report to a combined VP-administration position five years ago, but the department has been elevated in stature, and the VP-treasury reports directly to TargetCo's chief executive.

- *Consolidate related functions, wherever practical*   Combining two executive positions provides some budget flexibility to hire top functional skills while still reducing dollar costs and head count. Combining financial, accounting, planning, and administrative functions under a single senior manager is one opportunity that presents itself at many organizations. Another possible option in some organizations is to combine sales and marketing. Consider the actions of TargetCo. The industry's top marketing executive was hired as the new senior officer for both functions, replacing two current managers who had worked their way up the organization but were accustomed to managing in the years when TargetCo dominated the U.S. market. TargetCo now faced robust competition from both Europe and Taiwan. Two bureaucracies were replaced with one. A key driver from sales was promoted to vice president, reporting to the newly hired outsider. This long-time TargetCo employee understood sales and marketing from the customer's perspective and had resurrected sales programs in several TargetCo territories.

Benefits Adjustments

Calculate the percentage of total medical benefit dollar borne by current employees. In many companies, the percentage is significantly less than 20 percent. Modifying medical program coverage to pass on slightly more costs to employees saves dollars without involving head-count cuts.

The Financial Accounting Standards Board (FASB) has directed corporations to place liabilities for postretirement benefits on their balance sheet and to record these costs on an accrual basis. At McKesson Corp., the nation's largest drug distributor, chief executive Alan Seelenfreund has moved to eliminate those costs in total (estimated at $12.5 million annually) by substituting an employee stock option program (ESOP), which allows employees to pay insurance premiums themselves.

Department Reduction Analysis

Comparable in some ways to delayering, department reduction addresses the problem of proliferating administrative departments. First, the total number of departments are reduced, and then department budgets and related support costs are eliminated.

- Group separate acquirer and acquiree administrative departments according to categories. In one postacquisition program, sales and marketing departments were grouped together for analysis purposes. In another, financial analysis, budget, and internal analysis units were examined together.

- Examine the pattern of head-count and expense growth in the departments, and compare that pattern with the growth in revenue per administrative employee (total employees minus line employees). If the chart shows trends in two divergent directions, action is needed.

- Recommend some departments for consolidation, based on current staffing levels and the importance of that department's autonomy to critical customer or manufacturing activities.

- If consolidations are enacted, adjust support staff and expenses. Another bonus: the annual budgeting process is simplified because there are fewer cost centers to review.

Function/Position Full-Time Equivalent (FTE) Analysis

Responsibility for an overall function is often shared among several employees. At different firms, benefits administration, corporate financial analysis, and/or performance reporting may be shared among several different groups or individuals. This fragmentation reinforces overstaffing and erects barriers to needed head-count reductions. When responsibility for a function is diffuse, it becomes extremely difficult to calculate how many employee hours are spent in the company on that activity, much less compare performance with other companies. If individuals' job descriptions record activity in several areas, downgrading or eliminating one function results in no head-count reductions. The action eliminates only a fraction of the time of several employees.

One remedy is analysis of functions and positions through full-time equivalents, or FTE, analysis. Within the targeted department, individual interviews are conducted to examine the employees' actual and intended use of time, the functions performed, and any productivity measures. When all employees in the department have been examined, a functional full-time equivalent analysis is constructed, equating the head-count of the department with functions performed. External comparables are used as appropriate to establish FTE standards for those activities. If an activity is downgraded or eliminated, the specific number of head-count reductions should be readily indicated. The function reduction plan becomes a head-count reduction directive. The department head is informed of his or her FTE reduction requirement and that, for head-count purposes, one FTE must be interpreted as one full-time position.

Critical Process Analysis

Most acquirees have at least one major process that is a profit drain. Simplify or eliminate that process, and the MI team makes dramatic progress in creating new profits, cash flow, and value. The first step is to identify those activities and processes with high potential for future profit improvement. Read the president's letter. Learn about the activities in the acquired company that are most valued. These are also often the best opportunities for postacquisition profit improvement. "Protected" activities attract additional—and sometimes unnecessary—costs, staff, and complexity.

Kraft, Inc. has a well-deserved reputation as a sales leader in the packaged foods industry. Following acquisition by Philip Morris, outsiders examined Kraft's sales administration and deal accounting processes. The system was considered by several of these observers to be an automated expansion of the manual deal-tracking process used by the company for decades. Major design emphasis continued to be on processing and controlling merchandise deals at the individual store basis. The regional grocery chains of the 1970s had given way to the national megachain of the 1980s. A responsive deal administrative system for the 1990s would emphasize master arrangements with this new breed of customer. The system is now being simplified and used to further exploit Kraft's sales and marketing leadership as part of the Kraft General Foods organization.

Implementing Appropriate Centralization

Some companies swing back and forth between centralized and decentralized organization philosophies and structures. Ongoing profit-restructuring savings may be achieved by designating functions and departments for appropriate centralization. The resulting design may resemble a patchwork quilt, but that organization probably operates more efficiently than most pure centralized or decentralized organizations.

Volume-related activities—such as accounts receivables and payables processing, cash management and payroll processing—are centralized. These activities are combined with other, closely related activities to achieve scale economies. Key customer activities, that is, activities that involve direct contact with the actual customer, remain decentralized. Whenever possible, key client accounts and contacts are handled at the lowest possible point in the organization. Appropriate decentralization may allow acquirer company management to combine some activities of the two companies. The resulting savings also represent merger-integration profit improvements.

Outsourcing and the External Market Comparable

An acquired company department with exclusive authority for providing products or services within that organization presents a similar expense-reduction challenge to the protected activity. If charges to internal customers are calculated on a cost-plus basis, and if expenses and staffing are not tightly controlled, the cost of internal services may turn out to be considerably greater than the perceived cost of outside alternatives. Internal customers may complain that substitutes can be obtained from outside suppliers at higher quality and lower cost. The internal suppliers, in turn, warn that some of these outside deals are one-time specials and that those suppliers are here today but may not be around tomorrow. They warn that control and confidentiality are two advantages of an internal source and that costs are only part of the picture.

Yet cost reduction and new value creation *are* key concerns in the months following the close. Some organizations, such as Bell Atlantic, have attempted to develop the best of both worlds by creating a structure that reduces costs without automatically eliminating the role of the internal supplier. The key to such arrangements is an external value comparable. Outside equivalent prices are contrasted with selected internal services and products. If a significant value difference in favor of the external providers persists, the internal supplier faces a choice: either reduce department internal costs (along with intercompany billings) or face a possibility of losing the internal supply franchise to another supplier—internal or external. For MI purposes, the challenge is to identify those internal supplier arrangements where internal value supplied is below outside suppliers and to adjust budgets accordingly.

Organization Chart Analysis: The Informed Overview Approach

Statistical measures aside, an overview of corporate organization charts is sometimes the fastest and most reliable way to quickly identify head-count reduction opportunities. The staffing pattern of the department as indicated by the chart provides a basis for comparing functions between different companies. If TargetCo's financial analysis department is four deep and has sixteen full-time positions, excluding secretaries, and another company with the same number of separate business units has eight full-time staff, further investigation may be warranted. One-to-one and one-to-two reporting patterns in the department's organization chart indicate a probable candidate for consolidation with another department, particularly if the number of staff have been declining. Finally, span-of-control guidelines applied to the department charts often can be used to apply head-count reductions at middle-manager levels. If there are two one-to-four reporting groups in one of TargetCo's organizations, yet the pattern in other comparable companies is one supervisor to seven reports, the answer may both be a combination of groups or a replacement of two subperforming middle managers for one top performer.

Implementing the Core One Program

Equipped with an understanding of where to look, the merger-integration team leader can now proceed with implementing the core one program. The next step is to apply that understanding—to develop a quick but deep diagnostic in the first few weeks of the postacquisition period. The intent of the range estimate of the analysis is to set defensible upper and lower estimates for the value and net cash flow realistically expected to be achieved from profit restructuring, to help focus the postacquisition value process, and to anticipate the necessity for early action on the other three core programs. If core one will cover only half of the value difference, or half of the additional net cash-flow requirement to service acquisition debt, accelerated plans for marketing, manufacturing, and systems (cores two, three, four) may need to be accelerated. The diagnostic relies primarily on data analysis, with selective interviews when the data uncovers an apparent sizeable opportunity area.

Pursuing the Showcase Core One Target

Selection of the initial target of opportunity for the core one program is important. The percentage of proposed expense cuts to total expenses for that organization will shape the continuing expectations of the acquirer throughout the MI process. Similarly, the percentage of proposed position adjustments to total department positions will also take on continuing significance.

Identifying the Initial Opportunity:
Selection Criteria

The ideal initial target exhibits all or most of these characteristics:

- *Size, scope*   The target should have a large enough budget for profit restructuring savings in a 30 to 40 percent range.
- *Manpower intensive*   At least 60 percent of the target's expenses should be people-related costs.
- *Prospective centralized processes*   The attractiveness of the target organization jumps if activities are handled customarily in a centralized manner in other organizations but are decentralized within the acquiree.
- *Department management change probable*   Add another plus if a postacquisition change in the leadership of the target department is expected. A new department manager—particularly one from outside of the acquiree organization—has few ties and little allegiance to "the way that things have always been done around here." Ideally, that new manager will join with the leader of the merger-integration team to reshape priorities in the new organization.

Showcase Illustration:
TargetCo's Planning Department

This hypothetical example is an abbreviated version of an initial core one profit-restructuring analysis involving TargetCo's planning department. Several considerations went into the selection. The department was sizeable in terms of both budget and positions. Over the past four years, the department's annual budget had tripled to $1.67 million, while revenues only doubled. Staff had blossomed from six to sixteen full-time professionals over the period. The budget was highly asset intensive. About 80 percent of total expenses were people costs of some form. Cutbacks appeared to be overdue. Department head and long-range strategic planner John Vector was leaving. Vector had presided over the staffing increase, adding statisticians and internal analysts to help administer TargetCo's annual one-year/ three-year/ five-year planning process. Even before the closing, TargetCo figured that the company could survive without the three- and five-year looks. The long-range numbers were simply not reliable, in management's estimation.

The assigned responsibility of the MI team was to suggest which activities—and, in turn, which staff—would be part of any scaled-down planning organization in the future. Debt repayment pressures would become severe within months after the close. The MI team leader also saw the possible combination of the planning group with another TargetCo group to share overhead. In the analysis, the MI team considered two issues central to the future of TargetCo's planning department: (1) the value and need of current and prospective planning department tasks and responsibilities and (2) how current planners in the department spent their time. Answers to these two issues could help management better understand the tradeoffs between future activities and future costs. The analysis also would help determine whether the department was concentrating on issues of value to the corporation or, alternatively, whether workhours were being wasted.

The analysis approach was what the team called a top-down investigation. To MI team staffers, this meant that TargetCo's planning department would be scrutinized from two perspectives:

- *Top*   Assuming that no planning organization existed at TargetCo today, what are the tasks that a planning group should perform, and at what cost, expressed both in head count and dollars?

- *Bottom*   Starting with present activities and staffing, which are the activities that are the most likely candidates for discontinuation? What FTE (full-time equivalent) head-count reductions may be achievable?

Questions also were posed to senior managers of TargetCo and its new parent, AcquireCo. The chief executives of the two firms were asked to give their views about planning functions they saw as critical to TargetCo in the future:

- *Scope of activity change*   The long-range strategic planning function of the corporation should be discontinued for the next two years, except for the issue of the company's positioning and action in Europe following European Economic

Community changes expected to occur in 1992. This would result in ongoing staff and related cost reductions of $110,000 per individual times six positions (total of $660,000), less first-year transition costs of $100,000 to 130,000.

- *Process redesign, consolidation with other department* The annual budget process (run now by the planning department) was too complicated and began too early in the year. By beginning the budgeting process one month later each year and by reducing the number of submission and review iterations over the course of the planning cycle, three current positions could be reduced. The resulting profit restructuring improvements would be ongoing staff and related cost reductions of $90,000 per individual times three positions (total of $270,000), less first-year transition costs of $50,000.

- *Delayering* The planning department was four layers deep, which acquirer and acquiree management both thought was one and possibly two layers too many, given TargetCo planning's expected role in the future. Cropping back two layers in the planning organization would reduce eight additional heads, less four positions already counted in the two steps above. Ongoing staff and related cost reductions would be $95,000 per individual, times four positions (total of $380,000), less first-year transition costs of $75,000.

- *Department consolidation* By the time that the above three actions are taken, only three full-time positions remain, excluding secretaries. Those remaining positions were transferred to a new financial group.

In a bottom-up approach the MI team assumes that no preexisting planning organization exists at TargetCo. Assuming these assigned responsibilities, what would be appropriate staffing? Answer: none. The change in roles and responsibilities essentially reduced planning's function to a budgeting role. It was noted that two groups—AcquireCo's planning group and the new consolidated financial group in TargetCo—performed related functions and could be stretched to accommodate those tasks, resulting in the total elimination of the budget.

Documentation

The MI team's report covering the initial target organization sets the stage and pace for other analyses conducted in later weeks. Extensive, formal reports are generally discouraged for postacquisition work. Time is limited. The maximum percentage of this time should be spent on new value opportunities. The preparation of formal reports draws time away from analysis. The MI team's report on its initial organization is the exception, however. A comprehensive initial analysis provides hard evidence that progress is being achieved in developing postacquisition value. Approach and support data are revealed, as practical. A particularly complete first analysis may actually reduce subsequent documentation requirements, which does not mean, however, that such analyses are any less comprehensive than their predecessors.

Interview Sequence for Other Groups and Organizations: An Approach

The approach undertaken for the initial target organization cannot be duplicated for all other acquiree organizations without either inundating the company with a disruptive army of questioners or slowing the profit-restructuring process to a snail's pace. Yet interview data typically provides more than half of the input needed for the MI team to make reasoned judgments and analysis. A comprehensive approach is required. How should the MI team proceed with its investigation of other groups? The following three-round interview process is for organizations within the company. In most programs, these interviews would be conducted at the same time as the initial target organization analysis.

First Round: The Internal Client Interviews

The first round of interviews is termed the internal client interviews because emphasis is on gathering useful information about critical reports, information, and processes, rather than immediately probing for cost-reduction opportunities. The MI team arrives at the acquiree's headquarters. Top management announces that interviews will begin the next day. The internal corporate grapevine works fast. Within hours, virtually everyone in the organization knows who is going to be "first before the firing squad." Expectations (and fears) for those interviews are either that severe people and expense reductions will be announced at the meeting or that the interviewer will probe relentlessly for vulnerable spots through open-ended questions. Examples: "What are the critical activities performed in your group, and where would you look first to make reductions in the event of in, say, a 20 percent range in terms of both head count and expenses?" Interview responses to the anticipated areas of investigation are prepared in advance by the unit head. The department or business unit head may decide to prepare an expansion budget calling for even greater expenses and head-count than originally budgeted, justified by service requests from the executive office. Reports on key personnel, activities, and analyses and that productivity improvement report from two years ago may become misplaced.

But anticipated questions are not asked—at least not at the time of this interview. There are no direct questions about the operations of the unit or cost-reduction opportunities. Instead, the MI team leader or another senior member of the MI group asks the unit head to assist a special committee in developing a more complete understanding of internal services provided within the company and how the internal clients are served. The interviewee is asked to do the following:

- *Describe and rank the critical information and resource needs of his or her group* What do you need to get from others to achieve your goals, either formal or informal? The company acquisitions department may be expected to close two deals a year, although that is not written down anywhere. The leader of that group says that he needs more, and more frequent, competitive information reports from business unit leaders, since these help in surfacing possible new candidates. The benefits management group leader is evaluated on a cost and service basis. He states that his success depends to a great extent on receiving timely information from the various company units about changes in personnel, salaries, and benefits preferences.

- *Provide useful suggestions on how things might be done even better* This is the opportunity for the internal services client to put himself or herself into the role of being the provider of the information or resource—not just the client.

- *Repeat the process, but this time assume perspective of your group's clients* Having established a procedure for identifying, ranking, and suggesting improvements, the unit head is now asked to assume the same perspective as applied to his or her group. Questions must be carefully worded to avoid self-serving responses. Some suggestions: Among the improvement suggestions that have been brought to your attention before, which are the best? Why? What is being done about it? What will the merger-integration team be likely to hear from other organizations about what your group does and how they do it? Are there some considerations we should know about?

Conducted in the manner described here, the first stage interviews frequently yield a wealth of useful and usable information. The MI leader's deliberate change in interview topics and tactics (compared to the interviewee's original expectations) often proves to be worthwhile. In many instances, the interviewee opens up and provides considerably more information than might otherwise be expected. Relief about *not* being hammered on expense and head-count budgets loosens the tongue. Also, managers are always more eager to discuss deficiencies and opportunities for improvement in *other's* organizations. Sometimes the pace slows somewhat when the interviewee is asked to assume the role and perspective of his or her customers. Many managers have difficulty adopting another person's perspective. Others immediately draw back, assuming that any response works to their disadvantage.

Information from multiple interviews provides a solid indication for where to focus specific investigations. If these first-round interviews are all conducted at about the same time, the MI team has a valuable information resource for understanding the truth about company costs, people, and processes. Interview data are compiled into a format that allows comments to be considered by the MI team as a whole. Statistical and other data developed from other sources is combined with first-round interviews and the MI team considers this information in setting priorities for the next round of discussions.

Second Round: Contribution and Contributor Interviews

The initial round generally requires two to three weeks to complete, depending on the number of organizations involved and the number of senior interviewers conducting the discussions. Combined with other information, round-one interviews should suggest several opportunity areas for the next round of interviews, but the goal of those discussions is not simply to pinpoint possible future areas for further streamlining. The goal is also to identify areas of particular excellence within the organization and to ensure that these groups are properly situated in the new organization. If responses from the round-one investigation continually point to several third-tier employees as leaders in the corporation, a delayering opportunity may become apparent in the *second* tier.

These examinations are probing time usage and function examinations and are similar in approach and intensity to the target organization analysis. They consider the interviewee's specific time usage, contributions to corporate performance,and the availability of substitutes through consolidation or elimination of the activity.

Third Round: Follow-up Discussions with Unit or Department Leaders

Prior to presenting preliminary findings to the special committee, the MI team leader or another senior member of that group presents information from the proposed recommendations to the unit's leader. This minimizes the possibility of outright errors in analysis and interpretation, provides the organization's leader with an opportunity to suggest alternatives if, for example, a particular individual or function is viewed by the unit leader as being indispensible, and focuses attention and discussions on specific programs and actions, not on vague statements such as "working harder."

6

MI Core Two: Marketing and Sales

Expense streamlining paces the early merger-integration effort, but revenue side changes—that is, sales and marketing improvements—ensure competitiveness. Few leveraged acquisitions cover their value differences solely through expense reductions and cost eliminations. The acquiring group and its lenders usually need more sources of cash flow and sources of value for the acquisition to be fully successful. Figure 6.1 shows that overhead expense streamlining and administrative efficiency improvement restructuring are integral to acquisition success. The figure, which is based on an analysis of sixteen large corporate acquisitions by McKinsey & Co., shows corporate administrative expenses as providing about 42 percent of the new value created after the close. Operations changes in total represent a full 84 percent of postacquisition value enhancement, which leaves another 42 percent still to be explained.

Marketing and sales improvements stand out as an additional value source with 27 percent of the value-creation potential (Figure 6.1, source B1). Considered another way, the merger-integration program that excludes marketing and sales improvements is pursuing only 73 percent of the total available value sources. The additional value is needed. Although some acquisitions succeed by enacting administrative expense reduc-

182

Figure 6.1. Sources of Acquistion Value Enhancement

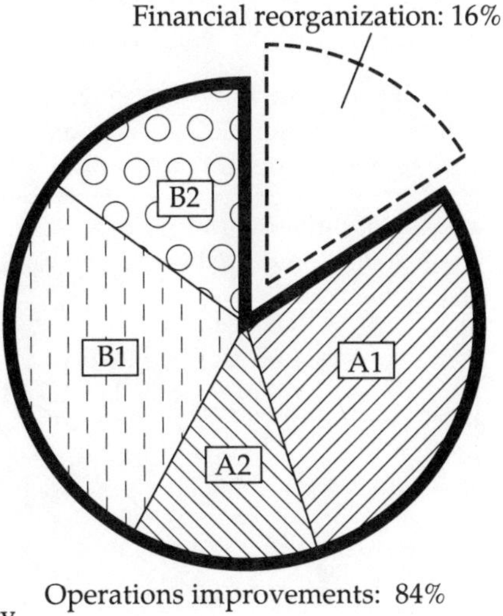

Corporate administrative expense and decision related – 42% of total

▨ A1 Efficiency and productivity improvements in corporate/ division overhead activities and functions: 29%

▧ A2 Improved capital expenditure and resource allocation decision making: 13%

Other value sources – 42% of total

▦ B1 Marketing and sales improvements, including sale productivity improvements, marketing support efficiencies and product line optimization: 27%

⊡ B2 Industry concentration and facilities consolidations: 15%

Financial reorganization: 16%

Operations improvements: 84%

SOURCE: Adapted from Gluck, Frederick W., "The real takeover defense," *The McKinsey Quarterly* (Winter 1988): 7–8, based on analysis of sources of value creation of sixteen large transactions involving changes in ownership.

NOTE: Percentages are based on total corporate value enhancement, including both financial reorganization and operations improvements.

tions and process changes alone, such instances are rare—and they have a tendency to become even rarer as the merger cycle matures. Figure 6.2 illustrates how the bargain-priced deal quickly disappears. In the initial few months of the new cycle, some acquirers may benefit from an underpriced deal. Some sellers remember the recent recession all too painfully. They listen attentively as the would-be acquirer suggests that "You're not likely to see a better price this soon in this uncertain economy." If the seller bites, the prize may be an advantageously priced acquisition—that is, an acquisition requiring not much more for success in the postacquisition period than common-sense administrative expense and process adjustments. Most,

184   Beyond the Deal

Figure 6.2.   The Requirement For Additional Postacquisition Value
Sources: The Short-Lived Bargain Purchase Period

Stage in Merger Cycle

Cycle Birth	Early Entrance to Growth	Cycle Boom Confirmed	Early Cycle Maturity	Advanced Maturity

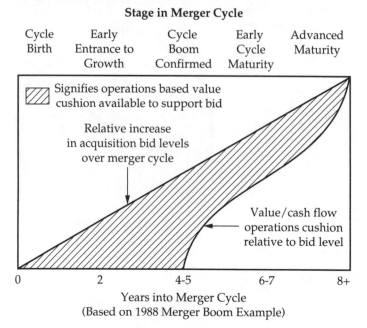

0   2   4-5   6-7   8+
Years into Merger Cycle
(Based on 1988 Merger Boom Example)

if not all, of the transaction's value difference is covered by
those sources alone.

In the earliest phases of the merger cycle, however, few
investors can take advantage of these possible opportunities.
Many would-be acquirers lack the requisite combination of capital and insight to act. LBO dealmakers of the early 1980s had
to confront many doubters, some of whom labeled the idea
of buying companies with debt in an economic downturn as
sheer lunacy. Unless these purchasers could back up their con-
victions with cash, the deal was likely to go unfunded.

It is also apparent that the brief bargain period disappears as
quickly as it arrives. New investors enter the bidding chase, bid
levels increase, and the range of purchase offers approaches or
exceeds the underlying worth of the target companies. Bargain
prices disappear unless the seller commits a fundamental error
in assessing the potential sales value of his ownership position
or unless other factors such as personal relationships prompt
a sweetheart transaction price on purpose.

Revenue-side postacquisition improvements differ from expense-side changes in terms of impact on the operating profits of the new combined enterprise. Many of the core one profit-restructuring actions described in the previous chapter drop directly to the operating profit line. Excluding one-time adjustments and transitional expenses, it is not unusual to see a well-planned and executed reorganization action that results in improved operating profits of seventy to eighty cents per each dollar of expense reduction. Elimination of unneeded positions or processes may yield an even greater percentage of expense reduction amounts, sometimes approaching 100 percent. Some postacquisition improvements in marketing and sales generate comparable impact on profits. Streamlining of marketing expenditures and increases in sales force effectiveness can result in a level of operating profit improvement rivaling the results from core one actions.

Not all revenue side actions affect operating profits in the same manner. New product introductions and some line extensions, for example, may yield less than thirty cents for each dollar of sales created because of related manufacturing, support, and distribution costs. The profit yield shrinks even further if introductory prices or special sales launch costs are required for an extended period.

Then there is the additional risk from a merger-integration strategy that is overdependent on top-line product innovations. Potential increased risks fall into two categories: new cash-flow development risk mounts as management concentrates on actions with comparatively low profit yield, and overall acquisition risk increases as well. Management bets its limited time and resources on the wrong choice—then discovers too late that there is not enough of either to save the floundering deal.

Table 6.1 provides an example of those additional risks. The figure shows key events in Robert M. Fomon & Co.'s acquisition of Cuisinarts, the well-known manufacturer of kitchen food processing appliances for home use. Cuisinarts retained its name but little else following the acquisition by an investor group formed by Fomon, the former chief executive officer of E. F. Hutton Co. Fomon's choice for CEO of the newly

Table 6.1.   Risks of Top-Line Revenue Strategies: The Example of Robert M. Fomon & Co. and Cuisinarts

Former E. F. Hutton Co. chairman Robert Fomon's investment company provided an example of the risks of a postacquisition program that is overreliant on top-line value creation: new revenue creation.

December 1987	Cuisinarts completes year of gross profits of $21 million on sales of $53.5 million but has negative cash flow of $3 million.
January 1988	Convinced that negative cash flow indicated attractive value-improvement opportunities, Robert M. Fomon & Co. acquire Company for $37 million.
February–August 1988	Despite knowledge of numerous cost-reduction opportunities in manufacturing and distribution, George Barnes, Cuisinarts' president, emphasizes new market opportunities virtually to the exclusion of other merger-integration actions. Barnes misses the market price points for his new small processor: a unit priced at about twice the level of comparable offerings from competitors.
Late summer 1988	New $3 million loan request by Barnes provides some capital for the Christmas season.
September 1988	Cuisinarts slips into technical default on its loan covenants.
April 1989	The board replaces Barnes with a new president, Donald Luke.
June 1989	Luke asks for more funds. The board opts for Chapter 11 instead.
December 1989	Cuisinarts sold to Conair, Inc. for $17 million, about 46 percent of the price paid by Fomon group.

Source: Nichols, Nancy A., "Why Cuisinarts' Motor Burned Out," *Corporate Finance* (January 1990): 44, 46–47.

acquired firm, George Barnes, pursued a headstrong new product course of new product introduction. This was in spite of the availability of other value-creation options and debilitating competition in the market segment chosen for entry. By the time the misstep was caught, it was too late to pull the acquiree out of its cash-flow nosedive. In November 1989 the board elected to file for Chapter 11. In December Cuisinarts was sold for less than half the price that the Fomon group had paid—two years after the original acquisition.

Avoiding Pitfalls in Marketing and Sales Postacquisition Value Creation

The lower profit yields and greater possible risks associated with some marketing and sales alternatives does not mean that this merger-integration core category should be avoided. Indeed, Figure 6.1 suggests that core two merger-integration actions *cannot* be disregarded—at least not if management wants the acquisition to work.

To realize full value from such opportunities, you first need to know where to look and what to avoid. Key pitfalls must be recognized so that they can be defused or sidestepped, and the diversity of MI core two approached in a systematic manner to optimize acquisition success. Five possible traps associated with core two merger-integration programs are listed in Table 6.2 and described in the paragraph that follows.

Succumbing to the Me-Too Product or Service Introduction

Anxious to make a splash in the marketplace, management may emphasize introduction of new products over less dashing—but possibly more profitable—alternatives. The Cuisinarts calamity shown in Table 6.1 is a good example of a "me-too" product introduction made at a hurried pace. Undertaking a low-success-probability market action at the time that corporate cash flow is the tightest might be explained by new owners' understandable desire to reassert the acquiree's

Table 6.2. Pitfalls to Avoid in Marketing and Sales Merger-Integration Programs

---

The sheer breadth of the marketing/sales category increases the potential for value miscalculations and pitfalls. These include

- Succumbing to the "me-too" product or service launch.
- Emphasizing new revenue creation over marketing and sales efficiency improvement.
- Assuming that pricing creates additional value.
- Failing to anticipate the liquidity trap.
- Introducing marginal new products or services, justified by incomplete cost assumptions

---

marketplace momentum. Perhaps the action is intended to indicate that the recent change in ownership doesn't mean a decline in innovation. Alternatively, the motivating factor could be management's and owners' egos. Whatever the justification, acquirers and operating officers are wise to first consider the market damage that a failed new product or service launch could mean in the marketplace before entering with a poorly differentiated product. Success is difficult enough for a new, moderately leveraged company saddled with a "me-too" service—or worse, one that doesn't meet competitive benchmarks. A new entity as of January 1, 1984, NYNEX promoted its Bell heritage of service in marketing to its downtown Manhattan customers. But an increasing number of technically sophisticated, cost-conscious customers abandoned NYNEX's local telco network when they perceived Merrill Lynch's Teleport to be a superior means of connecting to their long distance carriers' points-of-presence.

If the company introducing the "me-too" product is a highly leveraged acquiree, two additional debacles occur. The LBO's squeeze on cash flow reflects on the chances for launch success. The difference between a fully successful introduction and one that falls short may be a single promotion or that one additional distributor. The highly leveraged acquiree is especially unprepared to take extra steps (and spend extra money) to ensure that everything possible is done to achieve a successful introduction. Later, if the LBO's introduction flounders, the company may become particularly vulnerable to the cascading effects of negative expectations. Cuisinarts' miss with its low-end processor sent that company skidding toward Chapter 11. In retailing, rumors that ultraleveraged Campeau was on the ropes accelerated when 1989 fall season demand in the retail industry turned out to be lower than expected. To the rumor-propelled customer markets, it matters little whether the LBO scare has a basis in fact or not.

Emphasizing New Revenue Creation over Marketing and Sales Efficiency Improvement Actions

In choosing the actions for their core two agenda, management may fail to adequately consider differences in operating profit yield. By this, we mean the level to which a dollar improvement increases operating profit, cash flow, and ultimately, the acquired company's value. As described earlier in this chapter, elimination of undereffective marketing programs may drop almost a full dollar to the acquiree's operating profit line for each dollar of expenses dropped. By contrast, a flubbed new product introduction may actually lose money, thus eroding corporate value.

Assuming That Pricing Creates Additional Value

Sometimes, the positive corporate-value effects of upward pricing adjustments are overstated. Upward pricing adjustments made after the close usually increase short-term cash flow, but if that action is stretched too far, the acquiree's value may actually be eroded. An example is provided by an acquired company from the office supply field.

DeskCo was acquired by new owners in the late 1970s who wanted to increase their cash-flow draw from the company. They had correctly determined that their acquiree's customers were extremely loyal, which suggested, in turn, that sustained, gradual increases in prices could be made with little or no danger to DeskCo's customer franchise in its segment of the office supplies industry. The up-pricing policy was enacted year after year, and DeskCo's owners received their additional cash flow, but ultimately value of the acquiree was reduced, as loyal customers who would have otherwise remained single-vendor purchasers were forced to sample competitors. One long-time customer admitted, "We would like to continue to buy most of our supplies from DeskCo, but our budget pressures mean that we have to now spread the orders around."

The other shortcoming of upward pricing adjustments is that the action is deceptively easy and thus may cut short thorough investigation of marketing and sales merger-integration options with greater value potential. Why bother with the tough challenge of streamlining an acquiree's product line when the problem has already been solved by simple price action?

Failing to Anticipate the Liquidity Trap

The slippery path to Chapter 11 doesn't always result from poor management decisions. Hidden liquidity problems can also wreck the business of the new LBO acquiree. The liquidity trap problem is most commonly manifested in the "can't miss" new product. All concerned—acquirer, acquiree, senior lenders—agree that the potential of the new technology concept is outstanding, but enthusiasm wins out over tough judgment, and those same parties are surprised to find later that the new concept will require more time than originally expected to succeed in the marketplace. In the meantime the highly leveraged acquiree must, as one investment banker described, invest in losses.

For an established, moderately leveraged business, the effects of this liquidity trap may be so faint as to be imperceivable. Such a company's value may actually be *increased* by investing in such cash-flow absorbing that assumes that the accompanying "concept story" for public investors is sufficiently alluring. In the early and mid-1980s, Charles Wohlstetter's Contel Corp. earned nearly all of its profits from local telephone exchange revenues. Yet Contel maintained attractive price-to-earnings stock price multiples compared to other telephone utilities. One factor was that the telco had enough sizzle in the form of cash-flow–absorbing high-technology acquisitions to attract analyst attention.

The new acquiree, however, lacked Contel's solid base of other predictable operations to offset timing and cash-flow problems from *their* can't-miss technologies and concepts. The acquiree's pressure increases to the extent that demands for accelerated debt repayment draw away other cash reserves. Management of the highly leveraged acquiree make business decisions that are sound for larger and more stable companies but that may accelerate the LBO to bankruptcy.

Marginal New Products and Services Justified by Incomplete Cost Assumptions

A possible core two pitfall arises if brand managers, product managers, and marketing support staff attempt to preserve marginal product and services through erroneous and incomplete cost justification. After the close, talk quickly arises about the need to streamline products product lines while reducing or consolidating related support processes and staffing. In response, attempts will be made to rejustify some marginal products by assuming only partial absorption of some of the fixed manufacturing, support, selling, and distribution costs borne by other products. For purposes of product streamlining decisions, the argument arises that a fixed-cost infrastructure is already in place to support existing profitable lines. Thus, the logic goes, additional products that don't add to fixed costs should be assessed only on the basis of variable costs. Every CEO has heard this one: "These new products don't require any additional investment, so most of the sales drop directly down to the bottom line." Incomplete cost absorption helps make this happen. Product lines that once registered a 15 percent operating profit margin now bulge to a 25 percent operating profit margin when incomplete costing is substituted.

Although the underlying instinct of self-preservation is understandable, the new acquiree can ill afford to become victimized by the flawed logic of incomplete cost absorption when making important postclose decisions. With few exceptions, all products and services of the company eventually require full support of all resources of the corporation.

Setting Core Two Priorities: Price, Promotion, Product, and Positioning

In proceeding from core one profit-restructuring actions to core two marketing and sales initiatives, emphasis of the merger-integration effort shifts. In the core one analysis emphasis is on surfacing cash flow and value improvement as quickly as possible, building on a working understanding of the basic financial profit dynamics of the acquiree and the combined enterprise. As the acquirer's merger-integration investigation moves into core two territory, however, emphasis shifts to developing an applied understanding of the acquiree's basic business itself. This perspective is extended into the MI effort as cores three and four are addressed.

The number of possible core two alternatives is large, and the time for effective action is limited. How, then, should acquirer and acquiree management work together to set core two priorities? The approach suggested here is comprised of two elements: revisiting the building blocks of corporate marketing and sales strategy, which are referred to in this book as the "four Ps," and comparing and evaluating specific action options on the basis of the expected achievable new corporate cash flow and value creation.

The "four Ps"—price, promotion, product, and positioning— establish the foundation for a systematic understanding of the range of action options available to management. By organizing alternative actions by the four categories, the chances of myopic fixation on one course to the exclusion of others are reduced. It becomes tough for the acquiree CEO to undertake high-risk/low-return action such as a "me-too" product introduction when lower-risk/higher-return options are known to be available. A balanced and comprehensive core two MI effort includes at least some actions from each category.

Specific criteria are required to facilitate objective comparative assessment of action alternatives—both within and between the four different categories. *Value* is the present worth of the permanent improvement in acquiree net cash flows and corporate value expected to result from the postacquisition action. *Achievability* is the feasibility of achieving the indicated potential value improvement. The complexity of the proposed action, timing, the level and form of internal opposition, and competitive conditions in the acquiree's markets are all important parts of this criterion. Consideration of these factors is key to determining how much of the potential postacquisition value is likely to be achieved and when.

Price

The first P category—price—is examined in Table 6.3. In the discussions of this and the other three Ps in the following pages, criteria assessments are shown in relative terms. Management and merger-integration team leaders are encouraged to adapt this general framework to appropriate quantitative measures as they address their own MI core two alternatives.

Incremental (Spot Market) Pricing

Incremental or spot pricing are small changes in prevailing price to customers. These decisions involve pennies, not dollars, but if the acquiree's unit volume is large and customers loyal, such action may succeed in generating additional cash flow and value in the first weeks and months after the close. Achievability of this option is high because small pricing actions can usually be undertaken by immediate management action. The value combination is judged as medium because of the small size of the boosts and the limited period of time during which such pricing can remain effective; this option is not available beyond the first postacquisition year.

Changes in Sales Terms

Terms submitted to customers may be modified to accelerate cash flow, or incentives added to encourage earlier payment. This option is seen as being moderately achievable in the first

Table 6.3.   Postacquisition Marketing and Sales Improvement: Price

	Near-Term (6 mo.–1 yr.)		Beyond One Year	
	Achievability	Value Contribution	Achievability	Value Contribution
Incremental (spot) pricing	High	Moderate	Not applicable	Not applicable
Changes in sales terms	Moderate	Low	High	High
Inflation pass-through restructuring	Not applicable	Not applicable	Low	Low
Other value-directed price and terms restructuring	Not applicable	Not applicable	Moderate	Moderate

postacquisition weeks and low in actual value contributed because of the practical reluctance of signaling the mistaken impression that the LBO is encountering difficulties. Once time has passed and customers and lenders know that the change in terms is not a desperation move, however, this action can be a highly feasible means of increasing corporate value.

Sometimes the challenge isn't to introduce new terms and conditions to the marketplace but to hold customers to the terms that are already in place. One client indicated on its invoices that additional charges would be billed for any payments still due ninety days after receipt, but customers quickly discovered that charges were never actually collected. Not surprisingly, receivables outstanding began to lengthen. Customers were, in effect, being given interest-free loans after the ninety-day point.

Inflation Pass-Through Restructuring

This is a more complex form of pricing change and billing restructuring and requires time to implement. Customer retaliation and possible account loss are factors that the merger-integration group should assess carefully before proceeding.

Other Value-Directed Price and Terms
Restructuring

This spans a wide range of options for combining pricing and product to create a more attractive marketplace combination. For example, Bill Gates's software company, Microsoft, sells several types of software for the Apple Macintosh computer. The software is usually sold by single copy, but by bundling several of his most popular Mac programs at a special price while labeling the bundle as "The Macintosh Office," Gates extends the appeal of his products to well-heeled, first-time Mac purchasers who are looking to fill most of their software needs through a single purchase. Typically, such an approach is not available as a price action in the first few weeks after the close because of time requirements.

Conclusion: Price as Part of the Core Two Agenda

Pricing-based value actions are implemented most easily when the acquiree already lags behind competitive practices. Few customers can argue that the company should not be allowed to charge on the same basis as competitors. To support that approach, the acquiree must be prepared to make an investment into gathering intelligence on customer pricing practices on a continuing basis.

But management must know when to turn off the price-based core two program—not just how to turn that program on. Overreliance on pricing to generate new cash flow and value runs the risk of eroding the acquiree's customer franchise. Fewer and fewer customers remain. Unless the acquiree's product lines are so mature that a milking strategy is warranted, disadvantages may well outweigh advantages after a year following the close.

Promotion

As used here, *promotion* refers not just to in-store trade promotions (called *push marketing* by some) but also to *pull marketing*, including advertising and special events marketing (see Table 6.4).

Advertising and Promotions Mix Changes

Dollars budgeted for advertising are redirected to trade promotions after research confirms that push marketing is more effective than demand pull, or the reverse takes place, backed by analysis. Such mix changes requires a comparative assessment that allows management to switch major emphasis from one approach to another or to different timing.

Since many advertising and promotion budgets are set well in advance of enactment, the management and merger-

Table 6.4.   Postacquisition Marketing and Sales Improvement: Promotion

| | Near-Term (6 mo.–1 yr.) | | Beyond One Year | |
	Achievability	Value Contribution	Achievability	Value Contribution
Advertising and promotions mix changes	Low	Moderate	Moderate	Moderate
Advertising and promotions for expenditure reductions	Moderate	Moderate	High	Low
Channel strategy modification	Low	Moderate	High	High
Strengthen brand and product manager structure	Not applicable	Not applicable	Moderate	High
Sales productivity improvement: mgt., force	Moderate	Moderate	High	High

integration team leader may find that they have few opportunities to make such changes in the near term. This action option
is likely to become less effective with extended use, as competitors have time and opportunity to mount opposing campaigns
to neutralize the one-time advantage.

Expenditure Reductions for Advertising and Promotions

Particularly if the acquiree's products are well entrenched in
the marketplace, an outright reduction in advertising and promotions expenditures may be an effective near-term approach
for increasing cash flow and value. One client, part of a
packaged goods product company with a household name
consumer product, was confident that continuous television
advertising could be replaced with occasional saturation ad
campaigns with little risk to market-share erosion. Some acquirers, however, are reluctant to run any unnecessary risks
caused by starving the ad budget. Nabisco Brands, Inc.—a
part of RJR Nabisco, which was acquired by Kohlberg Kravis
Roberts in 1989—increased operating profits in 1989 by $220
million, from $530 million in 1988 to $750 million in 1989,
but Nabisco's consumer marketing budget was left untouched.
The annual budgets in both 1988 and 1989 were $465 mil-
lion. Through mid-1990, at least, such support was seen by
RJR/Nabisco management as being essential to preserving market share in highly competitive markets. Sales rose 7 percent
to $4.6 billion, and most of Nabisco's product lines preserved
their market shares.

Channel Strategy Modification

New sales channels are comparatively easy to add, but channel decisions are invariably sticky. Management or the merger-
integration team leader may encounter difficulty in discontin-
uing an existing channel without incurring excessive expense.
No company can afford an underperforming sales channel. Yet
LBO management may determine that it can no longer afford

the channel that it would otherwise select because of other demands for scarce corporate cash after the acquisition.

Consider TargetCo, which invested much of its research budget in three new products. Competitors already had existing offerings in these fields, and their products were sold through independent representatives who handled a wide variety of manufacturers and products. TargetCo management knew that selection of a superior sales channel approach would be critical to dislodging these entrenched market positions and creating market opportunities for their products. Accordingly, senior TargetCo management decided on a direct salesforce for the three new products, reasoning that a directly controlled and accountable sales channel was needed to help offset competitors' advantages. Once TargetCo was purchased by AcquireCo, however, everything changed. Expensive sales channels were out of the question—even if the new channel choice was better suited for the market challenge. In their first meeting after the close, AcquireCo's CEO advised his counterpart in TargetCo that "You had better make do with the channels that you have already."

Strengthening the Brand/Product Thrust

If the acquisition involves a consumer products company, new acquirers may be inclined to believe that strengthening the value of the acquiree means strengthening the program for managing product growth. Sometimes this results in replacing a committee approach to product management with the individual accountability of an empowered brand management approach. Correctly developed and implemented, the brand and product manager approach offers several potential advantages over group think:

- *Clearly delineated decisions*   By practice and necessity, committee management of products and brands gravitates to compromise and often is risk averse. The bold move is voted down because of group concern about excessive risk. The brand-manager approach is more likely to result in a clear-cut decision.

- *Urgency equal to the leveraged acquiree's* The up-or-out aspect of most brand-manager structures enforces a strong sense of personal urgency to make the right things happen in the marketplace. This spirit of overachieving in the marketplace parallels the leveraged acquiree's need to accomplish more with less.

- *Talent* The mere mention of a star system may make some senior administrators squirm, but few sustainable market changes can be achieved without the right personnel.

Admittedly, transition to a brand-manager approach may take too long to implement and be too expensive to receive serious consideration in the initial postacquisition weeks and months. For this reason, change to a brand-manager approach is classified as "not applicable" in the fourth line of Table 6.4. Yet over the longer term that transition may be the critical difference between the acquired consumer products firm that simply pays back its acquisition debt and the acquiree that emerges from the LBO process as an even stronger competitor.

For the acquirer, the best situation is when the acquiree takes action to change even before the deal. Consider, then, the example of Phillip Morris's acquisition of Kraft Corp. Kraft enjoyed a reputation in the marketplace as a sales leader, if not *the* leader, but in the late 1970s and early 1980s that reputation generally did not extend to marketing activities. At that time, Kraft rarely emerged as the top choice among marketing business school graduates—the lifeblood of a sustained effective brand- and product-manager structure. Through considerable work and expense, Kraft attracted the necessary talent for a first-class brand- and product-management approach. After the acquisition, the Kraft internal strengthening was put to good use by the acquiree's new parent, which had expressed dissatisfaction with the lackluster performance of another acquiree, General Foods, virtually since the time of that deal's closing. Kraft's Miles Marsh became the top officer of the newly formed Kraft General Foods unit, with a mandate to extend Kraft's sales and marketing effectiveness over to General Foods.

Sales Productivity Improvement

In many organizations, salesforce and sales management modifications do not even appear on the list of prime postacquisition value opportunities. This may be a mistake. The new acquiree corporation that increases the productivity of its salesforce and sales management makes great strides toward increasing postacquisition cash flow and value.

Efforts of an otherwise stellar salesforce may be neutralized if the salesforce's management underperforms. The acquirer's postacquisition assessment of sales management should search out appropriate opportunities for increasing the number of salespersons assigned to each manager or for replacing sales managers who have limited administrative and motivation skills with those better qualified. Imprecise or indifferently enforced standards are a recurring challenge. If the measures are unclear, unknown, or unenforced, prospects for optimal performance are dim. Alternatively, the key challenge is with the number and nature of the sales managers themselves. The manager post often is used as a reward for a past top producer seeking refuge from the field, which may result in too many managers for the size of the salesforce and poorly developed management skills. Salesforce longevity is often a poor qualifier for sales management effectiveness.

The postacquisition period brings the need to review the personal profit performance of each salesperson, and eliminate underperformers, and combine territories where merited. Using a modified contribution margin approach for measuring the salesperson's progress helps prevent missteps that may occur through reliance on revenue data alone.

Some new acquirees also have found the postacquisition period to be a fitting time to shift from straight salary sales compensation structure toward a structure based on incentive compensation. Properly implemented, such a change helps lower some fixed costs of a direct salesforce at a time when the leveraged acquiree needs such relief the most. A secondary benefit of a postacquisition change to an incentive structure involves selection. Many of the salespersons complaining the loudest about the impending change are also those who are performing under their potential; they complain and leave. The top salespersons welcome the change as an opportunity to make more money; they stay and thrive.

Conclusion: Promotion as Part of the Core Two Agenda

The possible promotion category opportunities for value enhancement are many. Acquirer and acquiree must develop a separate choice strategy for each. Because of the importance of marketplace support to future value of the acquiree, the choice usually involves efficiencies rather than outright elimination of positions, functions, or budgets.

Product

An advanced level of promotion effectiveness means little if the new acquiree has nothing to sell. The leveraged acquiree must balance decisions about product and service development and mix carefully due to intensified cash-flow constraints (see Table 6.5).

Product-Line Extensions and Feature Enhancements

During the latter stages of the due-diligence period or immediately following the close, acquirer management and the MI team leader should assess the extension potential of acquired product lines. Compared to a new product-line introduction, the product-line extension offers some advantages. The customer base exists already in most instances, and the manufacturing process and formulations are familiar. Those advantages, in turn, often translate into lower risks, compared to newly developed or purchased products.

The offsetting risk from inopportune extensions are twofold. First, the best opportunities may already be exhausted by the time the postacquisition period arrives. If some threatened marketing staffers bolstered marginal products by preventing cuts to the current marketing budget, the best extension opportunities may already be gone, only a few weeks into the post-close period. The second risk involves cannibalization. The line extension brings low development costs and an existing customer base, but an ill-considered extension may bleed profits and cash flow from an already established product critical to the acquiree's success. In these situations, the extension destroys rather than creates value.

Proprietary Technologies Developed and Introduced

Cost and lead-time requirements eliminate developing and introducing proprietary technologies as a near-term value option in most instances. As examined in greater depth in chapter 7, the postacquisition period may dictate greater selectivity in a new technology development due to the cash-flow pressure imposed on the leveraged acquiree from merger debt servicing.

Table 6.5.   Postacquisition Marketing and Sales Improvement: Product

	Near-Term (6 mo.–1 yr.)		Beyond One Year	
	Achievability	Value Contribution	Achievability	Value Contribution
Line extensions and feature enhancements	Moderate	Moderate	High	Low to moderate
New proprietary technology breakthrough	Not applicable	Not applicable	Moderate	Moderate to high
Major feature modifications and strategic affiliations	Low	Moderate	High	Moderate
Line-item acquisition	Moderate	Low	High	Low
Product mix change	Moderate	Moderate	High	Moderate

Major Feature Modifications and Strategic Affiliations

Developing breakthrough technology is not the only way for the new postacquistion enterprise to put rivals in the marketplace on the defensive. Major feature modifications or enhancements to the business' existing product lines can help swing the balance in favor of the newly formed company as well—and probably at a lower total cost than development of a proprietary technology advantage from scratch.

The critical balancing act is between cost and customer impact. Limiting the post-close modifications to too few changes, or the wrong ones—that is, changes unlikely to prompt any increase in purchasing—makes the effort a waste. For example, private branch exchange (PBX) manufacturers, the mid-1980s acquiree darlings of some global telecom giants, have traditionally been fond of overengineering features in their business systems. But no one asked the customer; in some instances the features were scarcely recognized by customers, and thus had negligible purchasing effect. By contrast, following its acquisition by Ford, Jaguar introduced a special feature package edition designed to attract the new luxury car buyer in the $25,000+ range—with favorable results.

Strategic affiliations emerged from the decade past with the dubious status of a pop business buzz-phrase—that is, something in which many felt they had to participate, but which few knew how to make work. For postacquisition marketing strategy purposes, the central affiliation issue is capture of additional advantage that could not be obtained through other business arrangements, such as technology contracts or outright purchase. In some instances, the loudly trumpeted "strategic affiliation" turns out to be little more than a posturing opportunity for the two companies' executives. But product/technology advantages sometimes *do* emerge if care is exercised before the affiliation to ensure the marketworthiness of the partnership. One positive example is provided by the Chrysler/Mitsubishi Diamond Star combination, which allowed both firms specific benefits that might not otherwise have been achieved—at least not as quickly.

Line-Item Acquisition

Line items may be acquired directly. Such additions may come from the new parent company, or the purchase may be effected through licensing or joint ventures. Normally, the acquiree encounters little difficulty in filling out its product and service line with rebranded products supplied by third parties, but these products are usually available to others, as well. That means that the most that the acquiree can earn is a merchandising profit margin. If the revenue-to-operating profit yield of the internally developed and produced product is twenty-five cents per one dollar of revenue, the comparable resale margin may be as little as ten cents per revenue dollar. It is not surprising to see why product acquisitions for resale are seen as stop-gap measures and are excluded from ongoing value calculation.

Product Mix Change

Modification of the acquiree's product line offering to customers—including elimination of products that no longer justify support—is an essential value-improvement activity. If the acquiree's product-line profitability analysis goes down only to the gross profit level—and does not consider "below the (gross profit) line" costs necessary to develop and support the product, then it is time to move to a contribution margin (operating profit) format. Once a product and brand manager is notified that a product's contribution to operating profit has fallen below targets, the options to the manager are simple: increase the contribution (or at least, improve the trendline to more closely approach the target) or risk elimination of the product and associated budgets.

Conclusion: Product as Part of the Core Two Agenda

New product and service development is expensive. The leveraged acquiree's limitations in supporting this development place the company in a catch-up role—particularly with competitors who recognize this Achilles' heel and accelerate their own development programs in response. Purchased and licensed products are at best a stop-gap measure for the leveraged acquiree.

Positioning

Positioning is the creation of new postacquisition value by accessing a new customer group for the acquiree's products or services (see Table 6.6).

Incremental Positioning Adjustments

Incremental positioning adjustments are the mirror image of incremental line extensions (see Table 6.6). On paper, at least, both actions are easy to implement. If repositioning positions the product or service better for the target customer group, additional cash flow may be generated in the first postacquisition year. Other than making the product available to a broader customer base through price reductions — downscaling — enduring

Table 6.6. Postacquisition Marketing and Sales Improvement: Positioning

| | Near-Term (6 mo.–1 yr.) | | Beyond One Year | |
	Achievability	Value Contribution	Achievability	Value Contribution
Incremental positioning adjustments	High	Low	High	Low
Lost customers recaptured	Moderate	Low	Moderate	Moderate
New customer group identified, acquired	Low	Low	Moderate	Moderate
Repositioning acquisition	Not applicable	Not applicable	Low	High

repositioning is often difficult to master. An example is provided by Chrysler's challenges with the acquired Eagle line of passenger cars following acquisition of Jeep/Eagle from Renault. Eagle had stylish lines and spirited performance, but the sedans were less widely known than the trendy Jeep, which made effective positioning difficult. Auto buyers wondered whether Eagle was a recreational vehicle or a European roadster. In an apparent move to increase Eagle showroom traffic—even at the risk of further blurring Eagle's distinct identity—Eagle was designated by its new parent, Chrysler, as the nameplate for a four-wheel-drive variant of the Mitsubishi Eclipse/Plymouth Laser sportscoupes. The Eagle Talon was manufactured by the Diamond Star joint venture of Mitsubishi Motors and Chrysler Corporation.

Lost Customer Recapture and New Customer Group Identification and Penetration

Recapturing a former lost account is often more profitable—and sometimes easier—than pursuing customers who are not yet familiar with the acquiree's products or services. Understandably, many salespeople are reluctant to revisit their lost accounts: the loss of an important customer is an embarassment, and few salespeople want to be reminded about those that got away. The benefits of lost-account recapture, however, should encourage management to overcome the embarassment.

Addressing the lost sales in earnest begins with management's refusal to accept the explanation that the reason for the earlier account loss was price alone. Established, long-term accounts usually don't become former accounts without a reason. Emphasis should be placed on identifying that nonprice reason: the *actual* reason for the loss. From there, the salesforce is one step from recontacting its old customer and jointly developing an agenda to reestablish account relationships.

Repositioning Acquisition

A repositioning acquisition may be viewed by the acquirer as the first step to a more desirable future. In the immediate aftermath of the closing, however, this is not to be a high-value opportunity. As many acquirers have discovered to their dismay, acquiring a company with desirable attributes does not necessarily mean that those characteristics are transferred to the acquirer.

The repositioning acquisition and diversification forays of AT&T illustrate the practical limits of the repositioning action. Broadening a version of the AT&T calling card to allow consumer charges doesn't move AT&T close to becoming a commercial bank because the administration of the new universal card is handled by a financial institution in Georgia. AT&T contemplated (but did not implement) acquisition of Electronic Data Systems during the height of the Perot/Smith feuding to create an instant third-party systems integrator giant.

Conclusion: Positioning as Part of the Core Two Agenda

Positioning is the most elusive of the MI core two categories. Care must be taken to enact the opportunities with greatest value potential and not merely those suggesting the loftiest future promises. Based on this consideration, recapture of lost customers is the most achievable postacquisition value action.

Implementing the Four Ps Agenda: An Approach

Table 6.7 shows one approach to shaping a coherent core two approach from these assorted opportunities. Five initiatives form a directed value-development agenda that results in additional cash flow, some of which may be applied to retire acquisition debt early. Ideally, some of the generated cash flow should be used to reassert the acquiree's product momentum in its market segment. Acquisition of a leadership caliber product corresponds to the third item in Table 6.7. Such an expenditure is critical to the success of the new company, for giving customers a hint of greater things to come, and for assuring

Table 6.7. One Approach to Creating Core Two Merger Integration Value

Concentrate on one channel.	Scale back three sales distribution approaches to one. Reinvest some in the remaining channel. Benefits: savings, greater effectiveness.
Review media.	Scale back continuous advertising exposure for the LBO's initial year. Make a transition to a selected advertising approach thereafter.
Reinvest some core one and core two savings in new products.	Top customers design the new product. Acquire the new product even if at a premium.
Rethink the combined marketing and sales organization.	Combine marketing and sales departments, with fewer total positions, for at least two years.
Pursue salesforce effectiveness.	Emphasize fundamentals rather than oversold technologies. The goal is same or more revenue with 10 percent leaner salesforce.

key employees that merger integration is not a disguised form of liquidation, in spite of the efficiencies pursued.

Acquiring the Franchise Nameplate Company

One revenue-side development that merits particular attention is the trend toward acquiring franchise name companies. The search for value in well-known brand names has characterized some of the more visible acquisitions of the latter phases of the great 1980s merger boom. Examples include Beatrice (multiple), Columbia Pictures, Butterick, Jeep, Kraft, and Tiffany. Even the Pillsbury dough boy didn't avoid an acquisition by Great Metropolitan.

Franchise name company acquisitions are the merger-market equivalent of the move to glamour issues in the big board. Rising concern about value as the boom matures leads acquirers to search for underlying value in the companies they pursue, and built-in recurring customer demand is an attractive source of value.

Some view the acquirers of franchise companies as insulated from the success rules that apply to less glamorous acquirees. According to many analysts' estimations, Ford overpaid for Jaguar in 1989 following a heated bidding contest for the British automaker with General Motors. Yet overpayment assessments about Ford's actions were balanced by other, more supportive opinions, the thrust of which were that Ford acquired a proprietary, upscale nameplate in the $30,000-plus luxury automobile market segment. Perhaps more important to Ford's shareholders, the automaker's move prevented that valuable property from falling into the hands of a competitor. The sheer magnitude of Kohlberg Kravis Roberts' acquisition of RJR Nabisco made merger-market watchers nervous that the multibillion-dollar financing might collapse the high-leverage junk bond market, but financing progressed smoothly.

If there is a rule concerning the purchase of the franchise brand company, it is to capitalize on, but not sell, the most important parts of that franchise—the branded products themselves. Mobilizing the potential brand value may take time. Until then, a continuing reserve of value exists for acquirers of the nameplates that back image with solid consumer revenues. Ford management may not yet have a plan for optimizing the franchise value of Jaguar in the U.S. market, but its future value exists.

7

MI Core Three:
Research, Procurement,
and Manufacturing

This chapter focuses on merger-integration opportunities relating to the basic product and service processes of the newly acquired firm or, if the acquisition was made by a synergistic buyer, the product and service process combination emerging from the transition from two firms to one. The product and service processes are the base activities and functions that directly provide products and services to customers—creating, developing, producing, and delivering products and services of the company in competitive markets. The continuum begins with conceptualization and ends with actual physical delivery to the customer.

The acquiring group's postacquisition challenge is to select a limited number of processes within that continuum that have an optimal mix of characteristics pertaining to postacquisition value creation. Such factors include total expenditure budget size, the portion of the budget that is discretionary, the timing of possible process changes, impact of those changes, offsetting costs, and implementation ease or difficulty.

Because of MI time constraints this process of narrowing down must take place quickly. If seven or eight different product and service processes are statistically evaluated with traditional analysis methods, the formative part of the postacquisition period will pass before the results are available. Some judgments are necessary, using factors cited above as guidelines rather than absolutes. For example, distribution is not emphasized as a process category in this chapter. The size of corporate distribution expenditures and the fact that some of these outlays are changeable argued for inclusion, but those factors are offset by some other considerations, including timing and costs. A comprehensive distribution approach must be in close step with new customer and competitor trends and also with related changes of importance in manufacturing. These multiple interrelationships argue against quick value-change actions. The transitional costs of change also may prohibit near-term action. Investment in the current distribution infrastructure is likely to be sizeable. Transition costs of a switch to another structure—even one that is superior to that now in place—may force distribution network changes to be assigned a lower priority.

Experience suggests that research and new product development, procurement, and manufacturing tend to emerge as the most consistent value sources in the limited postacquisition period:

- *Research and product development*   The R & D budgets are usually at least partially discretionary in many innovation-directed industries, and changes in the research priorities sometimes yield unexpected corporate value-improvement results.

- *Procurement*   In a manufacturing company, procurement of raw and intermediate materials is likely to be among the largest, if not *the* largest disbursements category. This in itself argues for inclusion. Yet the real MI opportunity may relate not just to the size of the purchasing budget but also to how the procurement function is conducted. Many companies exhibit an inherent conflict between the purchasing manager's responsibility to ensure continuation of supply and the responsibility to minimize costs. Such conflicts suggest opportunities for new value creation.

• *Manufacturing*   This comprises the major portion of total product costs in many companies. Because improvements in manufacturing efficiency and effectiveness tend to be evolutionary rather than revolutionary, this category may seem to represent a marginal value-creation opportunity during the tight postacquisition time period. That first look may be misleading. After manufacturing, management's priorities about the efficiencies to address and the value-creation change, as well. Furthermore, the acquisition's circumstances—such as additional plants and production workers—may force a faster pace of change.

Many of the efficiency and effectiveness improvement opportunities and actions described in this chapter could—and perhaps should—occur at times other than the postacquisition period. Without the sense of urgency exerted by the completed deal requiring new cash-flow and value, however, they rarely happen. The sheer magnitude of the dollar size of these processes and the size of staff involved reinforce a tendency toward inertia.

Postacquisition Research and Development: Toward a Market Focus

Near-term improvements in how a company conceptualizes, develops, and introduces its new products and services are a significant source new of potential postacquisition value.

The Underperformance Dilemma

An underperforming corporate development or research operation acts as a continuing drain on profits. Profit and cash-flow consequences of the underperforming development or research operations are severe. Some product-development functions consider too many opportunities to be successful. Without a concentration of staff and funding in market areas where the company is best positioned to succeed, few commercially viable products emerge, and the returns from those products that make it to market fail to offset the losses from unnecessary examinations.

Historically, different R & D departments have not been compared on a financial performance basis. How could, after all, a research operation in primary research be compared with a department concentrating on formula extensions of present products? Inappropriate comparisons remain a problem, but the potential gains from efficiency improvement have encouraged increasing use of competitive benchmark comparisons for assessing R & D efficiency and effectiveness. Expressed as a percentage of revenues, the difference between a well-managed research and development operation and one that is not may be two to three full percentage points.

Moreover, the effects of an underperforming development function spread throughout the rest of the company. If, for example, new products are developed with insufficient customer input, the newly introduced product misses the market. Manufacturing produces the wrong product, distribution delivers it, and salespeople discover to their alarm that competitors have been given a marketplace head start. If underperformance is allowed to persist, the product and service development or research function destroys corporate value by absorbing funds that could alternatively be applied to debt repayment or to other profitable investments.

If symptoms are recognized soon enough and problems are corrected quickly, however, the underperforming department may instead become a source for new merger-integration value. Consider the research performance efficiency of two competitors in the industrial filters field—Millipore and Pall. Millipore is a traditional research operation that combines general and applied research projects and expenditures as technologies emerge and recede. Indirect sources of market intelligence tell Millipore researchers whether their efforts are on-target or off. Millipore is reported as spending about 7.6 percent of annual revenues, or $47 million, on R & D. About 20 percent of Pall's product line are products in which the two companies compete, but Pall's research approach differs from its larger competitor. Pall concentrates on specific market opportunities where management believes the company can best succeed. Research facilities are adequately equipped and supplied but otherwise modest. A special extended advisory group comprising both Pall researchers and principal customers keeps the company close to its markets and helps pinpoint marketplace success of new product introductions. Yet Pall's research costs are reported as being significantly lower than its competitor both in absolute terms and expressed as a percentage of company revenues. Pall spends about 4 percent of revenues, or $17 million, on research annually.

Changing Course: Five Problems or Opportunities

Changes in R & D direction and priorities can yield significant value results. Five opportunity areas—the new technology investment imperative, the ivory tower research organization, the missing customer link, the staff-directed development program, and the ninety/ten dilemma—are discussed in the following pages.

The New Technology Investment Imperative

Research investment priorities are heavily influenced by the appeal of a particular technology to researchers. Company management is encouraged to invest in emerging technologies or risk falling behind our competitors. Nevertheless, the prospect of wasted expenditures and lost opportunities looms from a careless pursuit of new technologies. When several research groups all chase the same new technology, only early innovators earn an adequate return on their investment. Others— including late research entrants and companies without additional funds to develop a new technology—face a high probability of wasted outlays. Superior cost alternatives to direct participation in the technology often are not adequately considered. For example, licensing a technology after the technology has been perfected will likely be appealing to researchers that direct research. Such an orientation increases the prospects of waste. This investment in the new technology investment draws funds and staff away from less dramatic but higher-return-potential research opportunities.

Savings—and thus the opportunity to create additional value and cash flow—may accrue in the postacquisition period if opportunities are recognized and acted on. Eliminating a questionable research investment in a high-technology field, for example, frees up investable funds for other uses. To implement such action, however, the acquirer's first step is to undertake a rigorous review of all technology research investments of the acquiree. That assessment should cover the intended expenditure, plus the investment amounts and progress of competitive technologies of the technology, the realistic profits from such investment, and alternative research investment opportunities.

The Ivory Tower Research Organization

Over time, the self-perception of the acquiree's research group changes from the organization primarily responsible for new product and service creation to a department primarily concerned with its own perpetuation. Increasing layers in the R & D department's organization chart are a symptom of this situation. Maintenance-type research activities prevail over new products and services development. Parts of research budgets of established products are diverted to subsidize other research. Over time an increasing percentage of total department employees function in an administrative or supervisory role.

Value creation in the MI period starts with a thorough productivity review of the R & D function and the productivity of its employees. Unnecessary outlays should be eliminated, and authorized expenditures limited to activities directly related to new revenue creation. The development department is encouraged to return to its roots. Staff positions and responsibilities not directly related to new product development are scaled back, freeing cash flow for other investments and creating new value.

The Missing Customer Link

Research departments sometimes introduce a product that flops in the marketplace by following their own sense of what customers want instead of the market's. Researchers may feel that "This is the product that the marketplace needs—it is up to the salesforce to see that it is sold." The research staff at a telecommunications company may entrance the new owners of its company with the technological elegance of a new private branch exchange product line, but the technology may be irrelevant to customers. The company loses money, time, and opportunity because research efforts are misdirected.

Value creation in the MI period begins with development of a mechanism to directly verify product market potential with probable customers *before* expenditures are authorized. Elimination or scaleback of projects that are not supported by customer demand creates additional sources of postacquisition value.

The Staff-Directed Development Program

Research activities aim at keeping development personnel occupied; development department staffing and expenses are not adjusted to match high-priority, high-return opportunities. Because of this situation, development and research staff often are seen as free resources. Value creation in the MI period may require examining the profit contribution of development project work undertaken by borderline development employees. Adjustments can be made as necessary to increase cash flow and increase value.

The Ninety-Ten Dilemma

Two varieties of projects survive each year but probably should not. The almost-done project seems never to get beyond 90 percent complete, and the scaled-back (10 percent) project has a nominal budget but not enough investment to complete the project. Funds are wasted in both instances. To create value in the MI period, eliminate the underfunded 10 percent project and invest only in those 90 percent projects that have a viable return.

Procurement Changes and Postacquisition Value Creation

Untapped Value Potential

Some form of procurement process change is usually part of the merger-integration agenda. At a minimum, the acquirer and acquiree often succeed in securing some temporary breaks in prices and terms from some suppliers after the close. Yet the procurement category is often underutilized from a MI value-creation perspective. The cause of this underutilization lies in the difference between reactive approaches to the MI procurement issue and a systematic approach to that issue. Reactive approaches call for fast action but have little or no effect on the value-related characteristics of the acquiree's procurement function. Price breaks are visible and often achievable, at least for a time; but the value-improvement contribution is likely to be temporary because there is usually fundamental change in the procurement processes. After the break period has passed, customer and supplier usually revert to their former relationship.

In a systematic approach, however, the focus is on those purchasing activities and functions that appear to be most conducive to value-improvement change and to those companies and situations in which meaningful change—and thus additional value creation—looks to be achievable over the limited postacquisition period. This chapter therefore looks beyond the apparent postacquisition value opportunities to others that often are not pursued but perhaps should be. This means looking beyond immediate price breaks alone to three other possible opportunity areas, such as materials substitution, volume/vendor management and preferred vendor programs, and changes in the procurement officer's incentives and performance measures.

The Reactive Approach:
The LBO-Induced Price Break

One procurement category action almost always is undertaken after the deal is closed—attempting to secure relief in prices or terms from principal long-time suppliers to the company. Even a 5 percent overall price break from a principal supplier for the acquiree's first twelve to eighteen months as a subsidiary may mean the difference between viability and insolvency. If the supplier relationship is long standing and a flexible arrangement can be developed, the result may be additional protection against unforeseen business downturns. Moreover, the acquirer and acquiree may have no choice but to move quickly to secure such price breaks. If the original financing in the deal was a stretch, some level of supplier price breaks already has been incorporated into the official transaction projections. Between the time of financing authorization for the deal and the initiation of core three MI actions after the close, industry conditions may have eroded to the point that additional cash flow relief is required as an offset.

Widening knowledge of LBOs and the pressure exerted on acquiree operations by such financing works to the acquirer's and acquiree's advantage. Assuming that the acquiree or acquirer has maintained relationships with the principal supplier in recent years, and that the vendor wishes to keep either or both of those accounts, a request for some price or terms concessions after a high-leverage acquisition should not appear to out of line. This is particularly true if the industry has encountered other leveraged acquisitions in recent years. In that case, the principal supplier already may have faced similar concession requests from others in the acquiree's industry under comparable circumstances. The principal supplier who has granted post-LBO price and terms relief to previous LBO acquirees in the industry will probably find it difficult to refuse such terms to another company.

An effective concession request requires some preparation. The acquirer and acquiree should gain an accurate understanding of past LBO price and items concessions before approaching that vendor with its own proposition. This intelligence gathering must be swift and confidential. To avoid a premature signal of the intent behind such intelligence gathering, use outsiders. If an outside firm has been designated for the merger-integration role, a member of that team is a logical choice to undertake this assignment. The sources that are contacted in amassing this intelligence are as important as selection of the agent. Other suppliers that were damaged by the concession actions of the principal supplier in past LBOs are the most credible sources, if their information can be confirmed from multiple sources.

The Initial Concession Proposition

In constructing the concession request, more is at issue than just the supplier's past concession pattern. Changing business conditions (particularly following a major capital expansion by the supplier, the supplier's own financial strength, and changes in account relationships with other customers must be factored into the proposition. Deterioration of the supplier's own financial strength since the time of earlier LBO concessions may cause the firm to resist new concessions, but a supplier facing near-term difficulties can ill afford the loss of a major account. The appropriate tactic may be to stretch the length of a preferential supply arrangement. Moreover, the complete concession proposition reflects the principal supplier's concern about change in business conditions of customer accounts in other industries. The significance of this factor is likely to multiply if the supplier has undertaken a recent capital expansion: someone has to provide the orders to keep the plant going. Finally, the new acquiree's negotiation heft may be negated if other purchasers have already acted to increase the principal supplier's security, such as by enacting long-term preferred-vendor programs (discussed later in this chapter). Successful completion of a preferred vendor arrangement by a competitor in the acquiree's industry may be particularly damaging. A key supply source of the acquiree is less secure, and a competitor probably has some materials cost advantages.

The time for analysis is limited. The acquirer and acquiree must act swiftly to transform the principal supplier's sympa-

thetic intent into tangible savings. Typical concession proposi-
tions pinpoint a price concession from prevailing prices in the
10 to 15 percent range, with comparable concessions in terms.
Care must be taken not to use a base-price level that was recently boosted directly in anticipation of the LBO, however. If
the concession is based on a recently inflated pricing structure,
concessions may accomplish little more than return prices and
terms to pretransaction levels. Finally, what is not discussed
in the initial concession discussion conversation is probably as
important as what is covered. At the time of the initial discussions with a principal supplier, the effective length of time for
the concession must be addressed.

The Principal Supplier's Response

Open issues don't stay that way for long. If the acquiree's account is valued, the principal supplier will act quickly to eliminate areas of possible future misunderstanding. In addition to
the time length issue, other areas of concern are likely to be
reflected in the supplier's response. These considerations may
include one or more of the following:

- *Product span*   This refers to the breadth of products and
  services purchased by the new acquiree that are effected
  by the concession understanding. Does the proposed arrangement cover one, some, or all of the products sold to
  the acquiree?
- *Adjustments*   If the proposed arrangement is for more than
  a couple of months, the issue of adjustments often arises.
  The principal supplier has a strong self-interest in ensuring that changes in its own costs and productivity can be
  reflected in its pricing to avoid a profit squeeze.
- *Acquirer financial support issues*   The acquirer's direct financial support for acquiree purchase volumes beyond a certain size or under certain financial conditions, such as
  loan default, are issues that may be raised. Such concerns should be expected from a sharp negotiator. If the
  acquiree's requested concessions are sizeable and the acquisition transaction highly leveraged, this is much more

than a negotiating point. The supplier raising this issue will undoubtedly also request access to ongoing financial information.

- *Acquirer account access*   If the acquirer is in a related business, preferential access to the acquirer's business may be a counterrequest.
- *Volume*   This refers to dollar or unit volume of purchases. Volume is likely to be a key concern of the principal supplier and its counsel, particularly in a competitive marketplace involving the sale of identical materials to many buyers. Under such conditions, a supplier may be hard pressed to justify preferential terms based on changes in a customer's situation. In many instances, it is necessary for the spirit of the LBO-driven concessions to be translated into volume terms.

Limitations

Without conscientious follow up, the acquiree and its new parent may find that the gains from a postacquisition break in terms and prices are difficult to translate directly to the bottom line and turn out to be illusory. With too many exempted products or too many price situations outside of the arrangement, the arrangement becomes a mass of potential misunderstandings. The old arrangement is reestablished at the end of the term of the understanding, exerting an understandable temptation for the supplier to overboost future upward price adjustments to offset prior concessions. If most of an acquiree's supplies are designated by the acquiree's procurement officer as being in critical short supply, then these supplies and suppliers can be successfully placed outside of the bounds of any concession arrangement.

Procurement Processes and
MI Value Creation:
A Systematic Approach

In many postacquisition programs, price and terms concession negotiations are the beginning and end of the MI value-creation issue—at least as applied to procurement. Such a narrow scoping may overlook other opportunities in the procurement category, and by doing so, place unnecessary value-creation pressure on other merger-integration core programs. Realizing greater MI value potential from the procurement category requires that key value-related procurement processes be addressed. The approach for addressing these processes must be systematic and the full breadth of the procurement issue, including the characteristics of today's and tomorrow's vendors, key inventory issues, and production requisites. The examination scope also should be comprehensive. This means inclusion of a full range of value-related procurement processes—how the company buys, what the company purchases, in what quantities, and from whom.

Opportunity Targets

Certain procurement processes combine enough dollar size, improvement potential, and implementation characteristics to be sizeable MI value opportunities, particularly in manufacturing organizations where rigorous performance review of the procurement function have either been ineffectively applied, limited to too narrow a scope, or simply have not been undertaken in recent years. The potential dollar benefits of procurement-process change can be sizeable, and significant progress often can be achieved in the brief postacquisition period. In a merger-integration program involving a financial acquirer and an acquiree in a household goods field, enacting several simple changes in procurement procedures suggested by the merger-integration team yielded an ongoing savings opportunity in the $700,000 annual range, with additional opportunities indicated in an expanded program.

Advance Intelligence

Certain information first must be developed and assessed—quickly—for the systematic approach to work. Areas for advance investigation include the following:

- *Acquiree's critical resources* The acquiree's off-limits list of raw and intermediate purchased materials subject to special treatment must be reviewed and assessed quickly to separate special situations from materials and intermediate purchased products incorrectly placed in this category. This category sometimes expands to include other vendors and materials so that the purchasing officer can avoid rigorous purchasing negotiations with these suppliers on these materials or for reasons entirely unrelated to procurement issues. A raw-material category may be designated as sole source, but other suppliers are known to exist and have not been rigorously investigated, or the component is not critical to the manufacturing process, or manufacturing continually stocks out of a particular component because of a glitch in its process.

- *Production issues related to procurement* Production decisions are not made in a vacuum, and neither are manufacturing, inventory, and product design issues. Recurring stock-out items resulting in part from the idiosyncracies of the present production process must be known and understood—including the effect of modifications to that process on procurement practices. Possible targets for stock-keeping unit reduction and expansion must be understood so that the procurement process can be directed at future areas of purchasing emphasis and not just the present mix.

- *Vendors' key characteristics* The systematic approach requires advance knowledge of the importance of the acquiree's business to suppliers—both today's major vendors and companies that could become majors tomorrow. Intelligence also is needed on prospective or possible developments of present principal suppliers that change the acquiree's supply relationship, such as financial developments, long-term supply negotiations, and changes in management or capacity. Senior corporate and procurement officers in many manufacturing and assembly concerns can list their key suppliers, along with the percentage of their purchases supplied by each vendor by major category, but few officers can readily list the percentage that *their* business represents to their individual suppliers. Such intelligence is critical to developing and implementing a systematic procurement strategy, beginning with decisions made and actions undertaken during the postacquisition period. This knowledge is key to developing informed vendor programs: the present and potential importance of the acquiree's business to alternative suppliers primarily determines what can—and what cannot—be done to squeeze additional dollars from volume and vendor management and volume consolidation strategies. In reexamining the acquiree's list of supplies and suppliers, the merger-integration team will likely uncover some suppliers that are principal acquiree sources but have little reliance on the acquiree's business. Such a situation may indicate a growing area of vulnerability for the acquiree under certain conditions and circumstances. Unless alternative sources are known and available, the acquiree may find itself in a supply squeeze or unable to counter an exorbitant price increase with alternative materials or supply sources. The trend of the supplier's business with the acquiree is important; if the trend is decreasing, the major supplier already may be withdrawing. The opposite situation may arise: the capable second-tier supplier that is largely dependent on the acquiree's volume may be looking for more.

Although this kind of information is typically not available from any one source, most of the data can usually be pieced together from direct discussions with the smaller suppliers, public information (in the case of some large, publicly traded suppliers), and unconventional sources such as former employees and suppliers to the suppliers.

MI Procurement Process Analysis: Materials, Volume and Vendors, and Procurement

Key value issues and implementation concerns relating to materials substitution, volume and vendor management and preferred vendor programs, and changes in procurement officer incentives and performance measurement are three possible value sources.

Materials Substitution

Materials substitution can refer to both major materials substitution opportunities and elimination of redundant components and materials. Whole categories of potential materials substitute candidates and redundant materials eliminations may sometimes be uncovered in the acquisition of a manufacturing or assembly company—particularly if that company has never undergone a rigorous postacquisition investigation before. Opportunities for value creation from this source increase even more if design, procurement, sales, and manufacturing functions of the company have been poorly coordinated in the past. In one company, designers created a new product design that eliminated about one-third of the stock-keeping units of the old design and allowed less expensive materials to be used in many of the components that remained. The net cost appeared to be about 10 percent in volume. Manufacturing opposed that design (and the related major change in purchases) because existing equipment wouldn't be used and marketing expressed concerns that a design change could jeopardize existing customer relationships.

Few managers are willing to take on such entrenched opposition when the company is operating in its normal state, but when an acquisition occurs, the need to create more value from existing operations becomes explicit. If this process has been identified in advance as an area of opportunity, the merger-integration team works fast to uncover existing company research on possible materials-substitution opportunities already developed in the acquiree by dividing its effort into three categories—major possible product design changes with significant materials substitution implications, substitution opportunities involving present products and design, and key present and future manufacturing components and supplies. A second investigation following these three categories focuses on competitors, and if applicable, a third abbreviated analysis may be added to focus on other industries with process similarities. The leading prospects from each category and source are combined, and the resulting set is assessed on the basis of multiple criteria, including potential cost savings (and thus potential cash flow and value benefit), the continuity of those savings, offsetting costs, and expected implementation difficulty.

Volume and Vendor Management and Preferred Vendor Programs

Opportunities exist to achieve ongoing procurement expense savings—and thus MI value creation—through carefully planned and implemented changes in the company's purchasing tactics, followed eventually by development of one or more preferred vendor programs. Intelligence gathered in support of the systematic procurement process—specifically, data about present suppliers and their level of sales dependence on the company—provides the basis for commonsense changes in the acquiree organization about what is bought and from whom. Most changes are evolutionary rather than revolutionary, but cash-flow savings should result, unless product scarcity or exclusivity of a limited number of suppliers prevents this. The small but growing new supplier is willing to provide the acquiree with special prices and expediated delivery in return for a larger continuing share of the acquiree's volume of a component. If that component is presently purchased from a supplier with little dependence on the acquiree's account volume, a gradual transition in volume may well make sense.

A preferred vendor program is a more formalized extension of the evolutionary-change approach described above, with individual orders replaced with a structured contract relationship. Supply terms, quantities, and amounts are defined. The goal is to provide the vendor with sufficient continuing volume to achieve scale economies through long production runs of standardized components and then share those efficiencies between supplier and customer.

Procurement Manager Incentives and Measurement

Sometimes a deliberate change in the procurement manager's performance measures or incentives yields unexpected value as a source of postacquisition value. Performance of the procurement function—at any time, not just during the postacquisition period—depends in large part on the direction given to the manager held responsible for those processes. Many procurement managers must wrestle with two objectives that sometimes conflict—assuring continuing availability of supplies at all times and achieving the lowest possible total cost for purchased goods. Many procurement managers have both goals in some form in their evaluation criteria. The senior officer's challenge—and following an acquisition, the acquiring group's challenge—is to alter those directions in a manner that changes but does not confuse.

Since both goals are included in the procurement manager's formal evaluation, changes in action depend on informal signals. If the procurement function reports to manufacturing, and the vice president of manufacturing places great importance on avoiding any raw material shortages that jeopardize production, guess which of the two performance measures will be pursued by the procurement manager? Offsetting actions are necessary if top management wishes to swing the pendulum the other way—that is, toward the cost-minimization goal. A switch to a dual-reporting relationship and creation of a special bonus schedule based on specific procurement cost performance relative to production levels and patterns are two tactics that have been used in attempts to redirect the procurement manager's actions.

Combining the Opportunity Mix: The Example of Hypothetical Woodchuck, Inc.

This discussion of a hypothetical acquiree—Woodchuck, Inc.—incorporates many of the MI procurement value issues covered in the previous sections. Woodchuck is a manufacturer and distributor in a consumer products field that has become increasingly competitive over the past three years. Woodchuck was recently acquired by a West Coast merchant bank.

Action Steps

The merger-integration team plans to improve Woodchuck's postacquisition procurement results—and thus create additional sources of cash flow and value—by following several steps:

- *Gather facts*   The team will determine where Woodchuck now stands in terms of efficiency and effectiveness of its procurement operations and where the acquiree's procurement operation probably would end up without outside assistance.

- *Identify and develop benchmarks*   The team will identify appropriate procurement performance goals for Woodchuck from external sources, based either on functional or company comparables.

- *Select tactics*   The team will specify the programs that will help Woodchuck to more closely approach those stretch performance objectives.

- *Make adjustments*   Changes as necessary are made in operations to secure new value and encourage continuing improvements.

Industry Comparables

Table 7.1 shows how Woodchuck's hypothetical current and past procurement performance compares with a composite of comparable data from several of Woodchuck's competitors. For discussion purposes, assume that Woodchuck and "Competitor" are the same size as measured by sales and overall procurement expenditures. Further assume that the two companies purchase the same materials and supplies from the same suppliers. Competitor is assumed to have a preferred vendor program in place, whereas Woodchuck does not. Purchase terms offered by industry suppliers are identified under the terms column in the table. The data show that Woodchuck, the new

Table 7.1. Woodchuck's and Competitor's Purchasing Performance Percentages

| Terms | Major vendors paid at specified terms | | | |
| | Woodchuck | | Competitor | |
	Number	Percentage	Number	Percentage
1%/10 net 30	56	70%	50	50%
Net 30	12	15	5	5
2%/10 net 30	9	11	6	6
Net 10	3	4	9	9
Net 90	0	0	30	30
Totals	80	100%	100	100%
Key suppliers program?	No		Yes	
Percentage of top ten suppliers	40%		70%	

acquiree, makes a full 70 percent of its payments at 1%/10 net 30 terms when such terms are offered. This information suggests that Woodchuck almost always takes advantage of the best terms offered, but the information by itself provides no indication of Woodchuck's aggressiveness in fighting for even more favorable terms. Woodchuck could have pressed harder for better terms. Compared to Woodchuck, Competitor has made a significantly greater number and percentage of its purchases on a net ninety days' basis (30 percent versus zero).

Consequences of an Unbalanced Performance Measurement Structure

Following the retirement of Woodchuck's long-time procurement manager, Tooth, at the close, the new parent encourages top management of Woodchuck to place one of the acquiring company's officers in that position as a replacement. The merchant bank paid a heavy premium to acquire Woodchuck and indicates that cash flow to service acquisition debt is tight. Procurement is viewed as a high-priority area for new cash flow and value development, and they assign Bergenhut, senior procurement manager at a large East Coast corporation before joining the merchant bank, to the acquisition team. When Bergenhut asks Woodchuck's CEO, Dunner, for a copy of his predecessor's performance goals and measures, the senior exec explains "We gave only one instruction to your predecessor: Whatever else, make sure that Woodchuck is *never* without raw materials for production." Dunner was the company executive vice president for production before assuming his present post.

That instruction was certainly explicit. Other purchasing officers often had to juggle several goals such as ensuring adequate supplies and minimizing procurement disbursements. Bergenhut wonders about the hidden waste generated by a single-goal approach to procurement as he probes Tooth's vendor account data and attempts to trace the logic underlying his predecessor's purchase activities. With only a supply responsibility to fulfill, Tooth reacted to virtually every actual or potential purchasing problem with excess purchases and vendors. Production was never halted for lack of materials and supplies, but this assurance was achieved at great cost:

- *Financial support*   Additional corporate borrowing was required to support the overstock, which meant less cash for money-producing investments or for acquisition debt repayment.

- *Procurement expenses*   The prevailing purchasing practices meant unnecessary expenditures as well as unnecessary expense. Suppliers instinctively recognized Tooth's charter and took full advantage.

- *Questionable supply protection*   Woodchuck's former procurement officer spread orders around among seven or eight different suppliers on certain key components to protect tight supplies but small-volume orders placed Woodchuck at the bottom of most suppliers' emergency fill list. Allocated volumes were not enough for Woodchuck to be important to any supplier.

- *Actual problems obscured*   Excess procurement blanketed over other problems in Woodchuck that might otherwise have been recognized and corrected. Tooth purchased expensive, partially manufactured products at production's request that were inserted at the right point so that the production line appeared to be running smoothly. Purchasing was used to disguise a manufacturing process challenge.

- *Slow market response*   Woodchuck's overstocking slowed the company's reaction time to changes in customer preferences and trends in highly competitive markets. The piles of raw material inventory were a constant reminder of where Woodchuck's priorities lie. Requests for raw materials purchases for new product launches met with a curt response: "Why should we spend money for different supplies when we have all this here already?"

Action Target

In attempting to reverse Woodchuck's procurement direction, Bergenhut pinpoints and changes some of the most alarming consequences of past procurement practices through direct actions. Action targets include the following:

- *Out of control raw material inventories*   Woodchuck's raw materials inventory has ballooned to twice the level that Bergenhut figures is needed to support ongoing manufacturing needs. To contain the excess stocks, additional storage space had been constructed or leased. Unexplained theft loss also increased, and the materials volume in storage was so great that some spoilage occurred. Bergenhut's immediate response is to undertake an immediate disposal of excess stock—all the way down to the percentage level (estimations of actual raw materials inventories relative to production) suggested by the Competitor composite in Table 7.1.

- *Proliferating stock-keeping units*   The number and variety and stock keeping units jumped significantly over three years, fueling a corresponding need for new and different materials. Procurement personnel time and company funds were diverted to maintaining inventories that supported products that might never again be sold. A rigorous review of SKUs is undertaken with a goal of achieving a

30 percent reduction in the number total stocking items. Unless an SKU item was part of a minimum size order within the past month, the item is subject to cut.

New Performance Measures

At the recommendation of the MI team leader and Bergenhut himself, performance evaluation measures for the procurement manager are significantly changed. From now on, only 60 percent of the manager's bonus and salary review are based on availability of raw materials stock for manufacturing. The remaining 40 percent of his evaluation is split between pricing and inventory goals. An index group of certain items purchased both by Woodchuck and Competitor is established, and an independent outside group will track the comparative prices of the two. As procurement manager, Bergenhut receives a special bonus if he meets or beats Competitor's analyzed price level, adjusted for comparable volume. Bergenhut also will receive an additional bonus for maintaining raw materials inventory at low to moderate levels, measured in terms of two percentages—the percentage of manufacturing volume and the percentage of revenues.

Implementation Follow-Through: Enabling Programs

Changes in staffing, procurement philosophy, and the procurement manager's evaluation criteria are overdue, but such changes by themselves are limited in effectiveness without enabling programs—that is, specific actions to help achieve the planned performance improvements. Several enabling programs are implemented by Woodchuck:

- *First-year break in terms and prices*   Although many vendors anticipated a newly LBOed firm's request for easier terms virtually from the day that an agreement in principle was announced, Woodchuck's request provides a clear signal to vendors that a change in procurement management and approach has taken place at Woodchuck. Research by the merger-integration team indicates that Woodchuck consistently paid near the upper end of vendors' price range for most supplies. Bergenhut petitions each major supplier for a 10 percent across-the-board reduction in prices for a full two years and also seeks 120 days additional carry without additional fees. He would be happy to receive half of these terms. Bergenhut informs all vendors about his future plans to institute a key-vendors program.

- *Competitive terms* Woodchuck communicates to all vendors that it is establishing a price and terms market watch to help ensure that Woodchuck receives—at a minimum— the same terms as offered to its competitors for equivalent quantities and quality.

- *Substitutes: analysis and action* The company's holdover design process is replaced with a systematic approach incorporating low costs at the inception of the design process. The incumbent design process started with an overdesigned product model, using premium materials. This approach increased early customer interest, but changes to meet profit margin goals lagged. Only after prices slipped and margin goals sank below minimum gross margin target would the product manager call for less expensive materials. Now savings will be built into the product design from the beginning. Before any expensive models are built, the design will be conceptually configured using different combinations of materials and production processes, if applicable. Alternative demand projections will be developed for the most profitable designs.

- *Supplier evaluations and reductions* The MI team manager suggests that the total number of suppliers is too great, which draws precious negotiating time from the accounts that really count. Bergenhut agrees that the total number of suppliers needs to be reduced and recommends a preferred vendor approach. The new procurement manager will critically assess all present suppliers on the basis of terms, pricing, delivery, service, and communications. Low pricing will receive priority emphasis in the initial postacquisition months. Vendors with low total scores who also are small volume suppliers will be dropped.

Manufacturing Value-Creation Opportunities in the Postacquisition Period

Manufacturing costs comprise the largest portion of most companies' manufactured and assembled products' costs, and potential manufacturing changes represent a significant profit-improvement opportunity in the postacquisition period. Size alone does not always define a MI value opportunity, however. The postacquisition period is time bound, whereas many manufacturing improvement actions are evolutionary in nature—meaning that to implement basic improvements correctly, manufacturing management cannot be rushed by outside distractions. By the time that an automobile manufacturer has transformed its process from production lines to work stations, the formative part of the postacquisition period has passed. Accordingly, the acquirer must focus on manufacturing issues combining sizeable dollar (and value) potential with rapid change potential—manufacturing process rationalization, alternative production, capacity consolidation and flexible manufacturing, and manufacturing staff consolidations.

Manufacturing Process Rationalization

There is an opportunity to identify, pursue, and achieve a limited number of near-term efficiency improvements, focusing on frequently recurring areas of manufacturing process problems. If the change is directly linked to inventory and manufacturing costs, inventory investment requirements (cash flow) and profitability may be affected. Extend the simplification principle to its end, and multiple savings and value-creation opportunities may emerge: if the number of process review points has been reduced, why not scale back the number of positions, as well?

One path to improving the acquiree's manufacturing efficiency is to construct a new process from the ground up. A limited scope alternative is to begin the process that exists, then concentrate on a limited number of improvement opportunities that directly affect acquiree cash flow and can be changed or improved over a short period of time. This means that the merger-integration team actively seeks out a limited number of correction opportunities rather than conducting an overall process investigation. Some areas that receive early priority are consolidation or elimination of the unnecessary process points, elimination of bottlenecks and changes in the order, level, and type of supervision.

Alternative Production

For certain products and markets in which the product remains attractive but manufacture by the acquiree is no longer cost effective, a switch to alternative production or assembly approaches can be an opportunity. Major production facilities can be dedicated to products with cost-effective demand volume and production attributes. Outsourcing development and administrative positions, along with the product, is another possibility.

Capacity Consolidation and Flexible Manufacturing

Capacity consolidation and flexible manufacturing often are addressed as separate issues, but emergent global markets, consolidating capacity, and financial dictates of the leverage transaction are causing these two separate approaches to come together. When U.S. manufacturers focused primarily on domestic markets, decisions regarding plant location, capacity utilization, lines, and product mix issues tended to be straightforward. The plant was usually situated where the mix of labor, access to raw materials, direct labor, and production management skill blended together to make low cost and fast market response possible. Geographic representation emerged as an important principle to the manufacturing vice president. If the company wished to pursue a new product area or a new geographic territory, manufacturing departments reasoned that a separate facility in that area was needed. Sometimes the resultant manufacturing pattern resembled a patchwork quilt of limited-process, limited-product facilities. Many of the facilities deliberately operated below efficient capacity utilization levels: after all, excess capacity needed to be available for the next boom.

When the dual forces of globalization and high-leverage corporate financial restructuring entered the picture, limited-line and limited-process facility became increasingly more difficult for corporations to justify, either in technical process or financial terms. Management retrenched to fewer plants, with each operating at a higher utilization level. Consolidation of excess plant capacity represents a significant source of potential postacquisition value creation.

The Manufacturing Bureaucracy

The acquirer's and acquiree's manufacturing and engineering bureaucracies represent a significant staff category in some corporations. In many instances and organizations, this staff group may not be addressed by core one activities and analysis. When the total number of plants is reduced, there may be a tendency to simply reassign plant supervisors and on-site engineering talent to yet another layer of engineering administrators. Yet such action reduces the value improvement from manufacturing by swapping lower plant personnel costs for higher administrative position costs.

8

MI Core Four:
Systems Restrategy

Merger-integration core four—systems restrategy—applies most directly to postacquisition situations indicating a possible opportunity for partial or substantial combination of the systems or systems organizations of the acquiree and one or more of the acquirer's organizations. Although some of value-creation descriptions and examples in this chapter also may apply to other circumstances, systems-restrategy actions probably would not be high priority in the case of, say, the acquisition of a data-intensive distribution company by a passive investment holding group.

Postacquisition changes in acquirer and acquiree systems strategy—what is referred to in this chapter as systems restrategy—represent the fourth merger-integration core. Information and information systems issues arise in many transactions—particularly when consolidation of two systems organizations and structures arises as a possible value-creation opportunity. Comprehensive, cost-effective management information systems are central to the success of the acquirer's merger-integration program. This chapter examines some of the ways that an effective postacquisition systems strategy can contribute to MI success. The multiple layers of meaning of *system* are reflected in this chapter. To illustrate:

- *Computer hardware* In its narrowest application the term *system* refers only to physical computer hardware.

- *Geographic design and configuration* Hardware extended by facilities, software, networks, and skilled people to enable the parts to work smoothly together.

- *Information systems organization* The company's need for automated management information is continuous, and an administrative group with that support charter is needed. For practical purposes *system* is then viewed as synonymous with that company's information systems organization.

- *Output/paperflow* Sometimes a computer is not even part of the working definition at all—at least not directly. Noncomputer employees often consider systems primarily in terms of the reports and other output that are generated from the computer rather than the computer itself. To these employees, this paperflow network may well be the first thing that comes to mind when the word *system* is mentioned.

The balance of this chapter examines value issues and key analyses, restrategy opportunities, and a hypothetical integrated approach.

Value Issues and Key Analyses

Before pursuing specific systems-restrategy change opportunities, the acquirer and the merger-integration team first must understand relevant value issues and minimum information requirements.

Systems Restrategy Value-Creation and Destruction Issues

Despite the many kinds of systems, they share one unifying factor—value. It makes little difference whether the system change affects the paperflow jungle or the computer hardware vendor-selection decision, whether the composition of the ISO organization is at stake or the technical design of tomorrow's data center. The probability is high that the postacquisition company's cash flow will be affected and that, in turn, means a probable affect on value creation—or destruction—as well.

New value creation occurs, for example, if the postacquisition systems organization can fulfill the most important information needs of the new combined enterprise but at a lower total continuing cost than the sum of the costs of the acquirer's and acquiree's systems organizations. Eliminating unnecessary reports and nonpriority programming and maintenance expenditures are examples.

Value probably is reduced, however, if, for example, the ISO leader caves in to unreasonable new control-system demands in the wake of the close; if hierarchy rather than skill considerations prevail in staffing assessments assignments for the new combined systems organization; or if a clearcut decision is not made, resulting in a single postacquisition system design and information direction when acquirer and acquiree structures and approaches differ widely.

The multidimensional nature of the system issue indicates that numerous decisions will be made over the duration of the merger-integration program. Some restrategy actions will likely create value. Others will cause value decreases. Accordingly, the expected pattern is a mix. But the acquirer is interested in the net value effect. The purchasing group and its backers, after all, are concerned with whether systems restrategy—core four—can be counted on to help cover the acquisition value difference and, if the deal was a leveraged transaction, whether additional cash flow can be generated to repay or prepay acquisition borrowing. Instead of the net value balance, the critical core four value concern appears to be the timing and sequence characteristics of the postclose company's value trend:

- *Timing* The initial examination conducted by the merger-integration team uncovers two different systems restrategy possible opportunities. Several liaison and coordination positions appear to be likely candidates for consolidation or elimination. The MI team analysis uncovered a possible opportunity to cut hardware and software maintenance costs by bringing those activities in-house. The skills were found to be in place already, and such a change was recommended. These are tough decisions that affect the long-standing personal and professional relationship of the ISO manager, who cites other pressing postacquisition requirements assigned top-priority status by top management. If both possibles are deferred for a year, the acquirer and acquiree lose an early opportunity to help pare down the acquisition debt load to somewhat more manageable levels. Once the intensity of the early postacquisition change period is gone, those in the targeted positions have time to attach themselves to an executive-level system project to protect against this and other downstaffing attempts.

- *Sequence*   Taking actions that may be technically right and politically convenient first but that should follow other critical analyses or actions places the systems merger-integration process in jeopardy. At the time of the close, acquirer and acquiree information systems organizations exhibited substantially different systems designs and suppliers. The merger-integration team's analysis cited the multiple problems of continuing with two different systems approaches and recommends that both ISO groups converge to use the acquiring company's system. In order to establish his group as being in control and to maximize the number of staff in the new IS organization from his present group, the ISO head rearranges priorities and proceeds immediately with dismantling the acquiree's system. On paper, the result is a net cash-flow gain—or at least the avoidance of some of the perils cited in the MI team's investigation. But in the haste to move quickly some expensive mistakes are made: critical documentation needed to transform some acquiree ledgers to the acquirer's mysteriously disappears and several of the acquiree's top programmers quickly exit because of the abrupt reorganization.

The Postacquisition Information Systems Baseline Investigation

Before pursuing specific core four systems restrategy value and operational MI opportunities, it is critical that the acquirer has an accurate working understanding of the minimum management information reporting and data requirements, critical data processes, and proprietary databases, from both the acquiree and the acquirer organizations, as those needs existed before the close. Using those analyses as a base, the acquirer and the analysis team then devise a new analysis, referred to here as the postacquisition information systems baseline report, or IS baseline. The baseline begins as a subset of the earlier two company investigations and then is adjusted and modified to reflect the combined companies' postacquisition situation. Comprehensively developed, IS baseline includes the following characteristics:

- *Identification* From the two base analyses, the IS baseline specifies the most important data and systems-related needs based on present and potential estimated impact on the combined companies' profits, cash flows, and disbursements.

- *Adjustments* The number of elements identified in step one is either increased or decreased. Most adjustments are for one of four reasons: unmet systems-based needs relating to decisions and actions with major potential or actual cash-flow impact, consolidation or combination opportunities, eliminations resulting from changes in ownership status, additions required by financiers or investors that are not adequately met by elements in the current list.

- *Interrelationships: linkage backwards and forwards* The resulting list will likely include elements from several points along the management information origination/delivery spectrum (see Figure 8.1). Each list item influences other systems-related elements and is itself affected by other elements along the spectrum. Critical influences and interrelationships relating to each list element need to be understood—particularly in terms of possible repercussions if a list element is eliminated or changed in scope, timing, or other material performance characteristic.

- *Consideration of substitutes and alternatives* Total or partial substitutes for each list element, or for a critical interrelationship of a list element, are considered at this point,

Figure 8.1.   Systems Origination and Delivery Spectrum

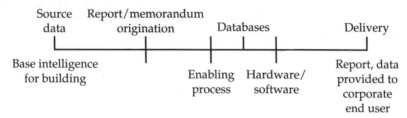

along with transition and substitution costs, in order to accurately determine risk of list item change.

- *Estimation of the possible negative effect of partial or total loss or a change in performance*   The results of the analyses and actions of the above four steps are measured and ranked in terms of theoretical potential loss. The orientation of the IS baseline investigation is to minimize possible loss by identifying those list elements that should not be altered under any circumstances because of the severity of the potential impact. Accordingly, elimination or significant performance change of each list item is calculated on an estimated economic loss basis, with that estimation including consideration of the financial impact of the business decision or activity related to the list element, the estimated correlation between decision or activity success and full availability and performance of the list element, and substitutes/alternatives availability and limitations.

- *Translation into action*   The analysis suggests what systems-related aspects can and should be examined for potential value-creating changes and which list items should be off limits.

The IS baseline investigation is needed to minimize core four risk. Without this knowledge in advance of systems restrategy action, the acquirer risks taking actions that could jeopardize mandatory information and systems process needs of the new postacquisition company. Alternatively, value creation from core four disappoints because aggressive action is not taken in the right areas.

To ensure objectivity, analysis should be conducted by an external group or individual with extensive input from the affected ISO organizations. Because many nontechnical considerations are involved, the selected analysis group or groups should be assigned a knowledgeable member of each company's ISO organization for the duration of the investigation, to help break through any information-access obstacles.

Restrategy Opportunities

Uncovering potential systems-restrategy opportunities involves defining the issue, recognizing the potential systems-restrategy opportunity, and considering implementation issues.

Paperflow Reduction

Creation and circulation of excessive written material—excess paperflow—is not always a computer problem, it is a systems problem. A thorough paperflow reduction effort, conducted at the beginning of the postacquisition period, helps accomplish three important objectives:

- *Spotlight expense reduction opportunities*   A review of reports and other written memoranda—including an analysis of who requests the reports, who develops them, how they are developed, and who uses them—helps to uncover paperflow waste. Tracking the flow and pattern of hard copy report data—beginning with the source of the information, to the memo/report developer or originator, continuing through to interpreters, compilers, and screens, all the way to the ultimate user—helps to identify change opportunities. Changes can involve the written material and the related development process in its entirety or just part of that process. If end-user sponsorship for the written material is weak or if near comparables are available, the entire daisy chain of support becomes a likely candidate for elimination. If the written material is essential, an under-stand ing of the development process can assist in identify-ing possible opportunities to shorten or otherwise modify the length and thus the internal cost of support.

- *Identify "empty suit" managers*   Managers with little real substance or ongoing contribution to value creation in the firm are prime targets for elimination in an active merger-integration effort. The paperflow reduction investigation may be exactly what is needed to bring these individu-als to the surface. A key skill of the superfluous manager is effective upstream communications. A separate paper-flow analysis should thus concentrate on unsolicited writ-ten material directed at top management from lower levels in the organization. Content and frequency of memos from subordinates in the chief executive officer's office may help flush out position-reduction targets that might otherwise go undiscovered.

- *Reveal excess review problems*   Excess paper doesn't merely reflect an overly complex set of corporate processes. The paper mountain may actually cause overly complex processes. Once information is set to paper, the inevitable bureaucratic temptation arises to broaden the circle of re-viewers. In some hierarchical organizations, the distribu-tion list may come to include virtually anyone who is a decision point in the process or who can conceivably be affected by result from that memo. Second-tier managers jockey to be included in the memo's circulation to gain or maintain internal political visibility.

Postacquisition Control Systems

The close of the deal sometimes brings more than just a signed document. The close also may bring an intensified demand for information control reports from corporate top management— presumably to assist top management in achieving merger-integration success. Some of these requests are reasonable and realistic, but others may not be so realistic. To the postacqui-sition ISO organization head, these are doubly dangerous be-cause of the near certainty of disappointment when 'blue sky' expectations are not met and the diversion of postacquisition systems organization resources from legitimate systems restrategy opportunities to a low or negative return task.

The investor/acquirer company chief executive senses the pressure even as the close is taking place. Lenders and others have supported a sizeable value difference through their actions, and for that trust to be rewarded, the CEO knows that the merger-integration program must pay off big, both in terms of value and in terms of additional cash-flow generation. Faced with this situation and pressure—possibly for the first time in their careers—some top executives overreach for a control-system solution. In times of anxiety, it is reassuring to believe in a decision mechanism that can be printed on a sheet of paper or displayed on a flickering monitor. The higher the officer's anxiety level, the greater the chances that the requested systems solution will exceed achievable expectations. The ISO manager's skill in gently deflecting or postponing such time and value wasters is important to the success of the other systems restrategy activities but also may be critical to his career.

At one firm in the retail industry an immense monitoring and control system was conceptualized by senior management in the aftermath of a series of consolidations and following finalization of new licensing arrangements. The design of this "management information and control system" was expansive and elegant. Predictably, however, there were problems. Several pieces of information that were required as input for the control system albatross could not possibly be made available in time to meet the near-to-on-line response expectations of management. In order to meet time limitations, estimates had to be substituted for compiled data. Without that change, support information quality was at best scarcely acceptable; with the change, the credibility of the control system's entire structure was undermined.

Combining Different Systems Organizations and Structures

An immediate issue confronting the acquirer and its merger-integration team immediately following the close is how to best combine and mix the acquirer's and the acquiree's systems organization and how to best combine the two entities' differing data center designs, database structures, service philosophies, programming and maintenance skills, and equipment.

Potentials and Pitfalls

Combined and coordinated astutely, the acquirer receives an opportunity to devise an altogether new systems organization from the roots of the two former information-systems organizations. The potential opportunity emerging from the combination of acquirer and acquiree systems organizations is to match new systems resources and capabilities with internal and marketplace needs. In the best situations, the acquisition means that one of the two companies substantially increases its systems capabilities. Information solutions that were once only dreamed about become realities.

Consider an East Coast manufacturer, merchandiser, and distributor of prepared foods, which received a subtle but nonetheless unambiguous message from two large grocery chain customers: develop and deploy an electronic data interface (EDI) capability or risk eventually losing some business. EDI represents the ultimate extension of the company's order entry, distribution control, and finished good inventory structure, with order terminal and order status available at the customer's location. Originally developed in other industries and with other customers such as hospital suppliers and auto parts retailers, EDI represents considerable promise—and for the systems organization that hasn't developed its version yet, considerable expense. Costs may exceed the resources of many companies—particularly firms facing intensified pressure from the parent corporation. In this particular situation, a second acquisition by that parent corporation suggested a possible answer to the EDI development challenge. The new acquiree had developed and tested a preliminary EDI design in recent years with grocery store chain customers.

Decisions: Aiming at the Right Targets

People, position, and organizational structure issues predominate when the subject of combining two different ISO groups arises. When the acquirer's end objective is to deepen the total pool of ISO staff talent, a combination can be positive, *if* the acquiring company and its senior ISO staff address the right issues in the right manner. In many instances, the acquiring company's ISO manager has broad latitude to dictate the composition and staffing of the combined companies' new information systems organization. Correctly applied, that latitude can mean an opportunity to strengthen and deepen the talents of overall staff. The ISO manager diminishes the potential talent contribution from the combination or consolidation of the two organizations if this staffing latitude is used only to reinforce a "spoils of war go the the victors" mentality.

The prospect of compressing two ISO organizations into one sometimes provides the necessary impetus to transform the underpinning of the ISO's organization structure from an approach based on promotions to an approach aimed at optimizing efficiency and effectiveness. Information systems organizations are not immune from the ravages of that disease that reduces productivity in many other functional departments— too high a ratio of supervisors, administrators, planners, and coordinators (combined) to actual staff codewriters. As the ISO organization matures, some programmers and systems analysts take on increasing supervisory responsibilities. By some point, positions are changed to be consistent with the individual's change in activities. Positions are made to accommodate these promotions, adding complexity to the ISO's job descriptions and new staff layers to the organization. If the codewriting workload of the department remains basically unchanged while this promotion cycle continues, a smaller and smaller percentage of the total ISO staff actually is doing the department's work.

Although this growing problem may be implicitly recognized, action is unlikely unless prompted by a change—such as consolidating two different ISO units into one following an acquisition. To combine the two groups on an equitable basis— while improving productivity—the indicated approach should be to designate the available ISO position slots in terms of functions performed, rather than years in the department. Applied rigorously, this can enable the ISO organization to reverse the dampening effects on productivity from years of position inflation.

An Integrated Approach Illustrated: TargetCo and AcquireCo

Several systems restrategy issues are brought together in an integrated approach in this hypothetical case of TargetCo and AcquireCo.

Before the Acquisition: Management Information Systems at TargetCo

TargetCo's systems organization could accurately be described as the information lifeline of that company. Key reports and processes were supported by a staff at the company's four United States–based data centers. The executive vice president for management information systems (MIS), Dave Datex, described TargetCo's systems capabilities as being "adequate to meet normal requirements within promised commitment periods and resilient enough to meet the important needs that arise."

Costs

TargetCo's budget had been $1.5 million when Mr. Datex first arrived at TargetCo three years ago—2 percent of the Company's $75 million revenue base. Datex noted that although the planned budget for the next year was now 1.7 percent of the Company's $100 million in revenues, or $1.7 million, TargetCo's MIS budgets were almost always missed. Based on past performance actual expenditures would likely be close to $2 million.

Even assuming that the planned 0.3 percent improvement for the next budget year could be achieved, TargetCo's MIS organization showed a disturbing tendency to continually require additional funds for reprogramming months after the original work was completed. Analysis by the MI team confirmed what the budget group within TargetCo has suspected: poor documentation, combined with high staff turnover in critical conditions, meant a soaring rewrite problem at TargetCo. The issue had been missed in the acquisition due-diligence process.

TargetCo's budgeters attacked the problem solely on a financial basis rather than through an understanding of both the numbers and the underlying operations. The budget group exerted continual pressure on analysts to whittle the percentage of systems expenses to company revenues even further, to 1.5 percent of revenues level or less. Members of TargetCo's budget department also noted that Datex's organization was five organizational levels deep, including one full layer of management at the four regional data centers.

An outside consultant once suggested that the ratio of MIS expenses to company revenues could be slashed by a full three-tenths to four-tenths of a percent by conversion to a single data-center structure. TargetCo's budgeters echoed the argument of MIS leader Datex and his senior people: key customers had become accustomed to having TargetCo's information located close to them. In their analysis, the consultants had noted that many of the budget analysts eventually became systems liaisons between Datex's MIS organization and the principal user groups. The MI team leader wondered whether this relationship could have anything to do with the persistent pattern of budget slippage.

Core Services and Other Department Activities

Datex contended that support of TargetCo's minimum data-processing services—that is, support of current operations but with no major development efforts—required a minimum budget of no less than 1.6 percent of company revenues. Datex, in turn, grumbled that this was a near-starvation budget that would force him to cut back severely on new activities—that is, of course, unless those activities were specified in the budget of individual user departments with dedicated funding. Datex used this poorly understood foible of the budgeting process for years to augment the budget for favorite projects.

Service Performance

Service performance of TargetCo's MIS organization had been adequate in most areas of operation and superior in an order-entry responsiveness and payroll, according to a recent independent assessment. That review report analyzed three areas—transaction support, reports and statements, and strategic decision information.

- *Transaction support*   Incoming mail and telephone orders from customers of Target Co's edible chemical products were recorded and processed, and those orders were, in turn, routed and tracked by the company's central processor network. Confirmations were issued and invoices transmitted. Adjustments to stock available for shipment were recorded.

- *Reports and statements*   Information prepared for regulatory agencies or requested by shareholders were compiled and transformed into reports. Some of these reports resulted from TargetCo's status as a publicly traded corporation. TargetCo's general and accounting information reports ranged from the general ledger and production reports at one end of the size and importance spectrum to a biannual report on the usage of electricity during the winter weekends at the headquarters building at the other extreme.

- *Strategic decision information*   The leaders of many of TargetCo's administrative departments viewed themselves as either originators, developers, or interpreters of data critical to the corporation's future. After all, if your department's information was *not* critical, how could you survive postacquisition downsizing? Within TargetCo there were significant differences of opinion about precisely what information was critical, but no one with sufficient clout ever intervened to define it. Each administrative group seemed to maintain its own set of programs, databases, and output reports. If they couldn't (or wouldn't) be handled by the systems organizations, a personal computer program was devised within the department.

*Advanced Systems Technology Investment in Key
Development Areas*

TargetCo made some significant investments in systems infrastructure and technology in areas of the business that top management spotlighted for special emphasis:

- *New order-entry system* The newly completed order-entry
  (OE) system was estimated by one MIS staffer as being 40
  percent more productive than the equipment and process
  that it replaced. The new system could handle more transactions, more accurately, than its predecessor and required
  fewer order-entry operators and supervisors.

- *Future OE expansion* The OE system could eventually be
  expanded into a preliminary electronic order entry system.
  A not-so-subtle hint from TargetCo's largest customer con-
  vinced the management that this was critical to retaining
  the corporation's most important accounts. The advanced
  form of such a system would link the customer's computer
  directly with TargetCo.

- *Sales productivity improvement* TargetCo's sales per salesperson dollar slipped badly over the past three years,
  and sales performance improvement was highlighted as
  an opportunity area one year before by TargetCo's outside
  consultants. The salesforce was already computer proficient; many salespersons had advanced degrees in molec-
  ular chemistry and computer science and used personal
  computers in their homes. TargetCo's selling circumstances
  appeared to be well suited for systems-technology improvement. Timely and complete information on formula
  changes, test statistics, and purification processes were important considerations in the purchaser's decision. Sales
  were essentially made on a white-coat basis—that is, one
  professional chemist speaking to another. Market research
  indicated that TargetCo's customers most valued the company's ability to develop small lot orders reflecting different
  formulation differences, but supporting that point of market differentiation required a considerable investment in
  data about formulation changes.

Customer information provided in the form of hard copy charts and tables had many drawbacks, such as transcription errors and out-of-date formulation changes— hardly the image for a company that wanted to be recognized for its market responsiveness.

The MIS department's solution was a personal computer program that allowed current formulation and test data to be downloaded to the salespersons's portable computer, directly at the client's site. A visually arresting sales presentation was developed. A prestige brand of portable—the kind that market research indicated that clients themselves most frequently purchased—became the delivery vehicle. The customers tended to drop everything when a computer screen lit up, retained more information, and ordered more. Systems technology came down to earth to solve a problem of increasing sales penetration.

Before the Close: Information Systems Organization at AcquireCo

For purposes of the illustration in this chapter, AcquireCo is assumed to be a synergistic purchaser of TargetCo. AcquireCo's systems approach and organization differ from TargetCo's in several ways—data center structure, staff structure, location, and effectiveness.

Centralized Data Center Structure

AcquireCo's information systems organization (ISO) was made up of a single main data center with nearby backup capacity. The central processing unit (CPU) actually combined two primary central processors plus a smaller unit used for front-end processing and data communications. Ben Quasar, executive vice president, winced at the suggestion that this was a supercomputer and instead called the combined units a binary central processor cluster. A centralized data-center design made great sense for AcquireCo, given the nature of industry information and how that information is used within by AcquireCo and its customers. AcquireCo is a commodity processor of edible and nonedible chemical compounds, and its processors must be capable of handling tens of thousands of buy, ship, and bill documents each day. Reports requested by most managers were simple and built on preexisting data and documentation whenever possible. Before receiving funding approval, any and all proposed new reports must first be fully justified, with an extensive written analysis detailing how that new information would be used to increase company operating earnings, why the report or the information contained therein cannot be developed from other reports and data that already exist, and the expected profit benefit to the company from the report, net of the expenses necessary to support that report, over a three-year period.

Shallower Staff Structure

Quasar was shown on the organization charts as the ISO senior officer, but he also has doubled as the chief operating manager for the company's data services center since top management decreed that there would be no more pure administrative jobs (with a few exceptions). The leader of the MI team noted that AcquireCo's system staff was four deep, compared to five organization layers for TargetCo's MIS organization.

On-Site Physical Location

AcquireCo's ISO operations are crammed into a corner of one floor at corporate headquarters. Admittedly, on-site location of ISO creates more space pressures at headquarters, yet this is partially by design to check the growth of other administrative departments. The ISO organization was recognized throughout the company as being lean. Faced with a request from another headquarters unit for more projects and additional staffing, the customary response was, "Which of the programmers supporting your department's systems do you want us to dismiss?" The proximity of services provider and users also cuts down on the need for coordinators between the two groups. Fewer reports are needed when a walk down the hall resolves many problems.

Systems Staffing Effectiveness

Quasar believes that there are some other payoffs from a centralized data-services-center approach, as well. More efficient
new program development can take place with development
staff located in one place, because assignment of tasks for
new assignments is faster. Coordination of the different parts
of a development assignment also becomes easier, and the
concentration helps ensure a critical mass for effective use of
automated codewriting tools.

In addition, a centralized data-center design provides Acquire-
Co's ISO organization with a sufficient critical mass for some
increased functional specialization between new development,
enhancement, and maintenance activities. In many systems organizations, development is viewed as the only fast-track activity.
Star status is seen as coming from a program that does something new and unique, not simply from maintaining someone
else's work. AcquireCo ISO leader Quasar tried to change that
attitude through assignments and the compensation structure.
He assigned programmers to development, enhancement, or
maintenance assignments on six-month rotations. Compensation, bonuses, and rewards were reconstructed as necessary to
make sure that the programmer who did the hard reprogramming work necessary to save the general ledger was rewarded
as well as the creator of the new program. There was another
consideration in Quasar's mind, as well. There had been some
discussion about the use of outside groups for certain codewriting
activities and for maintenance of certain standardized software
not fully supported by the manufacturer. Gradual delineation
of functions and activities could facilitate such a change, when
and if that became desirable.

After the Close: Combining
Different Systems,
Organizations, and Approaches

There is no single correct postacquisition combination strategy
and approach. An approach that works well for one business
combination may fail miserably for another.

Avoiding the Instant Postmerger Solution

The first step in developing and implementing a postacquisition systems approach that works is to avoid the purported instant solutions that do not. The transaction has been closed, and almost immediately systems and corporate management are deluged with advisors offering assistance with the integration effort. Sometimes these offers of assistance suggest that critical postacquisition action steps can be reduced to a checklist. Task lists have an important place in the MI process—but only after a successful futures strategy for reducing the two organizations into one has been devised:

- *Integration of operations*   First there's the issue of the ongoing operation of the two different systems. What should be combined? How? Which operations should be integrated? Which should remain as stand-alones?

- *Combining reports and processes*   Reports and processes must be reconciled and combined, but certain decisions need to be made first—postacquisition security policy, user access, vendor strategy, the number of fields in specific reports, hours of operation.

- *People*   Staff await the outcome of deliberations that will shape their futures. TargetCo's programmers and analysts wonder whether the decentralized data-center structure will survive. If it doesn't survive in total, will a part be preserved? Their systems counterparts at AcquireCo look at the cramped quarters at headquarters and wonder where all the new people will be placed. Will they move into TargetCo's MIS space?

- *Control/management information*   Senior management observes the seemingly endless march of changes and long for something—*anything*—to provide it with a greater sense of control. That insecurity becomes transformed into requests for new executive information systems.

- *The single-vendor issue*   Designation of a single systems vendor for the new combined systems entity often surfaces as an important issue. Sometimes its status is elevated to that of an answer for an entire collection of actual and perceived postacquisition systems challenges. Competent systems salespeople have long understood that a change in ownership is an ideal opportunity to promote a single-vendor solution. The acquirer's systems provider leads the charge, followed closely by the acquiree's vendor and a third systems integrator who promises an overall solution. The single-vendor issue is likely to be more critical to the vendor than to the client. Postacquisition systems requirements rarely dictate a single-vendor solution—at least not immediately after the close. Given the other changes that the new organization's systems group must withstand, the introduction of another system in the first postacquisition months is more likely to be a problem than a solution. The cost of software rewrites alone may cancel out any savings from a single-system approach.

Choices

Even if there aren't instant answers, there *are* choices among postacquisition systems strategies. Figure 8.2 shows three such choices—barebones, maximum/minimum, and strategic intelligence resource. They are not formula answers to be applied blindly to a new corporation's postacquisition circumstances, but they may help transform the acquirer's merger-integration goals for value improvement into discrete, implementable programs.

Alternative 1: Barebones Systems

In this approach, quick cost reductions are the overriding merger-integration goal. The objective is a systems structure that meets the minimum needs of the new systems organizations for the next twelve to eighteen months. Systems requirements beyond that point are for the most part disregarded. The reasoning is that unless operations of the organization work to establish a sound profit and cash-flow base for the new enterprise, there will be no host corporation.

Postacquisition support of critical transactions takes precedent over any other systems activities at TargetCo. Order entry

Figure 8.2. One Approach to Postacquisition Systems Strategy: Barebones, Maximum/Minimum, Strategic Intelligence Resource

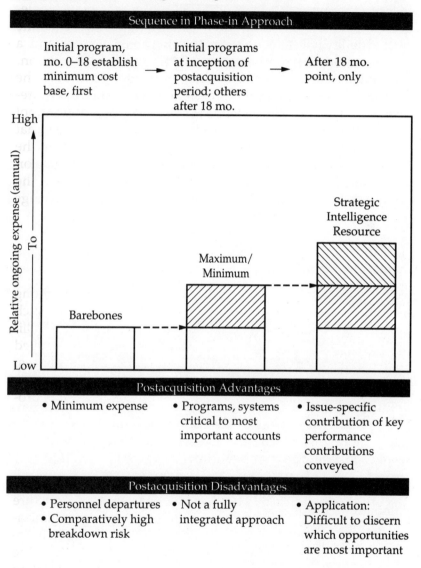

and treasury/cash management, for example, remain virtually untouched at the acquiree's systems organization. Today, support for those operations is split among several individuals. A quick full-time equivalent (FTE) analysis reveals that the time equivalent of five full-time employees is required at present for support. TargetCo's systems leaders are by the MI team leader to identify the *four* individuals who will be retained in the postacquisition period, based on the reasoning that concentration of responsibility will allow some productivity gain.

A moratorium is imposed on all third-party expenditures. The order is issued and takes effect immediately. Prior to the closing, TargetCo paid for equipment maintenance in advance through payments to an outside maintenance organization. Although that arrangement probably saved money over the long run, today's immediate need is for cash preservation. The contract is cancelled. Maintenance responsibilities are transferred to AcquireCo's internal staff. The payment moratorium also applies to software development by outside organizations and lease and rental payments.

New systems development projects funds are frozen. To close one loophole that sometimes arises when such announcements are made, management also specifies that the freeze applies both to future projects and to development work in progress.

Reports are reduced to the minimum needed to support TargetCo's most essential functions. The challenge is to determine the functions that are most essential and the most important reports related to that function. An initial request for voluntary action falls short. Only about 5 percent of the reports were cut voluntarily, and management figured that these would have been eliminated anyway. The second time around management takes more direct action. Systems allocations were deleted from each TargetCo user department's budget. From that point forward, all department-level development and maintenance requests have to be approved specifically by the MI systems committee group.

The most visible impact is on TargetCo's systems structure. AcquireCo's ISO group integrates some of TargetCo's hardware into its operations network, and the acquirer hires one or two development stars from TargetCo's group. The rest of TargetCo's systems organization is essentially put up for sale. In this case, systems merger integration means selective absorption.

AcquireCo's own ISO staffers began to breathe easier—until they realized that other adjustments remain to be made. AcquireCo top management had been been presented with several efficiency improvement recommendations over the past months, but there always seemed to be a reason standing in the way of implementation—a pending emergency project, possible disruption of ongoing programs, or tight resources. AcquireCo's top management sees this as the opportunity to take action, reasoning that some systems disruptions are going to be part of the daily life of the new enterprise for several months anyhow. The new enterprise might as well proceed with several of the best of the recommendations:

- *Department systems coordinator cuts* This represented a major cost-reduction action. Positions for sixteen systems coordinators in the new organization (sometimes their job titles read *liaisons*) were identified for possible elimination. This resulted in first postacquisition year savings of $1 million, with ongoing savings of $1.13 million per year thereafter. Ten of the fifteen coordinators were part of the staffs of the department user departments. The other six were from the two systems organizations. The liaisons had become increasingly important as complexity of the systems organization had grown, but now that the system was being simplified, fewer support positions were needed.

- *The hidden systems budget* Senior management of both companies encouraged management computer literacy. Virtually no constraints had been placed on computer purchases or usage. Unspent, discretionary portions of department budgets often were used for purchases of personal computers, work stations and minicomputers. This hidden systems budget was outside of the control of the information group and outside of the control of the corporation. Within TargetCo and AcquireCo the hidden amount represented about 30 percent of the formal systems department budgets.

More than just cost mattered. The computers used in these home-grown minisystems were made by several different manufacturers, there were no documentation requirements, and grossly different calculation assumptions were used. Each stand-alone program had its own set of assumptions and calculations. Even if the computers were compatible mechanically, the program of department A probably didn't tie into the program for department B. The barriers to free access to information protected the developer as a fortress king. The data were needed, but did the organization need to tolerate this approach to job preservation? Senior management did not want a return to the old days of a centralized systems monolith. They wished to encourage managerial computer literacy, but they realized that some changes had to be made. The following approach was developed as a compromise—to control without stifling innovation:

- Over a six-month period, all company personal computers would be returned. New computers would be issued by the systems organization: one vendor make would be specified for workstations, a second for minis and PCs.

- Secondary market sales of the old equipment would help offset the cost of new computers. There would not necessarily be a one-for-one replacement because new computers would be issued on an as-needed basis.

- Standard planning data—that is, common assumptions to be used in all projections regarding matters such as interest rates, revenue growth, and expense rates—were to be used henceforth for all calculations and projections. No more last-minute disasters to discover that one of the component subprograms assumed a growth rate double that of all the others.

- Standardized payroll and benefits administration software was selected to replace the separate payroll software of the two firms. While canned software lacked some of the fields and features of customized software, continuing maintenance support cost was less.

- AcquireCo had explored the opportunity for using outside software maintenance several years ago when ISO staff tasks were first segmented. Acquisition with TargetCo increased the potential return from such an approach.

Accordingly, management decided to proceed with a limited number of programs on an experimental basis.

The barebones approach succeeded primarily in financial terms. The system payroll of the two combined organizations was reduced by about 40 percent. Hardware sales provided some additional cash flow, and action was forced on other profit-improvement actions that had eluded action for years. Nevertheless, some argued that the barebones approach was penny wise and pound foolish. Top programmers from TargetCo's organization decided not to join the new AcquireCo/TargetCo systems group given its stark future. As one said, "It just doesn't look like it will be a fun place to work anymore." Position reductions resulted in some retaliatory vandalism, and some important programs almost crashed. Even the most adamant among the cost-cutters acknowledged that the systems organization would still need to be built back up again soon, limiting the cash savings to a couple of years at most. "The way I see it," systems chief Quasar admitted, "we're saving now but we'll just have to spend it back again later."

Alternative 2: The Maximum/Minimum Structure

The maximum/minimum approach adds selected customer systems to the barebones approach. *Maximum* refers to selective investment by the new systems organization in certain leadership systems that are critical to preserving today's revenue and increasing tomorrow's. *Minimum* refers to the continuation of a barebones approach for the major part of the systems strategy. The two keys are to make selective, deep investment of resources where they count the most in the marketplace and to finance as much of this expenditure as possible through reductions in other programs.

The cost of this approach is greater in relative terms than the barebones approach. Initial and ongoing savings are both lower, as are ongoing savings. The offsetting consideration is the protection against loss of customer revenues. There may be a temptation to use the max/min program to justify spending on a wide array of internal marketing and sales systems, but the central question remains, is that system critical to revenue creation? A system primarily designed for internal consumption that is not included in the barebones structure will probably not be part of the max/min alternative, either.

Federal Express has its worldwide point-by-point package tracking network. American Airlines has its SAABRE reservation network. Removing these systems would detract from the attractiveness of the company's service offerings to customers. In TargetCo's case, the key customer system has been the PC-based sales-support system, which allows salespeople to display and customers to download selected formula data. AcquireCo's key customer system has been its advance ordering system, which enables the company to fend off competitors. Although it originally appeared that an EDI system could be developed, the ordering patterns of the two companies' customer groups differed so significantly that the project was cancelled.

Alternative 3: Strategic Intelligence Resource

The third postacquisition approach alternative is called the strategic intelligence resource. As with maximum/minimum, this alternative is assumed to be additive—that is, the programs are in addition to those already part of the barebones and max/min approaches combined. Emergence of the corporate chief information officer (CIO) position designation, coupled with the concept of information as a source of competitive advantage, spawned a host of databases and programs. While differing widely in form and design, a unifying linkage was an assumption that the data would be used for executive-level decision making. These ultimate corporate information utilities, however, turned out to be about as useful (or as useless) as historical information. The old information was just reloaded into new relational databases.

Decision support systems (DSS), executive information systems, artificial intelligence—each has had its moment in the sun and some visible successes. Yet each seemingly has seen a decline in popularity as management looks beyond the impressive technology and considers whether this system and the information it generates helps it to manage better. Managing operations better in the postacquisition period frequently means focusing attention on the essentials and leaving behind or eliminating those things that are not critical. So it is for postacquisition intelligence systems. Intelligence becomes more than just a description of the resident memory of the processors. It also means a contribution by the new systems organization to the development of reasoned judgment about what are the most important tasks for the next week and the next month. A packaged food products company may use a combination of shipment order trends from its three largest customers, backlog data, and on-time delivery statistics as input to determining where—and how severely—different parts of operations need to be tweaked. The data is not oversold as a decision system. Indeed, the significance of the different data elements changes from time to time, as does management's interpretation of that data. But an intelligence system has been created in the broader sense of that phrase through the base data from the ISO group combined with interpretation by top management.

One Approach: Phase-In Composite

How should the new corporation proceed with its postacquisition systems strategy? Each approach has its own set of advantages and disadvantages. One approach is to utilize all three alternatives in a staged sequence following the close:

- *Barebones* For the first year to eighteen months of the postacquisition period, the barebones approach dominates. Completion of the deal provides a timely opportunity to put long-deferred productivity improvement programs into effect. The two organizations are leaned down to a minimum core. It is understood that new systems, software, and people will be added later with the new needs of the business.

- *Max/Min* Two customer systems are retained after the close of the deal. TargetCo's PC support system and AcquireCo's advance ordering system continue to be supported but as stand-alone systems. The new enterprise cannot risk losing the profits associated with these customer-oriented systems. Stand-alone systems will eventually be integrated into the new system structure as the new postacquisition structure is constructed.

- *Intelligence systems*   Intelligence systems do not receive serious reconsideration until after the eighteen-month period for the barebones approach has expired. Expenditures for integrative data are considerable, and in any event, the structure of the combined companies' new systems design will not be visible until after that point in time.

III

MERGER
INTEGRATION
AND THE 1990s

9

Extending Merger Integration

The degree and speed of postacquisition success often is a function of the accuracy and thoroughness of value-creation action undertaken *before* the deal is finalized. For example, the best way to take swift delayering actions and reduce ongoing costs after the close is to know where the target opportunity areas are before the close, and the best way to prevent a serious value loss from an unexpected exodus of critical people in the first days after the close is to identify the candidates for a stay-put bonus before the closing ceremony during the due-diligence investigation period.

Opportunities for effective application of merger-integration tactics aren't just limited to recently completed deals. One important application of MI approaches is to transactions completed several months or even years ago that are neither successes nor failures but that now require refinancing and new strategy to emerge from their stagnation.

The appealing LBO success model calls for lightning success and wealth creation, but such opportunities became increasingly elusive as the merger cycle matured. Instead of this dream, many other investors and lenders face a reality that is quite different—an uneasy survival coupled with stagnating operations. Actions taken to quickly repay initial acquisition indebtedness were wrong or ineffective or both. The acquired company has survived, but the extended time to achieve success endangers the deal's success as acquisition debt costs multiply. To move from stagnation back to success, additional financing is needed, and that, in turn, depends on market repositioning and financial streamlining to position the deal for stage two refinancing. Application of abbreviated versions of the four-core approach can help achieve such changes.

Resurrecting the "broke LBO" demands even more immediate action—and requires additional and replacement financing even more urgently, but refinancing may mean throwing good money after bad unless only salvageable operations are targeted and unless the right cash-flow and value-creation actions are applied—and quickly enough. A comprehensive cash-flow and value-development diagnostic—such as the four-core diagnostic in the merger-integration program—is critical to helping distinguish true turnaround prospects from cast offs and to taking corrective actions rapidly enough to make a difference in the deal's success.

For years, some leveraged buyout advocates attributed at least part of the improved performance of some companies acquired through high-leverage transactions to the deal structure's conditions—including the so-called disciplining effect that a debt-repayment imperative has on acquiree operations, costs, and strategies. If such a structure does have a positive effect, then it should not be restricted to completed deals. Applying certain MI techniques and approaches to an ongoing company's operations may hold promise for improved operations.

This chapter explores opportunities to apply merger-integration intelligence to increase corporate cash-flow and value-development opportunities that relate to the acquisition transaction. The focus here is not on the postacquisition period but rather on the phases of the merger time spectrum occurring before the close. The discussion examines the acquisition planning and analysis period that precedes a bid for an attractive acquisition candidate. For an operating company, this is sometimes even before the management has determined that an acquisition program is the best way to proceed in implementing the corporation's expansion directive.

This chapter also discusses MI considerations that lead up to and are part of the would-be acquirer's bidding process, including those situations in which timing and value-creation circumstances indicate that the best deal is no deal at all—at least not at the present time. It addresses value-creation promises and pitfalls of the acquisition due diligence period. The due-diligence period may be the prospective acquirer's first true opportunity to probe actual operations of the target company and not just those parts that the seller wants early bidders to see. The opportunity to boost chances for acquisition success, however, by preparing the agenda for the upcoming postacquisition MI program before the close is rarely taken.

Expansion and Acquisition Planning and Analysis

Ideally, the operating corporation's senior executive is an individual who understands and agrees with the critical importance of an orderly acquisition process in the corporation's ongoing business development process and who wants to establish a permanent corporate mechanism in recognition of that role. A balanced business development process is not predisposed toward any particular means of implementation, including acquisition. The beginning point is the operating company's expansion rationale—a blueprint for future value optimization of the company, reflecting marketplace opportunities and limitations. Acquisition becomes one of several alternatives for implementing the expansion course, if justified. Assuming that expansion is justified and further that an acquisition appears to be the optimal course, then emphasis may shift to the acquisition process itself. The supportive activities in that process include data gathering, criteria setting and screening, and control of the overall acquisition process.

The Continuing Operating Company A&D
Market Participant: Overview of One Approach

A systematic and well-ordered expansion and acquisition planning process is one mark of the corporate acquisition and
divestiture (A&D) market continuing participant. The continuing A&D market participant may just bring money to the
table, or the firm may provide operating synergies, as well. If
the company is a passive-investor group, the firm is probably
directed by an underlying philosophy that contends that continuing A&D market presence, analysis, and involvement are
necessary for wealth to be created for investors on a continuing basis. Trying to correctly time a speculative wave results in
whipsawing in many instances. An ongoing player avoids becoming emotionally or financially captured by either extreme
of the merger cycle—both the soaring optimism of a runaway
boom and the depressing aftermath of excessive expansion. In
doing so, this investor group is prepared to react to appropriate opportunities at virtually any point in the merger cycle.
The continuing operating company A&D participant, on the
other hand, shares the basic wealth-creation perspective of his
passive-investor group counterpart. The operating company
continuing A&D participant adds something else—a firm belief
that the company's shareholders are best served by continuing
profitable expansion into related areas of business interest and
the realization that one or more acquisitions are often the best
way to achieve that expansion goal.

The rationale underlying the operating acquirer's business
development planning process should not be to institutional-
ize a continual acquisition deal process. Rather, the underlying motivation should be to examine and challenge the expansion imperative of the company and then, if that expansion
urge holds up to challenging questions and close scrutiny, to
prepare to undertake appropriate value-improvement actions.
Those actions may or may not include pursuing an acquisition, depending on several considerations. Those considerations include prevailing interest-rate levels and trends, overall economic strength, capital availability, and competition—
both marketplace conditions in the field of possible business

expansion interest and the intensity of deal competition in the transaction marketplace. The telling factor in whether the expansion program becomes an acquisition program may be yet another comparative factor—the relative attractiveness of other expansion program implementation mechanisms compared to outright purchase.

The implicit assumption made by the ongoing corporate A&D market player and its leaders is that shareholders' interests are best served through growth, but this is not always true, and the consequences of a misstep can be serious. Expansion does not always mean additional value. In some instances, even a well-planned business development process will result instead in wealth reduction for acquirer company shareholders. Accordingly, the expansion imperative should be challenged before proceeding further. The following danger signals indicate a possibly flawed expansion rationale (see Table 9.1):

- *Emphasis on growth for growth's sake* When bigger is unquestionably equated with better, no one at either the board or executive management level is concerned with the acquirer's optimal size and limits of profitable growth.

- *Emphasis on revenue growth over profit growth* Attention focuses on the revenue size of the possible postexpansion company rather than the profit-generation potential. The acquirer blinded by outright size rather than effective size for the market and prevailing conditions may plunge the acquiring company into a fast decline.

Table 9.1. The Expanding Operating Business: Danger Signals of a Flawed Expansion Rationale

---

- Emphasis on growth for growth's sake
- Emphasis on revenue growth over profit growth
- Motivated by keeping up with competitors
- Agency management (little or no equity ownership by key decision makers)
- No postevent review procedure
- Underanalyzed entry and exit considerations
- Overestimated synergistic potential
- Overreliance on management improvement potential

- *Motivated by keeping up with competitors* Business expansion plans of others are continually cited as justification for the operating company acquirer's own reason for growth. If keeping up with others in the industry is the actual motivation, ego factors may be the expansion program's driving force, not shareholder value creation.

- *Agency management (little or no equity ownership by key decision makers)* Company management with little ownership stake in the acquiring company may have difficulty adopting a shareholder wealth perspective.

- *No postevent review procedure* Few or none of the operating company's prior business expansion forays are assessed in terms of the return realized by shareholders or other consistently applied measures of performance. This suggests that few will be evaluated on a profit basis in the future.

- *Underanalyzed entry and exit considerations* The company fails to give adequate consideration to the point in time in the product or service market's life cycle in pursuing expansion opportunities. An established market with many competitors and little remaining profit potential is misdiagnosed as new on the basis that the business would be new to that company. Conversely, opportunities for getting out of the business—and the associated cost of such exit strategies—are not included in the expansion justification.

- *Overestimated business synergistic potential* The acquirer has few confirmed attributes that can be applied to accelerate market penetration or reduce the risk of new business entry or both, but management believes otherwise and acts on those perceptions in designing and implementing its expansion approach. The potential pitfalls here are overestimation of leveragable skills or potential that can be applied to reduce the effective cost of the business expansion program or heightened business development risk—such as expansion into a market or product area mistakenly perceived to be related.

- *Overreliance on management improvement potential* Rumors suggest that some companies are poorly managed and that profits could be increased significantly by better management. The expansion-minded operating company relies on "managing better" to an excessive extent in justifying its expansion program.

Expansion Analysis Begins

Overview of the "Start with What You Have Already" Approach

The most defensible expansion and acquisition program starts with a thorough consideration of expansion and development in the operating company's existing markets and product service areas. The "start with what you already have" approach offers many potential benefits:

- *Spotlight on achieving full potential in existing market activities* An expansion investigation that starts with present operations prevents an expansion program that is continually distracted by the deceiving appeal of new markets. An objective, thorough assessment of present opportunities versus potential may even result in no new expansion at all, if better execution of present market plans turns out to have greater profit return potential than new adventures.

- *Related expansion emphasis* If expansion is justified, this approach encourages building on products and markets that the expansion-oriented operating company's managers know already. Key strengths, weaknesses, and needs within the existing business portfolio are considered at the onset of the acquisition process, rather than tacked on at the end of that process. One result should be fewer adventures into little-known markets in which the expanding company's chances for success are slim.

- *Department position consolidations* In applying this approach, the strategic planning process is simplified. The question of business direction and mission does not arise every year, slowing down the process and adding work of questionable worth and staffing requirements of questionable contribution. The chief executive at one company in a growing technology field applied a similar approach to

limit the growth of the corporate planning bureaucracy—
while increasing his own visibility and direct involvement
in the process at the same time.

Implementing the Approach

The logical way to apply the "start with what you know"
expansion-evaluation approach is to compare outside expansion prospects against existing opportunities that already are
known to exist within the company. A balanced approach is the
goal of the comparative process. Outstanding internal profit
opportunities do not suffer from familiarity; they are assessed
on a business investment approach as if they were new external development opportunities. External business development is not pursued until it can be proven that it provides
a better opportunity than internal reinvestment alternatives,
even when business risk factors are considered. The following
ground rules must be established for a meaningful comparative
analysis:

- *Internal: legitimate reinvestment opportunities*   Internal opportunities must represent distinct new opportunities that
  are comparable to external business development opportunities. Unless this is assured, corporate department heads
  and analysts skilled at the management of the company's
  capital expenditure system may succeed in using this process to resurrect and fund capital expenditure requests
  turned down in the past. To qualify for consideration as
  a reinvestment prospect, an internal opportunity must involve new capital investment that is integral to creation of
  new revenue and profits. Both potential revenue and new
  profits must be verifiable.

- *Internal: cost and performance assumptions*   To result in a usable comparison, the internal prospect must be assessed
  on a fully loaded assumed-cost basis rather than an incremental basis—even if some present facilities and ma-
  chinery would be used. This means that in addition to a
  portion of shared costs, the internal prospect's cost projections must reflect full direct and indirect expenses and cor-

porate allocations and full support costs, based on present rates. Projected profit performance must reflect presently achievable margins. Market entry and market-share capture costs must be supported by analysis, and additional expenses are to be added to projections to reflect these expenses. Increases in market share beyond nominal entry levels must reflect the additional cost of share capture.

- *External: expected economic return (EER) basis* An external expansion prospect is less familiar, so a greater level of variability is reflected in future projections. Using an expected economic return (EER) approach means factoring in the probability of achievement in the analysis. One approach is to project three different results based on optimistic, moderate, and pessimistic sets of assumptions and then call on the judgment of an outside source to establish defendable probability estimates for each. The weighed sum is the indicated return.

- *Both: comparative hurdle rate approach* Investment and expansion decisions are often made on the basis of an internal financial hurdle rate. If a proposed investment opportunity yields a return in excess of the operating company's weighted average cost of capital (WACC), the investment action is approved. But use of WACC sometimes leads to abuses, particularly when the hurdle rate return is known, and thus projection components can be tweaked to exceed the approval minimum. This consideration suggests the need for a different evaluative approach. The approach suggested here is instead to compare the expected return from the external expansion opportunity to the return from the best alternative internal reinvestment opportunity of comparative size—assuming, of course, that the indicated return from the best internal candidates exceeds the operating company's WACC.

- *Both: defined investment period* Entry and exit costs must be identified, assessed, and reflected in projections. Using an open-ended time period can distort accuracy because the compounding effect of large numbers can and does change a marginal investment to an unchallenged winner if the time period is stretched long enough. The suggestion here is to apply a seven-year investment period, even if the expected remaining market time available to the expanding company is longer. If the remaining market period is shorter than seven years, that should be reflected. The full costs of market segment entry and exit should also be indicated in that analysis for completeness.

Transition from Expansion Planning to Acquisition Planning

If the resulting internal/external prospect analysis indicates that some external business expansion opportunities may represent superior opportunities when compared to known internal opportunities of comparable size, expansion planning at that operating company probably moves from the concept stage to action. An acquisition program may be used to implement the corporate expansion program, if outright purchase can be shown to be better decision than other implementation options known and available to management.

Other expansion program implementation alternatives considered by management may include licensing, joint venture, and product purchase and resale. In certain markets and under certain circumstances, any or all of these expansion implementation approaches may be superior to acquisition. Some of these alternatives include the following:

- *Excessive acquisition prices*   Competition among bidders causes acquisition purchase premiums to rise to levels that management considers excessive. If the expansion-minded company is to be involved in this market, that involvement will not result from an acquisition.

- *Late entry into mature market*   The revenue and profit business opportunities of an established market are appealing. Management at the expansion-minded operating company figures that the market's present product can be sold at existing profits at high margins. If this pursued market is well along in years, however, present participants are well entrenched and fiercely battle new would-be competitors. Furthermore, the market could be wiped out if a possible new technology emerges. Such considerations encourage a shorter-term market entry approach than acquisition, assuming that interest in expansion into this market continues at all.

If prevailing acquisition prices are not entirely out of step with reality, acquisition may offer management some distinct advantages over other alternatives. Control—of the acquisition program and of the target company in the target market—is likely to be achieved more readily. Moreover, advantages over the other implementation alternatives emerge, as well. Exclusivity is likely to be superior with an acquisition compared to an affiliation effected through a licensing arrangement. Compared to mere purchase of the product and resale, the company expanding through acquisition can count on greater reliability of supplies for its markets. Avoid a joint venture by taking the acquisition approach instead, and top management of the expanding company may also be able to avoid the frustration and ambiguity of joint decision making by companies with differing interests and objectives.

Bid Preparation and Bid Submission

To the prospective acquirer, the submission of the acquisition bid represents the primary opportunity to ensure that acquisition price levels emerging from the chase for the attractive target company are at least somewhat in line with present value of the target and realistic postacquisition value-development potential. Earlier in this book, price and value dynamics in multibidder contests for an attractive acquisition candidate were described. Here, three challenges that emerge in the prebid and bid period and that confront both financial and synergistic would-be acquirers are examined. The "stretch dilemma" is the prospective acquirer's challenge of making finite purchase commitments based on very limited information. The target acquisition candidate may be attractive, but how far out on a limb dare the acquirer go without verifiable cash flow and value data? Add on overheated bid market and equally expansive egos to the formula, and conditions are ripe for someone to make a costly overbid. In the "sitting it out" approach, value may be created—or at least, value destruction avoided—by deciding *not* to proceed with a bid at the appropriate time. The acquirer decides to drop out—at least at this time and at these prevailing acquisition bid heights. But the knowledgable acquirer doesn't look at price alone in making the drop out/remain in decision. That investor also utilizes certain nonprice indications to anticipate overbid contests. Finally, the acquisition impulse often becomes a single decision: "I've decided that I want it (the acquisition target company), and there's no good reason not to proceed now." The bid is actually two decisions, however—a separate decision about the target of opportunity and another decision on the timing of the implementation action to secure that target. A comprehensive and complete bid process comprises both decisions.

The "Stretch" Delimma: How Far is *Too* Far?

Not much of substance is really known about the target acquisition company by any of the bidders, expressions by staff analysts and advisors notwithstanding. The auction format ensures the maximum bid intensity—with the least solid information about cash flow and value-improvement potential. The pursuit of the target acquiree by motivated acquirers raises prices, while increasing the possibility of an overbid. Bids for the hotly pursued corporation are high now—and apparently headed still higher. Each preceding previous maximum value ceiling is shattered by a higher bid and then by one that is even higher. The gap between these bid levels and the target's known value appears to be massive—certainly too high, one reasons, for a knowledgable bidder to risk. After a while, the bid contest takes on a life of its own, only incidentally related to value considerations. After the first round, the would-be acquiring company's chief executive officer is like the hunting dog that has picked up the scent of the game and will not be deterred. The CEO pressures advisors to justify a winning bid—irrespective of the obstacles.

Some of those in the acquiring company's boardroom or on the executive floor may watch the upward price spiral and harbor concerns—about acquisition debt repayment burden that would accompany the winning bid in a leveraged deal, the availability of time to create the additional cash flow and value to make this acquisition viable, and possible charges of fraudulent conveyance if the deal can later be proven to have been unworkable at these expectation levels. Such thoughts usually remain just that, however—unspoken thoughts—in the interest of self-preservation. No one likes to be told that they can't or shouldn't proceed with a deal. In a bid contest environment with both corporate and personal egos on the line, such outward expressions are particularly dangerous.

The consequences of a chronic overbid are potentially severe. In chronic overbids an acquisition transaction is so overpriced and structured that the deal is fatally unstable as soon as enacted. The chronic overbid is dead on arrival at the time of the close. Deal pricing is the primary culprit, although other considerations attract their share of blame. An inadequate level of equity in a highly leveraged deal's capital structure is one such consideration. A too-thin equity base escalates risks of managing the acquired firm to excessive levels. Acquiree management has virtually no room for *any* adverse performance or marketplace development. Poor structuring may result in the scheduling of debt-repayment terms with little regard to the time required in the acquired company to change operations sufficiently to boost internal cash-flow generation.

When the collapsed transaction's value difference is not covered, consequences described earlier result—missed debt payment dates and amounts, forced rescheduling and refinancing, and if the DOA designation is accurate, a painful collapse for investor and lender followed by liquidation. Even with a herculean merger-integration effort, the numbers simply don't work. The sum of current company worth and additional value added through four-core initiatives and other postacquisition initiatives do not cover the value difference. In June, 1990 federal bankruptcy court presiding over the 1988 collapse of the Revco DS leveraged buyout raised the issue of fraudulent conveyance in response to high-yield bond holders' claims that this LBO was so unstable at inception to be a failed deal at the close. That court action is continuing as of this writing, but irrespective of the final result as it pertains to Revco advisors and managers or its junk bond holders or financiers, this development expands the potential exposure net for parties involved in transactions that are later alleged to be dead on arrival.

This increased risk arising from the collapse of an overextended deal means that today, more than ever, acquiring company management must understand and act on the practical limitations of the transaction's bid range. Stretch bids must be subject to finite limits, even though such counsel is usually unwelcome when it comes in the heat of the bidding war.

In theory, the safeguards are already in place: CEO adventuring is held in check by the watchful eye of the acquiring company's board of directors; independent advisors provide their counsel without limitations that might arise if they were part of the acquiring firm. But theory doesn't always work. Board members hand-picked by the acquiring company may understandably be slow to rise up in opposition to their supporter, and the independent advisor may be that in name only—depending on the company's dependence or transaction or activity-based fees related to the acquiring company's account. If such a situation arises, the acquirer company is well advised to subject its acquisition value judgments to another third party with irrefutable independent standing insofar as the operations and activities of the acquiring company are considered. Company management gets to choose this time. Next time around, a judge could be making the selection.

Sitting It Out

Sometimes the decision that emerges as the best value result is to withdraw from a bidding process that has reached unsupportable—and unjustifiable—heights. But when should acquirer company management pursue the deal and the upward price spiral? When should management withdraw? The most readily apparent factor is the bid price itself, as compared with the sum of today's actual and tomorrow's hoped for value.

The full answer to the question of paying too high a price may not be available until years after the deal's close, but acquirer company management needs to make a decision about bid participation today. That means that other signals of an overheated market must also be watched and considered in combination with other factors in making a judgment about bid-process participation. Some of these signals are listed in Table 9.2. Other signals are described below:

- *Too-fast stock price appreciation*   If the acquisition target company's price has soared too high too fast, the prevailing market price may already take into account much of the postacquisition value-creation potential that the would-be acquirer had counted on to make the deal work. Assuming that the accepted bid *starts* with current market price or equivalent and proceeds from there, an important question arises: "Is there still enough untapped value potential in the target company to make the deal work?"

- *Adverse mix of rival bidders*   If the bidding competition is knowledgable about the realities of price and value, bids remain realistic. The opposite is also true. An adverse mix of overbidders may encourage the value-conscious acquirer to withdraw from the bid early. Too many inexperienced bidders drooling to finalize their first deal or too many acquirers pursuing strategic imperative dictates to acquisition leads to the abandonment of price sanity.

- *Price-to-earnings purchase multiples*   The combination of the price level of the general market, when combined with the prevailing acquisition purchase premium, provides an

Table 9.2. The Corporate Acquirer: Foundations of a Continuing Acquisition Program

No time-clock mentality	Eradicate the time-clock mentality so that deals don't have to be made within a set period of time.
Continuity	If necessary, maintain a contrarian perspective to sustain an aquisition/diversification watch when others have withdrawn.
Seniority	Avoid potentially destructive action biases by staffing with proven managers.

incidental indicator of the level of overheating in the acquisition market overall. A 40 percent acquisition premium may appear to be entirely reasonable when the Dow-Jones is at 1600. Should the some purchase premium percentage be seen as reasonable when the Dow is at 2800?

- *Exit of financial bidders*   The financial bidders by definition have no synergistic value potential: their bid must reflect the sum of present and prospective value of the target company, alone. When all financial bidders leave, bid price levels may be reaching unsupportable levels.

- *Deal origination mix shift*   The original source of the deal changes subtly, suggesting a change in the acquisition/ divestiture balance in the overall merger marketplace.

Bid Development, Preparation, and Submission

A candidate search process is now underway, but the search effort almost stops before it starts. The acquisition selection criteria are expanded so much that virtually no transaction can meet the standards. The president wants to avoid perception of overpayment. Accordingly, a message from the corner office comes over to the acquisitions officer informing him that acceptable deals must all fall in the lower one-third range of prevailing acquisition price-to-earnings purchase multiples. The acquiring company's chief financial officer has read about the problems of relying too much on future projections and has an opinion about minimum characteristics for acceptable deals, which he is not hesitant to share with the acquisition officer, as well. The CEO stipulates that the acquisition decision must be based on the target's prior year earnings, as future earnings projections are little more than speculative guesses. Then everyone on the executive floor wants in on the action. Even more quantitative and qualitative criteria are added to the lengthening list, ranging from the backgrounds of the target's senior officers to the current research expenses to revenue ratio.

A value-creation–based alternative is proposed as an alternative. In a heart-to-heart discussion with the president, the acquisitions officer suggests that multiple criteria will not ensure better acquisitions. Instead, an excessive list will merely ensure that no acquisition occurs at all. A scaled-down list of the most important criteria is suggested. General parameters for the acquisition will be set by industry and size guidelines. It is reasonable to insist that the acquisition be in a related field. A purchase size ceiling is also necessary to prevent an acquisition that is too big to be digested or that cannot be financed.

Beyond that, the decision to proceed to the next stage of fundamental analysis is to be based on financial-market (FM) value of the prospective acquiree, as compared with the prospective acquiree's operating-based value (OV). The value difference between the two measures—based initially on public data, observations of industry experts, and a limited number of competitor interviews—helps sort out those prospects that will advance to the next level of investigation from those on which further action will be deferred.

Fundamental analysis is the last action before direct bid contact with the candidate's officer. If the analysis process has focused on appropriate target segments, several candidates appear to be viable on paper. The on-site investigation provides an opportunity to test perceptions about the factors differentiating leaders from laggards in the segment. In the case of the railroad rebuilding client assignment, on-site visits determined which offers would next receive direct expressions of acquisition interest. Factory visits, combined with discussions with shared suppliers and customers, separated the viable operations from those that were merely capitalizing on recent positive investment comment.

Due-Diligence Period: Expanded Value-Development Role?

The due-diligence investigation is typically conducted as a fast-paced, limited-scope analysis. Preserve that pace, but deepen the scope to include postacquisition value-creation issues. Then due diligence might also signify an opportunity for uncovering new sources of prospective postacquisition value before the close.

"Let's Get the Thing Over".

If there's a shared resolve by both the buyer and the seller in the due-diligence period, it is to complete this interim with all possible speed. Both sides have made commitments. A visible retrenchment from the deal at this point would be embarrassing to one and in some instances to both. Back away on the sell side, and the seller appears to be hawking damaged goods. Back away on the buy side, and the acquiring team looks like they don't know how to close a deal.

Building Value over the Course of the Due-Diligence Period

After the offer has been accepted, the field of suitors is reduced to one. Now the acquirer's due-diligence groups have a limited time to reunderstand the business and to confirm the original value. During the auction period (preceding the agreement in principle), quality data was exceedingly scarce. The auction may include competitors of the seller or their agents. Accordingly, the cautious seller's attitude is sometimes that the less data provided the better.

The due-diligence analysis team gets organized and underway. The intent is not to concentrate on negatives but it is difficult *not* to bring up some possible negotiating points for the acquirer at a latter point, arising from new probing:

- The intended acquiree's cash management system is highly decentralized and virtually out of control. There are no lockboxes or concentration accounts and no centralized cash accounting. The proposed acquiree's treasurer must cipher out laborious manual estimates in order to arrive at some semblance of a cash figure.

- Some of the property adjacent to the company's Alabama assembly plant were found to be polluted, because of nearby industrial dumping. The acquirer's original bid assumed that the property would be sold at its greatest value use, which is for single family homes. This finding now means that residential usage is out of the question.

The due-diligence team identifies potential value opportunities for its client—centralizing certain processes, process simplification, and organizational delayering. As noted, the prospective acquiree's cash-management system as presently designed and operated is highly decentralized. The proposed approach called for a concentration account structure, with acquiree business units retaining local check-writing autonomy, but up to preassigned levels only. Prospective savings: 20 percent of the acquiree's overall cash management cost plus one-third of the positions field clerical staff.

New product decision making was slowed by an excessively complex approval structure, which included too many people in too many layers. The suggested alternative: establishment of a once-a-week coordinating group meeting including only the six departments critical for implementation and prelaunch work. With this approach management expected to accelerate pricing changes by two full weeks. Assuming current volumes, the annual recurring cash-flow improvement would be more than $8 million.

Finally, the target organization was analyzed as being two layers deeper than some other comparable companies. This issue would be revisited after the close. Also, the due-diligence team was continually on the lookout for possible stay-put bonus candidates—the key individuals without whom critical processes of the company would not work.

10

Fixing the LBOs That Broke

The dollar volume of leveraged buyouts that are broken–that is, those LBOs no longer capable of supporting their acquisition debt load—is significant and growing, and these known problems may be only the tip of the iceberg. Deferrals and asset sales can hide the troubled LBO from the scrutiny of the reviewer for months. Numerous other problem LBOs are buried in lenders' and investors' portfolios. This chapter describes a systematic process for problem discovery, classification, action analysis, and implementation. The initial imperative is to uncover emerging problem LBOs early enough for corrective action to be effective. Then to match the problem with a solution approach, it becomes necessary to quickly categorize the status of these deals: transactions are separated into those requiring only financial restructuring, those requiring financial *plus* operational restructuring, and those that cannot reasonably be salvaged. Finally, an abbreviated but intensive analysis is aimed at identifying actions and alternatives in the shortest period of time. Financial restructuring must be in place first to provide time for this diagnostic and implementation.

Discovery

The slip into problem status may be so gradual that it is almost imperceptible, and if financial measures are the sole means for assessing LBO progress, the problem LBO may be revealed too late to do much good. An alternative is to know what to look for in an LBO undergoing change. The two types of acquired companies described in this section are the declining competitor and the missed-timing victim.

The Declining Competitor: Is This Deal Still Working?

Even though the high-leverage acquisition has weathered the first trying months of its new existence, this acquisition is not yet a success. The financial numbers may still appear acceptable, but other problems—such as intensified competition—stand in the way of ultimate success.

The acquiree's limited financial resiliency is taking its toll, as competitors learn how to attack the LBO where it is most vulnerable—in its cash flow. Competitive factors were not a serious consideration in the LBO's initial months. The acquiree had enjoyed a high-quality reputation prior to being acquired, and an effective protective program was undertaken with key customers immediately after the close to head off rumors of instability before they arose. Over time, however, competitors were able to draw attention to the issue of the LBOed firm's staying power in other ways—through example, not rumors.

The more aggressive of the LBO's two primary competitors increased its total project and capital spending as soon as the acquiree's LBO was announced. More important, expenditure emphasis shifted from internal cost-reduction capital projects to expenditures with high marketplace and customer visibility. The competitor launched a computerized order-tracking system with great fanfare. A computerized remote-order-entry system was tried on an experimental basis with one large customer known to be particularly interested in such developments. Advertising emphasized the competitor's size and independence.

The competitor also disrupted the LBO acquiree's production schedules by tying up certain suppliers of components sometimes in short supply. Some customers of both the LBO firm and its competitor learned of these developments and began to shift their orders to the LBO's competitor in response.

The LBO acquiree ultimately threatened legal action, although management knew that it faced a near-impossible task in attempting to prove to a court that the competitor's actions were directed at them alone. It also could not match the competitor's expenditures due to the continuing pressure of acquisition borrowing.

Gradually, account losses began to be felt as revenue losses could no longer be replaced with customers of the same quality or who purchased the same high-margin products. As profit margins slipped, management's instinctive reaction was to scale back costs, but here they were blocked as well. Most of the available cost-reduction actions already had been taken in the first few months after the close. Other cuts were in areas that would have major customer impact, such as the delivery fleet, which the acquiree's management reasoned would only make matters worse.

The competitor's moves had succeeded in making some shared customers think of the LBO firm as a struggling competitor that could someday go under if things did not go right. Once introduced without opposition in the marketplace, the posturing began to become a self-fulfilling prophecy.

The Missed Timing Victim: The Need for Another LBO Model

The quick-entry–quick-exit LBO success model doesn't work for the company that counts the time to repay its acquisition borrowings in terms of years rather than months. Without an approach reflecting current conditions today, some LBOs drift toward problems.

Fast in, fast out was the key characteristic of spectacular LBO successes such as Wesray Capital/Gibson Greeting Cards, but such opportunities declined measurably as bid prices rose. Undervalued assets became not so undervalued, and initial public offering (IPO) markets disappeared, removing a source of liquidity and an ultimate buyer for the deal.

Structuring remained largely the same, however, long after the change in deal-market conditions pointed to the need for successor approaches. For one thing, the LBO structure was not designed to deal with the problem of a leveraged acquisition forced to stretch out its repayment arrangements. If the LBO cannot prepay its acquisition debt but instead must lengthen the repayment period, the acquisition and the deal's owners and lenders experience the other side of massive debt. Delays in repaying the borrowing levels accelerate the compounding effect of interest expense, exaggerating the LBO's financial challenge when that company can least afford it.

Left alone, the problem gets worse as financial obligations eventually choke off an otherwise successful business. Unless some financial restructuring provides relief, and quickly, the slow decline gains fast momentum.

Illustration: AcquireCo and TargetCo

AcquireCo's purchase of TargetCo closed more than a year and a half ago, but investors and lenders are beginning to feel uneasy. One asks, "Is it time now to restructure before TargetCo encounters *real* trouble?" If the answer to that question is yes, the related issue is whether financial restructuring—including infusion of additional capital—will suffice or whether operations need to be reworked and redirected.

The MI team left after six months. Profit-restructuring (core one) actions yielded a 30 percent increase in additional net cash flow. Ten percent of that amount saved was earmarked for new product launches (core two). Manufacturing consolidations and procurement improvements were substantially complete after four months (core three). The postacquisition systems strategy called for the barebones approach described in chapter 9 to minimize expenses (core four).

Then some problems arose, most of which were uncontrollable. Contaminants in TargetCo's manufacturing process slowed final consolidation and dropped TargetCo's total capacity by 25 percent for one full quarter. Strikes at two of TargetCo's largest customers caused inventories to bulge, which forced an investment in temporary warehouse space. TargetCo management celebrated when the strike at one key customer's plant was settled after ninety days, but then that customer decided to cancel the order anyhow, citing slower demand from all of *their* customers, along with some possible signs of a cyclical downturn.

Addressed individually, none of these unexpected events indicated imminent disaster. Nonetheless, the combined effects were severe—value and cash-flow retreat amounting to about half of what had been developed in the postacquisition period. Moreover, cash-outflow requirements would double in about a year. TargetCo could meet principal and interest payments but only by drawing down cash and cutting corners in marketing programs. The company was no longer generating sufficient internal cash flow to service AcquireCo's acquisition debt.

AcquireCo management didn't want to overreact by jumping in too soon or when there was no need. It was possible that cash flow would bounce back in a month or so as these obstacles were overcome, one by one, but there were still concerns. As one AcquireCo's director quipped, "I see a light at the end of the tunnel, but I can't tell whether it is an exit or a truck."

Using Early Warning Indicators Effectively

To help indicate whether intervention was needed or whether to remain on the sidelines, AcquireCo's chief executive developed a brief series of indicators:

- *Available cash*   Cash would be measured on a daily basis until the special watch period was over. Cash available for distribution has slumped to less than ten days' of projected commitments, extremely low for the industry and historically. Discussions were initiated to develop contingency cash sources—a sale and lease back of one of the plants, an additional line, deferral of bonuses for three months.

- *Source of debt repayment*   TargetCo's first sizeable debt-repayment obligation, a balloon payment, would come due next month. According to company projections, 45 percent of that amount would come from cash reserves and marketing project cancellations compared to projections of 20 percent before the recent problems.

- *Improvements in the unit sales per administrative employee* This sales ratio failed to keep pace with projections. The ratio test was developed to provide a quick look into whether additional staff cutback would be needed to offset sales. The ratio was behind projections, presumably reflecting sales softness rather than slow progress in headcount cuts. The cancellation by TargetCo's large customer was particularly troubling to management and suggested to the CEO a possible cyclical turn in the market. To test that hunch, TargetCo's marketing vice president would approach several other sizeable customers about longer-term contracts at very attractive prices. If no one accepted TargetCo's offer, additional staff would need to be cut.

- *Visible account churn* The account-churn indicator was designed to keep track of TargetCo's progress with its most important customers, but the indicator had other uses as well. High churn meant high administrative expenses. New accounts needed to be developed, established, and documented. Prolonged continuation of a high churn rate also suggested product quality difficulties.

- *Low transitional costs* Transitional costs in this instance are one-time offsets to head-count reductions. Below-budget spending here might indicate that positions scheduled for elimination were shuffled rather than cut.

- *Executive recruiters' signals* Executive recruiters have designated the acquiree as an area for concentration, which was disturbing. Several of TargetCo's key drivers—who had been given stay-put bonuses immediately after the close—were growing antsy. AcquireCo's CEO decided to have a couple of chats.

Classification

The challenge in this process is first to isolate the terminal transactions that cannot be saved. The other deals are then divided into two sets—those requiring only financial restructuring and those requiring both financial and operational restructuring.

Spotting the Dead Deal

The dead or dying company is sometimes difficult to spot. Keep in mind that Drexel Burnham Lambert's Fred Joseph was reportedly planning for the next budget year a couple of weeks before the firm's filing for bankruptcy protection.

The dead deal is first and foremost illiquid. The second and third request for infusion of additional cash is made to the parent and met, yet little seems changed. If the deal was originally overpaid—that is, if there is no chance of recouping the value difference between the price paid and preacquisition worth—and the company is chronically cash poor, then kill the deal quickly.

Often the dead deal acquiree has lost its way in the market. Key accounts are lost and do not respond to recapture attempts. Competitors are seemingly everywhere, and no new innovations are even on the drawing boards.

The Financial Restructuring (Only) Prospect

This acquiree appears to require only adjustments to the deal-financing structure to become viable and remain that way. Adjustments may be as simple as an accrual extension or as involved as a total new financing structure led by a different banker. The prospective opportunity to keep acquisition activity high by refinancing the LBO deals of others (presumably, they're redoing your transactions, while you're refinancing *their* transaction) has resulted a new phrase—the "failure boom."

Financial Restructuring Combined with Operations Restructuring

The acquiree has found that its cash position dictates a new and different financing structure—one with more money. The logical complement to the financial restructuring is a quick but deep reconstruction of the corporation's business along the lines of the four-core program. The diagnostic used for an accelerated financial/operational restructuring is essentially the same two- to three-week multiple-issues analysis that precedes the postacquisition action. The financing restructuring action must precede the operations-based program to buy sufficient time to allow the operations changes to work. Unless the financial restructuring can ensure the viability of the acquiree for at least six months, the operations restructuring should probably not be started.

Action Analysis and Implementation

The action analysis begins with compilation of specific tasks and alternatives that will accomplish the goal. Once that agenda is set, the developer of the analysis also becomes the implementer.

Disadvantages of a Reactive Approach

Operational and financial restructuring of an identified problem transaction is often approached on an ad hoc basis, with the reaction developed as the problem becomes visible. There are several distinct disadvantages to such an approach. The most important advantage involves timing and reactions. If you wait to act until the problem manifests itself fully, chances for fully resolving that problem decrease significantly. By the time the problem arises, is understood, and is analyzed, there may no longer be enough time to make a difference—whatever the acquirer's actions.

An Anticipatory Approach

An alternative approach attempts to anticipate the need for corrective action before that need arises, with the continuing program involvement of an examiner. Standard financial performance indicators are combined with some of the early warning indicators discussed in this chapter. Those, in turn, are combined with operations key factors developed by the examiner for each portfolio investee or borrower. Quarterly visits of the examiner to the acquiree provide a means for following up on trends and new developments indicated by the statistical data alone. The on-site work also assists the examiner in better understanding the quality and predictability of the portfolio company's numbers and observing how management reacts in crises. Finally, the periodic tracking report grades the condition of the acquiree in terms of operating and financial criteria. Special problems and opportunities—including turnaround emergencies—are raised immediately as they arise.

11

Becoming Your
Own Raider

This chapter addresses the issues and challenges that the operating company management faces when it attempts to apply mergers integration principles to improve ongoing profit performance. As managers and owners strive to increase the value of their businesses, they discourage unwarranted acquisition interest.

The "becoming your own raider" approach calls for simulation of the performance-enhancing characteristics of some high-leverage transactions within the corporate environment. The goal of BYOR is to help achieve breakthrough improvements in corporate cash-flow generation and value creation that normally occur only under intense periods of structured change, such as during the aftermath of a completed LBO. The difference is that this raider isn't an external threat but rather is the company itself, and this raider doesn't change the ownership of the company, charge transaction fees, or unbalance the company's balance sheet and financial structure. Effectively applied, with measurable performance goals and safeguards, the BYOR approach can help bring performance improvement advantages to the daily world of operating company decisions.

The seven suggested steps for implementing what is referred to here as the continuous corporate turnaround attempt to replicate the conditions of productive intensity that accompany fundamental changes in activities and operations and a corresponding increase in value. The goal is to move the operating company away from a structure and underlying culture that tend to cause the company to oppose change and toward a structure that helps the company to be responsive to change—ideally, to anticipate and welcome productive change.

Becoming your Own Raider

Factors underlying LBO Performance

The goal of the becoming your own raider approach is to achieve performance results attributed in some leveraged buyouts to the characteristics of that structuring approach and the manner in which it is applied, but without the debt or ownership change. The effective BYOR approach begins with development of an accurate understanding of the performance factors of successful LBO acquirees that, when properly developed and managed, can help improve corporate performance and then separates these from apparent factors with little performance impact.

Acquisition Debt: Indirect Performance Effect
at Best

Some LBO advocates have noted the disciplining effects of massive borrowing arising from a highly leveraged transaction in explaining the dramatic performance improvement after some LBOs are enacted. The postacquisition LBO is envisioned by some as a leaner, more responsive competitor. We do not see acquisition debt as being a performance improvement influence per se. Rather, massive debt in an LBO can become an enabling instrument related to the actual key motivating factor. It makes little sense to suggest that the infusion of massive amounts of debt by itself stimulates the performance of the affected company's key employees. Faced with a massive debt that may appear to the employee to be too much for the company to support, the manager's instinctive reaction may instead be to stop trying rather than to try harder. Nor does massive debt make the postacquisition LBO a healthier company. Massive borrowing increases financial risk of the company while reducing or eliminating access to conventional capital markets—at least until much of the borrowing is paid off or appears headed in that direction. Until then the presence of excessive debt may destabilize the firm and its ongoing operations.

Direct Factor: Scheduled Performance Obligation

The LBO's true motivating factor is the imposition of an obligatory, scheduled performance requirement that is time bound and has rewards and penalties for principal participants. Such a scheduled obligation program contains the potential to motivate the manager to top performance, assuming that key interests of management and company can be made to coincide. That motivating potential arises from the following characteristics of such a structured obligation:

- *Obligatory, unavoidable* If the performance program is designed correctly, the performance measure is clear, and obligation to pursue that objective cannot be avoided easily. Managers will be hard pressed to explain away poor performance with a memo: they either succeed in reaching the goal or fail.
- *Rewards* Assuming that the effected acquiree manager is part of the buyout group, the rewards for full success are extensive.
- *Penalties* The consequences of failure are great, as well. Miss an interim goal the first time, and the consequence is vigorous encouragement. Miss a second time, and there may not be a third chance.
- *Time-bound* Change must occur quickly. Because the achievement goal is time bound, the manager has no choice but get to the right answer as quickly as possible. The ever-

ticking time clock lessens the tendency toward excessive analysis (paralysis by analysis) or consideration of extraneous factors.

- *Scheduled* The obligation should be of a recurring nature, to reinforce new behavior through repetition.

Acquisition Debt as Enabling Vehicle

In the LBO, the transaction's acquisition debt serves as the means by which the obligatory schedule approach is implemented. Debt requires repayment, and the presence and high profile of a scheduled principal and interest repayment schedule establishes an unavoidable incentive for improved corporate performance. The manager's personal stake in the new enterprise activates that potential. A corporate obligation cannot become a personal commitment until and unless the manager has a personal interest in achieving the corporate goal.

Developing and Implementing the Company's BYOR Program

The becoming your own raider approach begins with understanding the true motivations underlying LBO performance. Next comes the realization that few operating corporations know how to combine leverage and performance motivation to outperform their competition. Although corporate chief financial officers are keenly interested in new, emerging antitakeover approaches, they are skeptical about high-debt-percentage financing. Many CFOs admire the apparent performance improvement that many acquired companies show after using high levels of senior debt and a set repayment schedule, but they certainly don't welcome the prospect of seeing their companies in an LBO raider's gunsights. The principal feature of the BYOR approach is the simulation of an acquisition directed at their own firm and not an external target, under the following controlled conditions (see Table 11.1):

- *Calculate a theoretical raider purchase price* The BYOR approach begins when top management assumes the role

Table 11.1.   Becoming Your Own Raider

Calculate a purchase price.	Calculate a theoretical raider purchase price based on prevailing acquisition-purchase multiples, realistic cash-flow and risk assumptions, and prevailing capital market costs.
Convert to P&I amounts.	Convert the purchase price to principal-and-interest debt-servicing amounts. Then make adjustments for predictable cash receipts expected from asset and business-unit divestitures.
Allocate debt-servicing costs.	Allocate the period debt-servicing costs to company revenue, expense, and profit centers. Use a formula based on factors such as head count, operating-profit contribution, and expenses.
Reallocate debt-servicing burden.	Reallocate the debt-servicing burden to business units and departments. Adjust the allocations to encourage future corporate performance in areas of greatest emphasis.
Insist on improved performance.	Insist on improving performance by each unit despite the added debt burden. Scale back operations that are not capable to carrying their fair portion of the acquisition debt.
Develop standby financing.	Optional: Develop standby financing to position the company to convert potential acquisition debt to an actual management buyout financing arrangement.

and perspective of an outside acquirer and constructs a winning bid. Develop a winning bid—but for your own company. Prevailing acquisition price-to-earnings multiples and the company's three-year projections provide a competitive baseline for management estimating the current market bid level for the company. To win the bid war, figure that the bid must be 10 to 15 percent above those levels. For the BYOR process to work, the theoretical raider price cannot be pushed arbitrarily to levels that deliberately place the company out of range.

- *Convert the winning bid into debt servicing* This simulates conditions of high-leverage acquisition financing for the transaction. Now the company must develop additional sources of net cash flow to meet servicing requirements.

- *Allocate debt service to appropriate company departments and units* The purpose of BYOR is to stimulate effective *voluntary* corporate action, aimed at creating new value. Thus, instead of a centrally directed program, the decisions of what to consider, how, and how soon are addressed by the company's managers.

- *Insist on achieving performance commitments* This is where top management's resolve to direct and support the BYOR program is critical. The expected initial response of the department or business unit head will be to dismiss the additional obligation as theoretical. In the same way that corporate allocations for shared administrative services may be treated as costs for "someone else, but not me," the BYOR numbers may be brushed aside unless the approach is supported from the top. Top management can correct this misperception at the monthly operations review meeting by automatically including BYOR allocations in the monthly budgets for all areas of the corporation. The chief financial officer makes "below the line" reversals to accurately reflect actual performance for external purposes, but all *internal* reports—all management performance reports, profit programs, and budgets—reflect the special corporate charge. Profit, revenue, and expense leaders who dismiss this as a numbers game and miss their commitment goals first receive a reminder and then a firmer warning. The delinquent manager's choice is either to improve performance within sixty days or receive assistance from an outside merger-integration advisor. If results are still disappointing after that point, even more severe action may be needed. Performance measurement simplicity systems and approaches specify numerous goals. But achievement of the individual goals may still not assure that the major objective—in this case, the corporate cash-flow improvement objective—is achieved. By contrast, a companywide goal in a BYOR program is seen and recognized by all.

As with LBO debt repayment, there is no ambiguity about success or failure. The additional net cash-flow–creation obligation is either achieved or not.

- *Standby financing put in place (optional)* If management introduces and implements the program in the spirit intended, and if the net cash-flow creation increases are achieved without damaging the base business, why not make the full transition to reality? The following three actions need to be take in such a transition: (1) establish a standby financing facility (when BYOR is initiated, company management announces that the program will be tied to an actual acquisition defense standby commitment from a sizeable financial institution); (2) initiate an actual management buyout (having seen what can and cannot be achieved on a voluntary basis, management decides to go ahead with a buyout; information from the BYOR program is used to set initial priorities for the postacquisition value creation effort); and (3) repurchase stock (the savings generated by the program are reach dollars, not dreams; savings are used to buy back stock reducing the target for possible raiders). The standby arrangement provides the clearest possible signal to potential suitors that the company has the program, resolve, and resources to ensure its independence. The financing, if activated, may be used to implement the buyback or used in whole or part in the stock repurchasing program.

The Continuous Turnaround Corporation

Eclipse of the Paternalistic, Underperforming Corporation

The 1980s merger boom meant the end of publicly traded company independence for many firms. Kraft Corporation became part of Philip Morris. Burroughs acquired Sperry, and the two became Unisys. Bank of New York removed Irving Trust from the ranks of the independent banks. As this pursuit and capture of familiar names began to mount, one could almost sense the melancholy. The sense of loss was discernible, as if voices were asking, "What happened to that company that used to care for me?" Good old Venerable Corp. was sliced into little pieces in the merger-integration process. The company was squeezed for profits until a more delectable target came along. After a suitable mourning period, however, the tears must end. If the underperforming, paternalistic company couldn't save itself in the acquisition market shark fight, what form of corporation can?

The Resilient Corporation: A Change-*Anticipating* Corporation?

The becoming your own raider company provides one answer to that question; but BYOR calls for a conventional company (which is perhaps also a paternalistic and underperforming company, as well) to alter its future priorities through LBO-type performance motivation. The continuous turnaround corporation response to this question is different: it emphasizes process change as the key to effective performance change.

The elements of the continuous turnaround approach are drawn from corporate turnaround strategy, marketing program resurrection efforts, and plain common sense (see Table 11.2). They focus on the most important things needed to build in the corporate design, assuming an intent of creating an enterprise that not only reacts but also *anticipates* change.

- *Seize the cash, then track it*   If cash flow creates value, then cash ensures liquidity. If the future is expected to be fast-changing, at least figure out where the cash comes from and goes so the captain of the corporation always has the sense that his hand is on the tiller and also on the till.

- *Learn from loss sales analysis*   Lost sales can provide one of the fastest means for learning about future change opportunities: if the lost accounts were profitable in the past, find out what has to be done to resurrect the relationship; if the accounts aren't profitable, see how many more like that are still active customers—and should be eliminated.

Table 11.2. The Continuous Turnaround Corporation

Seize cash and track it.	The turnaround experts' first action also is the top priority for CEOs seeking to improve ongoing corporate success.
Analyze lost sales.	Gain insight from an objective assessment of where, why, and how sales have been lost. Determine what is important to correct and what should be left alone.
Develop new strategies.	Develop a new market strategy with your top ten customers.
Concentrate effort.	Place most of your eggs in a few baskets, and undertake actions based on 80 percent data.
Understaff and overreward.	Faced with the alternative of two bureaucrats at $30,000 per year or one operations manager at $50,000, go for the latter.
Educate.	Create a companywide understanding of the most important aspects of the corporate cash-flow/value-development model. Managers shouldn't become modelers, but they should understand which actions create corporate value and which destroy that value.
Shake up the organization.	Periodically shake up the organization. Reward new leaders, and ceremoniously dispose of corporate empty suits. Mobilize positive tension.

- *Develop a new market strategy with top-ten customers* The chief executive of a Canadian company presently in the process of being acquired also operates as an internal turnaround expert for the parent's many industrial subsidiaries. To the CEO, a Canadian by birth and background, the American term *strategy* means marketing— not marketing in the sense of scanning customer lists at headquarters but as a process of breaking down and then building up the company's product/market approach and enlisting key customers to get it accomplished. As those customers' needs change, you change. Ten top accounts often represent 40 to 60 percent of sales.

- *Place (most of) the company's emphasis in a small number of baskets*   As competition increases, size barriers rise to effective market entry and penetration. Resources are normally limited and even more so with emphasis on additional net cash-flow generation. Dividing resources over too broad a base wastes company resources, as no project or activity can get sufficient backing to succeed.

- *Understaff and overreward*   Competent, well-paid people somehow find a way to accomplish their multiple responsibilities and roles. Amid the continuing movement of the continuous turnaround, these key employees must come to view themselves as a part of the small solid core that will drive the company forward in the future. The job security of past decades is over. In its place arises the individual's partnership with the corporation borne out of shared dependency.

- *Create a companywide understanding of the most important aspects of the corporate cash-flow/value-development model*   Develop a workable understanding of how the company *really* operates, and reflect this in a value-operations model. Quantify that approach, but insist that the explanation be simple enough for employees to clearly understand actions that build value and those that destroy value.

- *Periodically shake up the organization*   Even the continuous change corporation eventually begins to function as a bureaucracy if allowed to become static. Prevent that from happening, by awarding the outperformers who thrive in change.

12

Emerging Board
of Director Issues

High-leverage transactions were the hallmark of the great merger boom of the 1980s, and despite some recent developments, HLTs in modified form should remain important financing instruments in the 1990s. The resilience of HLT financings means new challenges for acquirer and acquiree directors and managers, however. The time appears right for boards to review the adequacy of their high-leverage transaction acquisition and divestiture policies and procedures.

Changes in Acquisition Financing and Merger-Market Conditions

If HLT policies exist at all, they tend to reflect conditions from an earlier era—a period in which equity financing of acquisition transactions predominated. But those realities have changed, largely because of the transition to debt-based acquisition financing. Leverage causes acquisition results—whether success or failure—to happen sooner. In the early 1980s some of the early-phase leveraged buyouts created wealth in months, but the time between the closing of the deal and the acquiree's Chapter 11 filing has in some instances been reduced from years to months.

Does this acceleration mean additional exposure for selling organizations and the boards of directors that authorize their actions? A transaction that failed five years after the close used to raise no special concerns or attention, but the same is not true of an LBO bankruptcy that occurs within months of the close. The federal court investigation of the Revco DS collapse—a $1.3 billion LBO that failed within two years of the deal close—has raised new concerns about the extent and severity of possible exposure for deal principals, brokers, intermediaries, and advisors.

Merger integration was once viewed primarily as a people issue. MI was pursued at a deliberate, if not outright slow, pace. Today merger integration starts with cash-flow and value-improvement issues and is often mandatory if the acquisition is to succeed. During the equity-based transaction era acquirers and acquirees worked out their integration problems, opportunities, and processes, often over an extended period. The pace of postacquisition integration was deliberately slowed in some instances to allow related departments and functions to "work out the integration process among themselves."

But laissez-faire evaporated with the change in acquisition-financing approaches and debt servicing's resulting effect on transaction success. The meaning and significance of merger integration changed dramatically. MI became a requisite activity for helping generate enough sources of additional, continuing cash flow to meet new servicing demands resulting from the deal debt load and to generate sufficient added value to cover the value difference separating the price paid for the acquisition target company and that firm's conservatively estimated worth at the time of the transaction.

People issues remain a part of MI. The selling company's board may approve a sale, and the new owners immediately lay off skilled people never categorized as redundant or surplus before the leveraged transaction forced downsizing. For board members in both the acquiring and the selling firm, a new concern arises about possible new exposure as otherwise capable employees lose their jobs because of the dictates of a volatile financing vehicle.

The new acquisition order also means a larger net of possible deal exposure in terms of the number of participants and intermediaries approached. Particularly in the case of a spectacular LBO collapse occurring shortly after the close, potential exposure can extend beyond the directly interested parties to the transaction, all the way to the seller's and buyer's advisors. Deal principals become possibly subject to charges of fraudulent conveyance if a bankrupted LBO transaction can be proven as having been intrinsically unstable at the time of the close. Even transaction fees are potentially at risk as debt holders attempt to salvage whatever value they can, from whatever source they can.

Board Issues and Actions in a Fast-Changing Environment

Three important board and special committee issues are examined in this section—the future of high-leverage-acquisition transaction financing and possible resulting exposure, effective and early exercise of acquisition supervision and control by the board, and development and implementation of board-level postacquisition success assessment of the company's completed deals.

Leveraged Acquisitions Are Here to Stay

A growing body of support data suggests that HLTs in general, and leveraged buyouts specifically, have lapsed into decline (see Figure 12.1). That does not mean that highly leveraged acquisition financing is to become a relic of the past. HLTs perform an important function within the full spectrum of the acquirer's financing options. Furthermore, such financing may actually create value if combined with financial-risk-reduction actions.

Figure 12.1.   General M & A and Leveraged Buyout Trends, 1986–1989

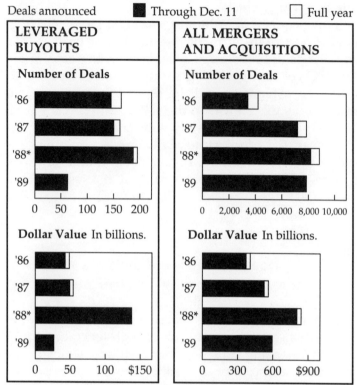

* Includes the $25 billion leveraged buyout of RJR Nabisco Inc.

SOURCE: *New York Times,* December 17, 1989 (data from 100 Information Systems).

High-Leverage Transaction Financing under Attack

As the new decade begins, the pace of acquisition activity has not matched the torrid pace of the 1980s. What caused this difference? Some point to the Delaware Supreme Court's indications in the Time Warner/Paramount Communications battle. Others point to the collapse of the junk bond market, which reduced market liquidity. The pivot occurred so quickly that alternative sources of liquidity could not be developed (see Figure 12.2). Because of the merger cycle's long expansion, certain transitional changes must be anticipated as the merger cycle ma-

Figure 12.2. High Yield (Junk) Bond Debt Trends, 1988 and 1989

Percentage of trasactions using junk bonds

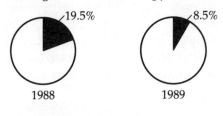

1988   1989

Junk bonds issued
(dollar figures in billions)

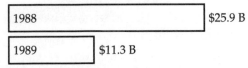

SOURCE: *Mergers and Acquisitions* as reported in *USA Today*.
NOTE: Statistics reflect periods from January through September 30 of each year.

tures. The 1980s merger boom, after all, celebrated its eighth birthday when the new decade began on January 1, 1990.

The decline in the volume of HLT deals and thus financings has coincided with increased attention from two other interested bodies. The controller of the currency made debt-based deals highly visible (and thus, more subject to some form of future control) through the designation of high-leverage transactions along with requests to major leverage deal lenders to indemnify their qualifying loans. In the U.S. Congress legislation aimed at curtailing interest deductions for some or all LBOs has surfaced again.

Will HLT Financings Survive?

HLT financings will adapt and eventually thrive once again. High-leverage transactions add a needed dimension to the acquirer's overall financing spectrum. Arguably, many acquisitions before 1982 were made with excessively high percentages of equity in their acquisition capital mixes. Management wasted precious (and expensive) equity capital if they used only equity to acquire a growing concern with excess cash flow.

High-leverage transactions also may result in increased corporate value under certain conditions. If the subject company's capitalization is altered to increase the percentage of debt in the subject company's capital mix, and if that change can be made without causing offsetting increases in risk perception, new value may be created. Key points in that logic sequence follow:

- *Change in capitalization means decreased funds costs* An increase in debt as a percentage of total capital reduces the cost of funds, also known as the weighed average cost of capital (WACC), since the after-tax cost of debt is usually considerably less than the cost of equity.

- *Lower discount rate increases the value of the present cash-flow stream* The lower WACC means a lower discount rate and that, in turn, means an increase in the present value of the subject company's future expected stream of earnings and cash flows, assuming that all other things are equal. Calculate present value using a 12 percent rate, and then redo the calculation using a 10 percent rate. Watch the present value increase—without any change in the projections.

- *Potential value offset: increased risk* If there is a perception that the added debt escalates the risks of the business, then the source of value may be cancelled out by that risk. That greater risk is also a component in the value determination formula—an increase in perceived risk adjusting the value of a constant stream of profits and cash flows down.

- *The importance of perceptions* If the recapitalization does not result in added risk as perceived by others, the net effect remains positive—a net increase in value.

A third development supporting the continuation of high-leverage forms of acquisition financings is the resiliency of the acquisition market and the adaptability of merger-market participants to change. Acquirers and intermediaries are remarkably innovative when it comes to overcoming obstacles, and the collapse of the junk-bond market represents quite a challenge.

Financing availability contributed to the strength of the 1980s merger boom, but where will tomorrow's leveraged deal liquidity come from? One guess is that the financing market will evolve from the broad-based, total-company financing mode of the junk exchange to a more limited financing secured by groups of assets.

Directors of the Divesting Corporation: The Ongoing Entity Issue

Survival and growth of HLTs means that corporate directors and top management must meet specific challenges that arise from high-leverage deals. A particular problem is the ongoing entity issue: the potential for exposure increases when the transaction results in a failed business. The company's operations come unraveled in the aftermath of the deal, leading some to contend that the seller failed to convey a viable business to buyers.

What, if any, obligation does the board and its special committee have to help ensure that the business unit that is sold survives as an ongoing business entity? The threat to the ongoing-entity status contemplated here is the assumption of a level and percentage (of total capital) of acquisition that endangers the divested company's future existence. Consider the following examples:

- *Gross overpayment: equity deal* The issue of gross overpayment usually doesn't arise with an equity acquisition. Even if an acquirer using equity funds grossly overpays, that mistake is reflected the acquirer's own financial return and earnings per share numbers.

- *Gross overpayment: high-percentage debt transaction* If the overpayment is fueled by excessive borrowings, the financial risk of the divestee may increase so dramatically that the seller later finds itself accused of contributing to the eventual demise of its former division.

When the time between the close and the Chapter 11 filing is less than one year, a cautious director figures that *some* potential financial exposure to the selling firm may result. The members of the board's special committee should realize that *caveat emptor* prevails. Risk-averse directors should consider the ongoing status of the divestee as a minimum protective action.

Directors of the Acquiring Corporation

Prebid Supervision and Control

The acquisition market has begun to stagger. Deals are coming undone. Transaction financing is extended, then withdrawn, apparently for no reason. A growing chorus of analysts predicts the imminent end to the current acquisition expansion cycle. Nevertheless, management may argue that this turmoil—and the related price break that goes along with it—represents an opportunity for action. In a leveraged buyout, as the directors are reminded once again, the burden of meeting the acquisition debt obligation relies primarily on the operations and assets of the acquiree. Some directors are concerned about what they perceive to be a plunging market. The prospect of a deal that is finalized just days before an acknowledged turning point in the M & A market would not just be a matter of embarassment; potential exposure to shareholder suits could result, as well. There are no instant answers, but careful directors are well advised to factor the consideration of the acquisition market's life stage into their proceed/don't proceed decision.

Postacquisition Deal Performance Review

Empirical analysis of the financial rate of return achieved by shareholders in the acquiring companies encourages the board to establish a permanent structure for assessing whether the deal worked or not, with reviews occurring at predetermined points in time following the close. This issue may become a board imperative. Without a mechanism for assessing whether the deal has succeeded or failed, directors and management are without means for determining the benefit to shareholders from acquisitions already completed. If it later becomes evident that past deals were failures but the board continued to give management a free reign in pursuing yet more deals, some exposure could result. Table 12.1 shows some suggested parameters for establishing such a review process.

Table 12.1   Establishing the Acquistion Performance Review

Scope	All acquistions completed by the company or subsidiaries during a predetermined threshold period
Review dates	First: three years after the close; second: five years after the close
Reviewing organization	Acquisition performance review committe of the board of directors
Evaluation criteria	Estimated performance of acquired company on a freestanding basis; total return to acquirer company equity holders compared to other alternatives

About the Author

Developer of the first integrated approach to postacquisition corporate integration, Peter J. Clark reveals the secrets and explains the techniques of bringing acquiring and acquired company together in *Beyond the Deal: Optimizing Merger and Acquisition Value*.

Mr. Clark is managing director of Maplestar Consulting Group, Inc., Manhattan-headquartered management consultants concentrating on corporate strategy, expansion, acquisition, and divestiture opportunities. As the outside consultant integrator in corporate business combinations in the 1980s, Mr. Clark pioneered development of the multifaceted Four Core methodology and other approaches critical to success in the after-deal stage.

In addition to his active consulting and advisory agenda, Mr. Clark has also been a chapter contributor to other leading books on corporate development, acquisition, and divestiture strategy; and he has served as an expert panelist for *Mergers and Acquisitions* magazine. Mr. Clark's upcoming book (1991 publication) for Harper Business, *Deal Masters 100*, will focus on the captains of American corporate transition in the 1990s.

He resides in New York with his wife, Dee, who heads her own executive assessment and career development organization.